‘Ane end of an auld song?’

HISTORICAL SOCIOLINGUISTICS

Series editors

Vol. 8

PETER LANG
Oxford - Berlin - Bruxelles - Chennai - Lausanne - New York

'Ane end of an auld song?'

Macro and Micro Perspectives on Written Scots in Correspondence during the Union of the Parliaments Debates

Sarah van Eyndhoven

PETER LANG
Oxford - Berlin - Bruxelles - Chennai - Lausanne - New York

Bibliographic information published by the Deutsche Nationalbibliothek
The German National Library lists this publication in the German National Bibliography; detailed bibliographic data is available on the Internet at http:// dnb.d- nb.de.
A catalogue record for this book is available from the British Library.

Library of Congress Cataloging-in-Publication Data
Names: Van Eyndhoven, Sarah, 1993- author
Title: "Ane end of an auld song?" : macro and micro perspectives on written Scots in correspondence during the Union of the Parliaments debates / Sarah van Eyndhoven.
Other titles: Macro and micro perspectives on written Scots in correspondence during the Union of the Parliaments debates
Description: Oxford ; New York : Peter Lang, [2025] | Series: Historical sociolinguistics, 2296-1909 ; volume no. 8 | Includes bibliographical references and index.
Identifiers: LCCN 2025412025 (print) | LCCN 2025002345 (ebook) | ISBN 9781803745015 paperback | ISBN 9781803745022 ebook | ISBN 9781803745039 epub
Subjects: LCSH: Scotland--History--Union, 1707--Public opinion | Politicians--Scotland--Correspondence | Scotland. Parliament--History--18th century | Scotland--Politics and government--1689-1745 | Scots language--Political aspects | Scots language--Variation | Historical linguistics--Scotland | Public opinion--Scotland--History--18th century
Classification: LCC DA807 .V36 2025 (print) | LCC DA807 (ebook) | DDC 941.107--dc23/eng/20250408
LC record available at https://lccn.loc.gov/2025412025
LC ebook record available at https://lccn.loc.gov/2025002345

Cover image: 'View over Loch Ossian in wintertime'.
Photograph by Sarah van Eyndhoven.
Cover design by Peter Lang Group AG

ISSN 2296-1909
ISBN 978-1-80374-501-5 (print)
ISBN 978-1-80374-502-2 (ePDF)
ISBN 978-1-80374-503-9 (ePub)
DOI 10.3726/b21846

Published by Peter Lang Ltd, Oxford, United Kingdom
info@peterlang.com – www.peterlang.com

This publication has been peer reviewed.

For Lynn, for sparking my love of Scots, encouraging my academic dreams and cheering me across the finish line.

Go Little Book, go spare no pains
Go take thy Fate 'mongst Great and Small:
Go Smite, go pierce them Heart and Reigns
Convince, or then, Confound them all.

—*A Copie of the Baron's Court* by Patrick Anderson (1574/5–1624),
Scottish linguist, mathematician, philosopher and divine.

Contents

Figures

Tables

Preface

This book is based on my PhD thesis, which explored the use of written Scots features in the personal correspondence of Scottish politicians active during the Union of the Parliaments debates. This period was an interesting and unique period of time to investigate, given that written Scots by 1700 had steadily retreated from most text-types in the face of ongoing anglicisation, but simultaneously the Union debates sparked heated discussion around questions of nationality and Scotland's separate identity. It seemed plausible that Scots features may have been influenced by such discourse, and moreover could have become indexical markers used to lay claim to these ideologies, but previous research on this time period, particularly from a sociolinguistic perspective, was thin on the ground. I thus sought to don both my historical and sociolinguistic research caps, drawing from the frameworks of First, Second and Third Wave perspectives on variation, and combining quantitative, macro-social methods with micro-social analysis, to explore both broad sociopolitical factors alongside plausible stylistic intentions in conditioning or influencing the linguistic behaviour of these writers. After three years of navigating the archives, frustrating delays and dealing with the headaches of transcription and statistical analysis, it was to my great delight that results were obtained, and exciting results at that. Scots was found to correlate with certain political factors, though in complex and multilayered ways that reflect the composite nature of the historical figures operating in the Scottish parliament. The narrative presented here suggests use of Scots features was both influenced by, and contributed to, the political and ideological loyalties these writers harboured. It also tentatively suggests that a process of reinterpretation was underway, in which Scots features were becoming a resource that could be selectively employed for particular indexical and communicative purposes. It is my hope that the story presented here can be at once enlightening to the historical Scots community, and informative for historical sociolinguistic research in general, conveying the novelty and promise of this methodology and its results, and encouraging more scholars to seek out local archives to explore the treasure trove within.

Acknowledgements

This volume and the thesis it draws upon are the product not of an individual, but a whole team of supportive, motivating and inspiring people whose time and patience saw me through the highs and lows of self-directed research and carried me over this finish line. This book would not have been possible without the guidance and advice from my PhD supervision team: Dr Lynn Clark, Dr Alasdair Raffe and Dr Warren Maguire. That it eventually came to completion and furthermore has a story to tell is a testament to the brilliance of this incredible team of researchers. Thanks are also due to Dr Lauren Hall-Lew and Dr Rhona Alcorn for their academic support in the initial stages of this project, as well as Dr Joanna Kopaczyk and Dr Pavel Iosad, whose advice and critique helped strengthen the overall narrative. In particular, Joanna's encouragement and enthusiasm for Scots inspired me to keep going and to publish my results in this very book. I am forever indebted to Dr Stefano Coretta for his statistical creativity and advice, which enabled me to explore this dataset and uncover the story presented here, and to all the input I received from members of the Historical Sociolinguistics Network. In addition, my gratitude goes to the staff of the National Library of Scotland, the National Records of Scotland and the archivist Keren Guthrie at Blair Atholl Archives for their assistance in locating and providing the records I needed to consult, and to the various collection holders who kindly granted me permission to photograph their ancestors' correspondence.

Research of this kind is nearly impossible without essential financial support, and I am sincerely grateful to the Angus McIntosh Centre for Historical Linguistics (AMC) for both their generosity, and for their great team of researchers, from whom I have learnt so much. I cannot overlook the team of champions that was the postgraduate student community I was lucky enough to be surrounded by, and I am very fortunate to have had so many wonderful people see me through all the ups and downs on the way to completion. In particular, heartfelt thanks have to go to my pals: Lisa Gotthard, Alex Lorson, Mattia Zingaretti, Stephen McNulty and Tobias

Ungerer, as well as the friends who saw me through to the other side – Vilde Reksnes, Gilly Marchini and Ian Hajnosz. In addition, appreciation must be extended to Vicky Watson, Sarah Janac, Gabrielle Budd and Thomas Stephen, for their consistent support and the valuable skills I learnt from them along the way. Finally, my simple and honest gratitude has to go to my family, who so patiently supported me throughout this incredible odyssey. Thank you for all your love, care and support, for always being ready to cheer me up and on, and for never, ever giving up on me.

Abbreviations

Language

OSc	Older Scots
SSE	Scottish Standard English
OE	Old English
ME	Middle English
SStE	Southern Standard English
RP	Received Pronunciation
GVS	Great Vowel Shift

Dictionaries and References

OED	Oxford English Dictionary
DSL	Dictionaries of the Scots Language
RPS	Records of the Parliament of Scotland to 1707
ODNB	Oxford Dictionary of National Biography

Sociolinguistic Terms

CofP	Community of Practice
SIT	Social Identity Theory
L2	Second Language
D2	Second Dialect

Archives and Corpora

NLS	National Library of Scotland
NRS	National Records of Scotland
SHS	Scottish History Society
CSC	Helsinki Corpus of Scottish Correspondence
POLITECS	Political Opposition, Loyalty and Indifference in Eighteenth Century Scottish texts

Statistical Modelling and Techniques

HTR	Handwritten Text Recognition
OCR	Optical Character Recognition

CER	Character Error Rate
LIWC	Linguistic Inquiry and Word Count
VNC	Variability-Based Neighbour Clustering
brms	Bayesian regression models using Stan
MCA	Multiple Correspondence Analysis
PCA	Principal Component Analysis
GLMER	Generalised Linear Mixed-effects Regression
SD	Standard Deviation
CrI	Credibility Interval
MCMC	Markov Chain Monte Carlo

Other

East CB	East Central Belt
West CB	West Central Belt
UK	United Kingdom

Introduction

When Lord Seafield, Chancellor of Scotland, signed the Act of Union between the Scottish and English parliaments in 1707 and handed it back to the clerk, he famously exclaimed 'now there's ane end of an old song'. Or was it an *auld* song? For the linguistic situation in Lowland Scotland had complexified and undergone a dynamic change by the turn of the eighteenth century. Scots, both in written and spoken form, had seen a meteoric rise in use and status following its development within the medieval burgh system, and its spread throughout lowland Scotland. Independent transformations from northern Middle English, and the adoption of the variety within every genre of written work, and by every social order from royalty to tenant farmers, suggested that Scots was headed for nationwide standardisation. Yet this trajectory was cut short and reversed, through a series of historical events that led to the increasing adoption of anglicised variants, as Scotland and England were brought into the same social, religious and political orbit. The shift to high-prestige southern English variants affected the writing system in particular, and by the time of the Union of the Parliaments in 1707, written Scots had largely disappeared from most genres. Yet written Scots did not disappear completely, and it resurfaced with considerable vigour during the *Vernacular Revival*, some decades later. The roots of this backlash can in many ways be traced to the Union process itself, which suggests this particular moment in history had a tangible effect on the language of lowland Scotland.

For, against this backdrop of ongoing anglicisation, the Union debates (1689–1707) took place. They capture a turbulent, unpredictable and at-times chaotic period of Scottish history, in which economic, religious, constitutional, patriotic and personal tensions all came to the boil. Grievances, concerns, ambitions and desires all contributed to the dynamic political landscape that led, ultimately, to the unification between the Scottish and English parliaments. Following this agreement, the Scottish parliament was dissolved and subsequently a new British state and parliament formed, with its administrative capital in Westminster. Yet negotiating this agreement was by no means straightforward, nor was the Union itself the teleological endpoint of the deliberation. The ensuing debates leading up to the final ratification of the Union treaty sparked heated and intense political discussion, in which concepts of national identity, the patriotic defence of Scottish liberties and interests, independent sovereign status, and ecclesiastical and dynastic legitimacy all informed and constructed the discourse around incorporation, though these were matched by more pragmatic approaches concerned with the security of Scotland and safeguarding her institutions. Then, of course, there was the inevitable role of personal interest and political ambition characterising the desires of many ruling elite at this time. The narratives emerging from the debates tentatively suggest an increased awareness of an emerging Scottish national identity, and they informed the ideology and rhetoric of the three parties operating within the Scottish parliament.

It is not implausible that the use of written Scots among the politicians at the heart of the Union debates may have been consciously or subconsciously influenced by these political developments and their consequent discourse. Scots had become increasingly associated with 'domestic' and 'local' use, and such associations might lend themselves to representing a 'national' agenda that aligned with particular political identities. There is an instinctive or intuitive link between national identity and greater use of the vernacular, and indeed contemporary studies into written Scots use have identified such links (Shoemark et al., 2017; Shoemark, Kirby and Goldwater, 2017). In addition, salient and repeated patterns of linguistic variation within political settings built around local or pan-regional loyalties have been found in contemporary sociolinguistic analyses. In such scenarios, variation is not just responsive to but actively indexes identities, ideologies or membership of particular sociopolitical interests, suggesting the tangible role that political change and nationalist discourse can play in their occurrence and use. Given these findings, and the tense political environment in pre-Union Scotland, a similar relationship could well exist, suggesting the universality of certain sociolinguistic trends.

Moreover, while written Scots had retreated or was transitioning out of most text-types, correspondence might encourage its continuation, considering the lack of an economic incentive to anglicise personal writing (Robinson, 1983; Meurman-Solin, 1993, 1997; Corbett et al., 2003; Bugaj, 2004). Correspondence also tends to be less formal and planned relative to other text types such as legal contracts (Meurman-Solin, 2000: 158; van der Wal and Rutten, 2013: 2), and reflects the social relationships between correspondents to a very high degree, in which the vernacular can index social standing or familiarity (Görlach, 1999). However, this particular time period has received comparatively little attention within Scots scholarship, and the tentative link between eighteenth-century written Scots and political identities in personal correspondence has not yet been explored in detail (though see van Eyndhoven, 2018, 2021 for a small-scale study). This is partially attributable to the lack of appropriate, easily accessible resources to investigate such links, given that a digitised corpus of political correspondence from this time does not exist. Moreover, huge volumes of letters are stored in libraries, archives or private collections, yet research has 'only just begun to scratch the surface of this extraordinary mine of manuscript or typescript sources, especially as far as Late Modern times are concerned' (Dossena, 2012b: 13), and Scottish letters are no exception. They thus represent an untapped resource of hitherto unseen data that awaits digitisation into text-searchable files. As a result, the form, function and extent of early eighteenth-century written Scots features is still largely unknown, as is their potential as political and national identity indexical markers.

Accordingly, the thesis this book is based upon sought to address this gap, by building a novel corpus of correspondence from politicians – or commissioners as they were known at the time[1] – involved in the Scottish parliament as they debated the Union agreement. Alongside their correspondence, the writings of a politically active clergyman were included, to explore whether the politicians behaved uniquely as a community of

1 Commissioners were active members of the Scottish parliament, whereas those who were not returned for their constituency could still be politically active during interim periods. In the context of this book, these labels are used interchangeably, but both refer to the ruling Scottish elite debating the Union articles in the Scottish parliament.

practice of their own, or whether they shared significant overlaps with another highly educated and socially connected writer through their common political agenda. In addition, correspondence dating either side of the key debating years (1700–1707) was included to assess whether these crucial years behaved differently in particular. Details on how such a corpus was compiled and built are given in Chapter 4.

Following the methodological process, the following chapters detail how this correspondence was analysed. Firstly from a quantitative perspective, utilising different statistical modelling methods that approach the data through the First Wave framework within sociolinguistic investigation. Change over time is explored in Chapter 5 using a hierarchical clustering model. This assesses how the Union years may have influenced relative frequencies of Scots and identifies a promising change in frequencies during the key Union years. This is followed by a series of statistical analyses modelling the effect of various extralinguistic (particularly political) factors in influencing the probability of using Scots, in Chapter 6. These first two investigations hereby investigate whether this time period was unique from a linguistic point of view, and whether writers' affiliations with different parties and their ideological platforms had a measurable impact on their likelihood of choosing Scots features. Complementing these broad-based, macro-social investigations into the patterning of Scots across the corpus, the data are then explored through a close-up, micro-analysis, informed by Second and Third Wave sociolinguistic perspectives in Chapter 7. Four selected individuals and their intra-writer behaviour across recipients and specific letters are analysed, drawing on sociolinguistic notions of accommodation, style-shifting, identity and indexicality to consider plausible motives for their variation. This complements the quantitative analysis in suggesting the extent to which the statistical patterns are reflected in individual behaviour, and whether their behaviour might accumulate ideological associations to construct those patterns.

The book is accordingly structured as follows. Chapter 1 gives a brief historical background into the Union debates and the state of Scotland in the early eighteenth century. The historical events that took place generated or contributed to salient ideologies motivating certain groups of politicians to associate with one another, shaping and informing the political parties in the parliament. These parties and their ideologies will subsequently form the extralinguistic factors included in the quantitative analysis. Chapter 2 then outlines a history of Scots up to and including the turn of the eighteenth century. The development of Scots from its early northern English origins into a distinct and widespread variety across lowland Scotland, before the events leading to its reduction within the written sphere as anglicisation took hold, are both outlined. This provides a background to the linguistic situation by 1700, suggesting what we might expect in terms of written Scots in correspondence, and how these elite writers may have interacted with it.

Following this, Chapter 3 provides the theoretical framework through which patterns and instances of variation will be explored. The plausible relationship between political identity and linguistic variation that criss-crossed political lines of allegiance and opposition at this time period naturally lends itself to concepts within sociolinguistic frameworks. Accordingly, the insights offered by the 'Three Waves' of sociolinguistic variation are considered in line with their application to the data, while previous historical and contemporary Scots research bordering on this time frame or theoretical approach is summarised. Chapter 4 describes the methodological process involved in building a novel corpus of political writings and defining the Scots features to be included in the analysis. As a novel dataset and time period hitherto untouched by quantitative analysis, this section both highlights the challenges of historical correspondence research and eighteenth-century Scots features in particular, but also attempts to provide a potential blueprint for other researchers contemplating corpus research derived from these kinds of data sources.

These background chapters set up the historical, linguistic and theoretical context in which this analysis takes place, while the methodological chapter outlines the people, texts and features that comprise the analysis. These are then followed by three analysis chapters. Chapter 5 covers the temporal analysis of written Scots, exploring the frequencies of Scots relative to English across the timeline included in the corpus, using Variability-based Neighbour Clustering or VNC (Gries and Hilpert, 2008). The presence of a perceivable change in Scots variation is good evidence that this time period was unique, and worth investigating further from a sociolinguistic perspective. Following the temporal analysis Chapter 6 undertakes a statistical sociolinguistic exploration of the corpus using Bayesian regression modelling (Bürkner, 2017) and Multiple Correspondence Analysis (Kassambara and Mundt, 2017) to examine the influence of various extra-linguistic factors upon the probability of Scots occurring. The combination of these two techniques provides a compelling new insight into the influences, including political factors, operating on the variation demonstrated by these political figures.

The last chapter (Chapter 7) takes a micro-perspective, analysing the letters of a representative from each of the three political parties within the Scottish parliament, and a politically active clergyman. Variation is analysed at the level of individual letters, to consider plausible stylistic factors contributing to differences in Scots use between recipients, drawing on concepts from the Second and Third Wave frameworks. In particular, influences derived from the recipient themselves, including audience or accommodative designs, are contemplated, as well as stylistic and agentive causes deriving from the author and their wish to position themselves or claim in-group membership(s) by foregrounding a shared or common background. Through these behaviours, the analysis suggests the extent to which the Scots used by these politicians reflect their belonging to the wider social identities identified in Chapters 1 and 6, and the extent to which they demonstrate a creative and stylistic repertoire of their own that serves to reflect their political and ideological concerns.

The insights and findings of Chapters 5–7, both in combination and individually, and their relation to the ideas put forward in Chapter 3, are discussed in more detail in the Chapter 8, before being summarised in the Conclusion (Chapter 9). This also considers what such results mean for an understanding of eighteenth-century Scots, and the role of political change and identity on linguistic variation more generally. This book thus seeks to illuminate the time period, features, and individuals that comprised the linguistic climate surrounding the Union debates, shedding new light on early eighteenth-century Scots and the role of political change in its progression.

CHAPTER I

'For the Union makes us strong?': Cause, concern and consequence in the lead up to the Union of the Parliaments

An understanding of developments underpinning the sociopolitical, temporal and cultural climate within a diachronic window of time is crucial to recreating the environment in which language is being written. No doubt these changes influenced individuals in their ideologies, identities and relationships, but potentially in their language use as well. There has been a wealth of literature written about the Union of the Parliaments, and this chapter does not intend to cover the various debates and schools of thought in any great detail, nor does this book seek to propose a new interpretation of the passage of the union. Such a discussion is better left to research examining the event from a more narrowly historical or political perspective. Instead, a general discussion of the events that gave rise to the idea of the Union, the progress of the treaty itself, and in particular the concerns of the main groups and parties involved, is examined in this section.[1] Specifically, it provides a brief time-line of events that influenced and informed the Union debates (1689–1707), a discussion of the parliamentary process, the nature of the agreement itself, and the different political parties involved in the Scottish parliament. Collectively, these sections highlight the complex cultural dualism facing Scottish politicians in the early eighteenth century as they sought to balance local loyalties and identities with supra-regional and socioeconomic demands, a conflict that may have influenced their language choices.

1 For further literature on this area, see Ferguson (1964, 1977), Riley (1978, 1979), Young (1999), Whatley (2006) and Macinnes (1990, 2007).

The pre-Union years

The lead-up to the Union of the Parliaments in 1707 was by no means a smooth and orderly progression of pre-meditated discussion and measured debate between two equally positioned nations. Neither can it be seen as the ultimate conclusion to the dynastic Union of the Crowns in 1603, and any understanding of the time period should avoid making teleological assumptions about the inevitability of Union (Ferguson, 1964: 89; Raffe, 2012b: 266). Yet the idea of an incorporating union – a union of two or more states merging into one political whole – was not a novel concept; proposals for union between Scotland and England had surfaced several times since 1603. Already early on, some Scots believed that a peaceful, negotiated alliance with their southern neighbours would be strategically more sensible for a small island such as Britain (Mason, 1994; Whatley, 2006, 2008; Macinnes, 2007; Jackson, 2012). From 1699 onward this idea gained momentum, and union with England became part of an ongoing debate that sought to improve trade and the relations between the two countries (Ferguson, 1964: 93). However, the conditions leading to union being placed once more on the debating table were different for both nations involved. For Scotland, the question of union emerged in light of the evolving succession crisis arising from Queen Anne's childless state, coupled with ongoing constitutional tensions plaguing the nation since the dynastic union of 1603. This created stark divisions within Scottish society, at a time when social, political, religious and economic tensions ran high, and internal fissures ran deep. Yet they were crucial for a discussion concerning closer union to take place, and the following outlines some of the causes that gave rise, eventually, to the Union of the Parliaments.

Economics and the Darien scheme

The deteriorating material condition of the nation by the end of the seventeenth century became increasingly pertinent to the discussion around an incorporating union (Macinnes, 2007: 243; Raffe, 2012b: 253). The years immediately prior to the Union saw a series of harvest failures, famine and dearth, while trade was affected by French privateering on Scottish ships, English interference in Scottish shipping, tariff walls erected by rival powers, the Nine Years' War (1688–1697) and the War of the Spanish Succession (1702–1713) which disrupted Scottish trading links with France in particular (Whatley, 2008; Young, 1999). Such economic woes increased ten-fold in the aftermath of Scotland's colonial experiment, known as the Darien scheme (1698–1700). First established under the Company of Scotland in 1698, Darien was an ambitious enterprise to establish the colony of New Caledonia on the Isthmus of Panama. It was intended to revive Scotland's economy by providing a unique opportunity for economic growth, prosperity and modernisation, and a chance to break free from economic dependence on England (Whatley, 2006: 5; Stephen, 2007: 16). The national venture saw widespread support, and many Scotsmen invested considerable sums of money into it. However, the grandiose scheme was plagued by organisational incompetence, compounded by the harsh conditions of the location, and finally crumbled two years later when the colony was attacked by the Spanish (Douglas Watt, 2014). Despite pleas for assistance, the English government refused to send help, and the subsequent failure of Darien took with it a quarter of Scotland's liquid capital, significantly exacerbating the economic plight of the country (Jackson, 2012: 342).

The abandonment of Scotland's national enterprise led to considerable emotional shock and high levels of resentment towards the Crown (Bowie, 2007: 28; Stephen, 2007: 17). Its failure added yet another blow to Scotland's competence in economic affairs, and while internal reasons and mismanagement played as much a part in its collapse (Jackson, 2012: 354), it was easy for the opposition to stir up nationalist anger and direct blame at the English ministry, elevating Darien to the status of a nationwide disaster that had damaged Scotland's honour (Whatley, 2006: 203, Raffe, 2012b: 264). Yet it also had the counter-intuitive effect of bringing an incorporating union back to the table. The Darien venture added to the feeling that the considerations of the Court did not align with Scottish interests (Whatley, 2008: 3), and there emerged a growing group who argued for closer union to resolve the diametric interests of Crown and nation, as well as repair the damage to Scotland's economy.

Tensions between the two nations were compounded further by the fallout of the *Worcester* affair, which came close to imploding relations between Scotland and England. An English merchant vessel, the *Worcester*, was seized by the Company of Scotland in August 1705 while sailing off the coast of Fife, in retaliation for the seizure of the Company's last ships by English customs officers. The captain Thomas Green and his men were accused of piracy and charged with murdering the crew of two other Company vessels which had disappeared in the Indian Ocean (Whatley, 2006: 200; Macinnes, 2007: 271). The following year, the innocent captain and two of his crew were hanged in front of large crowds who gathered on Leith Sands (Graham, 2005: 153–190). The roots of this extreme reaction can be traced in many ways to the anger surrounding the Darien aftermath and the rising dissatisfaction with Scotland's economic situation, but it also played a decisive role in shaping the parliamentary process during the critical years of the Union debates (1705–1705), influencing the motives of several key commissioners who began to seriously push for incorporation as a solution to the failing two-state situation they found themselves in. Advocates of union were not necessarily motivated by a sense of pan-Britannic nationalism, but rather took a pragmatic perspective that sought to redress Scotland's economic plight and constitutional woes. Alongside pragmatism, however, ideological motivations stemming from the aftermath of the Revolution of 1689 played an equally crucial role in the lead-up to the debates and informing the discussions themselves. These religious factors had their roots in changes occurring well before the economic issues described above, but came to a head at the same time as Scotland was suffering acutely from financial distress, weaving through the rise of tensions described here and adding another layer to the Union debates.

Religious factors

Presbyterians, Episcopalians and the Revolution of 1689

Many of the interests underlying the political groups within the Scottish parliament stem from the profound religious changes that took place during the seventeenth century, particularly the 'Glorious' Revolution of

1689 and the subsequent rise of Jacobitism (Raffe, 2012b: 259). By 1700 Scottish society was religiously fractured, having experienced changes in Episcopalian and Presbyterian forms of government several times since 1560. The Episcopalian settlement of 1661–1662 created a major rift between Presbyterians and Episcopalians, who together encompassed the majority of Scotland's population. This would go on to have lasting consequences during the Union debates and beyond (Raffe, 2012a). Episcopalian control was overturned following the invasion of England by the Protestant Dutch king, William of Orange, in 1688. King James VII and II was forced to flee to France upon the invasion, where the French king Louis XIV offered him shelter. A few months later, William's Convention of Estates overturned the previous ecclesiastical settlement with the Claim of Right. Enacted on 11 April 1689, this stated that no Roman Catholic could be monarch or hold public office, and that a government by bishops was contrary to the general inclinations of the people. This essentially declared the throne vacant as James VII, a devout Catholic, was denied his role as monarch.

Episcopalian bishops refused to recognise William and his wife, Queen Mary, continuing to uphold their theological ideals including divine right monarchy and indefeasible hereditary succession, which would only accept the exiled James VII as the divinely ordained sovereign. Accordingly, William turned to the Presbyterians, and in June 1690 parliament officially re-established Presbyterianism (Glassey, 1987). The Glorious Revolution gave political and legal legitimacy to the return of Presbyterianism, yet this was by no means accepted uniformly across Scotland, and in areas such as the North East Episcopalians continued to have a stronghold (Whatley, 2008). The monarch's endorsement of Presbyterianism as the only true church of Scotland flew in the face of Episcopalian ideology and establishment, entrenching hostilities between the two groups (Raffe, 2010: 323), and the Revolution settlement would go on to play a significant role in the Union debates, as religion and politics became inherently linked in Scotland throughout this period (Raffe, 2012a: 180, Raffe, 2012b: 259–260). Politicians of all stripes sat in the parliament, but the developing chasm between Presbyterians and Episcopalians led to ideological clashes between them. Commissioners were profoundly informed by their denominational adherence, and this had significant ramifications for the formation of parties and the debates around the treaty itself (Macinnes, 2007: 257). Most Presbyterians saw Union as a key means to protect the Kirk[2] and the monarchy, while Episcopalians largely aligned with the opposition Country party in a bid to prevent the Union and restore the exiled Stuart[3] dynasty on the throne (Raffe, 2012b: 260).

While the influence of religious orthodoxy on political actions is difficult to quantify, faith wasn't simply a convenient banner adopted by political members to disguise their more immediate motives (Raffe, 2012b: 259). The principles of doctrinal ideology were a force that drove political action across the unionist – nationalist spectrum, and their choices went beyond personal ambition and top-level management, guided by genuine conviction and principled support (Patrick and Whatley, 2007: 111). The safety of the Kirk was a crucial component of the Union package, so much so that several members of the opposing side voted against their fellow party members when it came to the Kirk Act within the amended union treaty.[4] Nor were Scottish politics differentiated from the ongoing religious controversy in Scotland – the sharp divides in Scottish society were echoed in parliament (Raffe, 2012b: 258). Ultimately, unionism within parliament appealed most to those who were pragmatic in their religious convictions – those who saw the Union as the best way to preserve their establishment from the risk of a French-sponsored, pro-Catholic restoration (Riley, 1979: 53; Patrick, 2008: 173; Whatley, 2008: 11; Jackson, 2012: 346), rather than necessarily upholding their particular strain of Protestantism (Bowie, 2007, 2008; Stephen, 2007). The central principles of the different confessional cultures guided the arguments and decisions of commissioners from across the political spectrum, and religion forms one of the key extralinguistic

2 The 'Kirk' refers to the Presbyterian church of Scotland, while 'the Church' can refer to various denominations (such as Episcopalian).

3 The Scottish royal bloodline was originally spelled *Stewart*. The family name comes from the *Office of High Steward of Scotland*, which was held by the founder of the noble house, Walter Fitz Alan (c.1150). The spelling *Stewart* and its variations had become established by the time of his grandson Walter Stewart. However, Mary, Queen of Scots (r.1542–1567), being brought up in France, adopted the French spelling of the name as *Stuart*, which became the regular spelling from then onward.

4 Voting lists available at <https://www.rps.ac.uk/>

factors examined here. These principles also had the consequence of causing various Episcopalian members of the ruling class to join the *Jacobite* movement that emerged out of 1689.

Jacobitism

The Scottish Jacobites[5] were a collection of mostly Episcopalian (and Scottish Catholic) individuals who sought to reinstate the exiled King James VII and II on the throne, following the 1689 Revolution. Scottish Jacobitism was primarily influenced by notions of an indefeasible hereditary monarchy that was sanctioned by political ecclesiastical legitimacy or divine right, under which the deposed king James VII was rightful heir (Kidd, 1999: 135; Raffe, 2012b: 260). The Union, by seeking to secure a Protestant successor on the throne, was thus unacceptable to the Jacobites. Jacobitism was concentrated largely in the Western Isles, Highlands and the North East, and these areas became the Jacobites' stronghold throughout their multiple attempts to overthrow the existing political order through armed rebellion. However, alongside clan chiefs there were considerable numbers of Lowland Jacobites as well, and the movement was sustained and more subversive in Scotland than either England or Ireland (Macinnes, 2007: 246).

Although considerable numbers of the political elite in particular disguised their Jacobite sympathies in order to advance their political and personal interests, others utilised parliamentary means to oppose Union, which allowed them to play more subtle cards than mere plotting. The Jacobites became a central plank of the Country party platform up until 1707 (Macinnes, 2007: 250, 255), and formed a major political and ideological force operating at all social levels. Jacobite activity, with its clear political and nationalist overtones and decisive links to the Union agreement

5 There were also Jacobites in Ireland, Wales and England, though they are not discussed here. For further reference, see Monod (1989) for an introduction to English Jacobitism, and Ó Ciardha (2002) for more information on the Irish Jacobites.

even after its passing, suggests a potential political identity that could have influenced written Scots use, and this is explored in more detail in later chapters. This also motivated the decision to include correspondence up until 1745 (the last major Jacobite rising) in the corpus. The issue that was to act as the catalyst for Jacobite activity throughout the eighteenth century, however, was the *Hanoverian Succession* put forward by the English in 1701.

The Hanoverian succession

Not just confessionalism, but also sovereignty, became a key consideration in the debate around the Union, triggered by the death of Princess Anne's last surviving child, in July 1700. As Anne was soon to be Queen, this left no immediate heir to the English and Scottish thrones. The War of Spanish Succession (1701–1714) furthermore opened up the potential for the return of the exiled Stuart dynasty, since Louis XIV of France favoured a Catholic restoration of the exiled Jacobite dynasty under James VIII and III,[6] the son of James VII, who had died in 1701 (Ferguson, 1964: 90). The English parliament thus wished to settle the succession on Sophia, widow to the elector of Hanover and the granddaughter of James VI, but also, crucially, a Protestant. This would not only prevent a northern military front from opening up, but removed the potential for Louis XIV to launch an attack from a Stuart-restored Scottish base (Young, 1999: 42; Jackson, 2012: 342), and this became known as the Hanoverian Succession.

While the Presbyterians within Scotland similarly desired a Protestant successor, the hasty passing of the *Act of Settlement* in 1701 by the English parliament, which stipulated that the future heir must be Protestant, was seen as an infringement of Scotland's national sovereignty, particularly as it was passed without Scottish consultation. Although the act did not specifically regulate the succession to the Scottish throne, it was difficult to think of a peaceful scenario in which the two kingdoms had different kings

6 Also known as the 'Old Pretender'.

(Ferguson, 1964: 91). Hostility increased in momentum through a series of 'tit-for-tat' Acts, the first of which was Scotland's *Act of Security* in 1704, which asserted Scotland's right to choose its own Protestant successor, of the royal line of Scotland, unless Scotland's grievances, including English interference with Scottish liberties, religion and trade, were dealt with (Ferguson, 1964: 97; Macinnes, 2007: 259; Stephen, 2007: 35; Whatley, 2008: 3). The English perceived this as an act of open defiance, given the Act risked the possibility of a Catholic France takeover, and countered this with the *Alien Act* in 1705. This stipulated that if the Scots would not accept the Hanoverian succession, or agree to appoint commissioners to negotiate for an incorporating union by 25 December 1705, then Scottish traders would be treated as aliens and their cattle, linen and coal trades would be banned (Ferguson, 1964: 101). For an economically struggling and militarily weak Scotland, this represented a significant burden to everyday Scottish livelihoods (Bowie, 2007: 79). Scottish parliamentarians did concurrently agree to negotiate an incorporating union, though this came at the cost of political relations between the two nations, which naturally had a bearing on the sentiments of factions within parliament.

It was against this backdrop of incredibly tense Anglo-Scottish relations that the Scottish Estates were recalled on 28 June 1704, primarily to respond to the idea of an incorporating union. While the atmosphere was decidedly hostile, the dynastic question reignited debate around the existing connection between the two countries, and the emerging constitutional crisis was seen as part of a wider problem of sovereignty. Certain voices began to voice increasing support for an incorporating union – whilst preserving Scotland's prosperity and religious freedoms – as the best option available (Macinnes, 2007: 272). Eventually, the Hanoverian Succession was accepted and Union treaty began its progress through parliament in 1705.

The progression of the Union treaty

While early attempts at unification during William's reign had been unsuccessful, negotiations finally began in earnest under John Campbell, second Duke of Argyll in 1705, in which the Queen was to nominate commissioners, as well as the time and place at which the treaty could be debated. The group of commissioners chosen were largely favourable towards an incorporating union, selected to reflect party dominance rather than a balanced representation (Young, 1999; Macinnes, 2007; Stephen, 2007). The debates that followed generated widespread and sophisticated deliberation, in which a variety of voices took part, though unionist perspectives dominated the field. As they intensified, they became a complex and intricate mixture of economics, nationalism, xenophobia and ecclesiastical and constitutional politics. A range of options were explored, and three core principles of the union – incorporation with a common monarchy and parliament, freedom of trade, and the Hanoverian Succession – found majority support, though with powerful opposition. Yet commissioners were not merely looking out for their own interests and political ambitions, often standing firm in their defence of Scottish interests (Whatley, 2006: 245). As a result, among other concessions the English offered the *Equivalent*, a payment that compensated Scotland for their future participation in interest payments of the debt accumulated by the English state since 1689, and for the standardisation of the currency. Opponents of the Union attacked the Equivalent as clear bribery, yet many political players who did not benefit from the compensation package still voted for Union, suggesting it did not create the pro-Union majority in parliament (McMillan and McLean, 2005; Macinnes, 2007: 294, 301).

The outcome was a modified incorporating union that preserved some of the Scotland's key institutions, in particular the Kirk, educational system and Scottish law. The final terms of the Treaty of Union were agreed upon by 22 July 1706, and the treaty as a whole was ratified on 16 January 1707, by a majority of 110 votes to sixty-nine. The Act for a Union of Parliaments took effect on 1 May 1707, and the parliament of the United Kingdom met for the first time in October 1707.[7] On most levels the treaty seemed to satisfy, essentially preserving the most important elements of Scottish sovereignty, suggesting an attachment to a perceived form of historic

7 See <https://www.rps.ac.uk/> for details of the votes and dates up until 1707.

nationhood was prevalent at this time, to the extent that it was especially catered for in the Union agreement (Whatley, 2006: 10; Macinnes, 2007: 280). While attitudes toward the agreement were complex and multifaceted, a prevalent sense of 'Scottish' as separate from 'English' does appear to have infused the discussion, and the question now remains whether this would have filtered into the linguistic choices of the individuals involved in that discussion. First, however, the political groups informing the debates must be understood, particularly the concerns or ambitions binding these groups together, in order to recognise salient influences on language use.

The Scottish political parties

The Union debates saw three parties become involved in the Scottish Parliament: the pre-existing *Court* and *Country* parties and a new, emergent party who would become known as the *Squadrone Volante*. It would be too simplistic, however, to simply split the party lines into a binary division of unionists and nationalists, as 'players in the making of Union were both polemicists and politicians' (Macinnes, 2007: 9). The Union saw a wide range of perspectives and the language of Scottish nationhood was appropriated and advanced in complex, multifaceted ways between and within these three parties, often driven by principled ideologies. Even their religious identity was amorphous – while the Presbyterian – Episcopalian divide gradually came to overlay Court and Country party alignments, there were exceptions and outliers in each camp, contributing to their multifaceted composition.

The Court party

The Court party represented the main body of politicians supporting incorporation and advocating ratification of the treaty. This group was largely monopolised by a small group of powerful Scottish magnates who had dominated the Scottish parliament since the Revolution of 1689 (Riley, 1979: 55). By 1700 the Duke of Queensberry had emerged as leader, subsequently forming the 'Court' interest (Scott, 1981: 277). A major role was played by former Presbyterian emigres who had fled during the Stuart reign, and their personal experiences of the late Stuart rule and the Revolution itself continued to inform their stance (Whatley, 2008: 26). They were characterised by their staunch Presbyterian values (though some, such as the Earls of Mar and Kinnoull fell outside this circle as Episcopalians), as well as their commitment to the Hanoverian succession. Consequently, they were acutely suspicious of Jacobite intrigue and the motives of the exiled Stuart dynasty, though several were more moderate in their approach and a small number of Court members were even sympathetic toward the Jacobite cause. Yet, while Court figures were rewarded for their loyalty following the conclusion of the Union (for example, with a peerage), they were also aware of the national aspect of their political activity within the new British state and continued to see themselves as Scotsmen (Murdoch, 2006). Some even changed their stance towards incorporation, such as the Earls of Seafield and Ilay, and the Duke of Argyll, who became increasingly disillusioned with the Union in the face of the proposed malt tax to be imposed on Scotland in 1713. Ilay wrote to William Carstairs in 1710 that 'I was always of the opinion that it was obviously our interest not to mingle ourselves too much with the factions here [Westminster], I mean as Scotchmen, for it being very plain that no party here has our country much at heart' (MacCormick, 1774: 786–787).

The Court party advocated union for a number of interlinked reasons, but the ongoing economic difficulties in the lead-up to the debates influenced many of its most articulate proponents (Whatley, 2006). The dynastic Union of 1603, and the Darien failure of 1700 in particular had proven that the Scottish government did not have the means to successfully undertake operations in ways unacceptable to the English government, which made the distinct sovereignty of the queen of Scotland theoretical rather than practical (Ferguson, 1964; Stephen, 2007). Incorporating union, they claimed, would place Scotland in an equal partnership with England, providing new avenues for acquiring status, prosperity and participation within the British Empire, while the security offered by the Hanoverian succession safeguarded the monarchy, the Scottish church and the Revolution Settlement (Macinnes, 2007: 277–284; Kidd, 2008). This highlighted the genuine concern of many to secure and support Scottish liberties and institutions, and throughout the Union debates the Court party advocated its position for reasons that were not necessarily antithetical to nationalist thought, but were imbued with a pragmatic undertone. Their role in guiding the treaty through parliament can be seen as an act of managerial sophistication, rather than crude political bribery (Macinnes, 2007: 11). Of course, supporters of the Union were aware of the potential to realise their political ambitions and did exploit the opportunities accessible to them, but their support stemmed from more than just political expediency (Whatley, 2008: 25). Many demonstrated a principled commitment to the Union for a range of ideological and deeply national reasons, like their oppositional counterparts (Ferguson, 1977: 186–88; Riley, 1978: 274–81; Macinnes, 1990: 11–25, 2007: 9).

Unionism itself is a complex term in Scotland, and despite its connotations does not suggest those who identified as unionist necessarily embraced the social, cultural and political dominance of their southern neighbour. Whilst themes of assimilation with, and emulation of, England certainly played a role among particular lines of thought, much more often unionist ideas were about the maintenance of semi-autonomy or nationhood within the Union (Patrick and Whatley, 2007: 162; Bowie, 2008: 114; Kidd, 2008: 4). Indeed, it is a category error to think of nationalism and unionism as complete opposites (Kidd, 2008: 6), and to categorise historical actors as such fails to take into account the deep-rooted loyalties on both sides of the political spectrum (Jackson, 2008, 2012: 2). 'Principle and patriotism were not the exclusive properties of the Anti-Unionist opposition' (Patrick and Whatley, 2007: 184), and strains of Scottish unionism were often highly sensitive to claims of Scottish nationhood, developing as a *counterweight* to English imperialism through proposed incorporation. Some such as Lord Seafield were even convinced that outright rejection of Union would prove Scotland's 'ruin' (Macinnes, 2007: 285). Several Court politicians also maintained friendships and alliances with opposition figures and as the parliament was comprised of men drawn from a small pool of leading Scottish elite, it is perhaps not surprising that cross-party allegiances existed. This, however, suggests a firm polarisation into 'opposing camps' is not a realistic perspective of pre-Union Scotland, and language use might consequently be less clear-cut as a result.

In terms of their personal histories, most Court members were highly educated at prestigious universities in Scotland or abroad in Leiden, Utrecht or Paris, and members of the landowning class also frequently went on a 'Grand Tour' of Europe (Heal and Holmes, 1994: 243–275; Raumolin-Brunberg, 1996a: 28), visiting various fashionable and intellectual capitals across the continent, as well as spending considerable time in London. Court politicians were thus high-status, well educated, multilingual and operated on local, national and international lines. These factors will have increased the likelihood of adopting the emerging prestige standard and shifting towards a more anglicised writing style. Yet, while increased use of the emergent standard might be expected given their upbringing, experiences and a possible political desire to converge both socially and linguistically with the norms of their southern neighbours, this section has also made clear that this assumption is by no means a given, and we will see this complexity return in the analysis chapters.

The Country party

The Country party formed the key opposition body to the proposal of an incorporating union. The party originally consisted mostly of a rather fractured collection of constitutional reformers, who were part of an initial Country-Cavalier opposition to the Court party. This included several leaders from Scotland's powerful ruling families, who jointly led the weak coalition while cynically competing with the Scottish magnates from the Court party (Scott, 1981: 277), though not all members were drawn from the peerage. However, the party became more organised post-1700 around a series of issues related to Union, including religion and sovereignty (Macinnes, 2007: 284). Following the death of King

William in 1702, Jacobites began to participate more actively in electoral politics, with the hope of furthering the Stuart cause under Queen Anne. The failure to obtain toleration for Episcopalians encouraged those of Cavalier[8] sympathies to join the Country party, and the result was a considerably larger presence of their numbers in the 1703 elected parliament, in which they represented an alternative national interest in Scottish politics (Jackson, 2012: 344). A number of prominent Presbyterians also joined the party, out of concern that the proposed Union would break the Covenants. These were national oaths to God, in which the Scots were bound to a holy duty to effect a religious union with England (Raffe, 2012a: 36). The Incorporating Union, as a pluralist arrangement recognising the distinct Presbyterian and Anglican establishments of Scotland and England thus flew in the face of the Covenants (Kidd, 2008: 76; Bowie, 2015: 237).

The severe differences between the Jacobite-Episcopalian Cavaliers and traditional rank-and-file Presbyterians within the party, whose ultimate goals fundamentally differed, caused tensions that prevented the fragile alliance from improving (Young, 1999: 27; Patrick, 2008: 111). Presbyterianism had become central to or even synonymous with Scottish nationhood for many people, which clashed with the Jacobite tendency within the Country party who saw themselves as representing historic legitimacy derived from Scotland's ancient, unbroken past, reinforced by Episcopacy (Wallace and Kidd, 2018: 194–195). As a result, the Jacobites opposed an incorporating union and a Protestant establishment, whereas most of their Presbyterian counterparts wanted the Hanoverian Succession and some form of equitable connection with England, preferably in the shape of a federative union (Ferguson, 1964: 103).

The opposition party was thus hampered both internally and externally by their composition of two ultimately incompatible wings, leaving them unable to maximise their support (Macinnes, 2007: 295). Differences within the party eventually led to the breaking-away of a group of politicians, who would later become the *Squadrone Volante*.

8 Cavalier referred to the Jacobite (and naturally Episcopalian) clustering of commissioners within the Country party.

What united the disparate group was their opposition to the Union, with emphasis on the subjection of Scottish interests to the English following the dynastic union of 1603 (Bowie, 2007: 67). They wanted to be sure that the English saw them as sovereign equals, rather than a 'wayward vassal nation' to be reabsorbed into the 'English pan-Brittanic imperium' (Kidd, 1999: 133). Their major points of contention against the idea of an incorporating union included the loss of political rights, privileges and hereditary offices among the landed classes, a drain of people and funds to the south, the level of Scottish representation proposed for the new British parliament, and the sentimental loss of an ancient, sovereign kingdom. Through such grievances they managed to create a flimsy scaffold of unity behind a secularised form of Scottish patriotism, from which to attack the government. It remained nonetheless an uneasy alliance, and this could surface into open tension when agreement was required on more than just the rejection of incorporation (Bowie, 2008: 48, 75).

The 'nationalism' of the Country party was as complex as the 'unionism' of the Court party. Members did at times feel the Union treaty directly challenged a deep-seated sense of Scottish national identity, but often unity to the cause was filtered through loyalty to divergent forms of church government and monarchies (Bowie, 2008: 51). Andrew Fletcher and George Lockhart, for instance, were characterised by contemporary (and current) accounts as 'Scottish patriots' (Robertson, 1997), noted for their dedication and intransigence to their 'unwaveringly patriotic, political agenda' (Whatley, 2008: 11). Yet their reasons differed fundamentally – Lockhart was fervently Jacobite and focused on Episcopalian toleration and the Stuart restoration, whereas Fletcher was largely latitudinarian in his outlook and pushed for a federal union. The Country party frequently appealed to an idealised version of Scottish history, and many of the principal arguments for Scottish independence were historical and mythological in nature (Finlay, 1999: 123), but like their Court party contemporaries they were also pragmatic and opportunistic (Ferguson, 1977: 190–192; Macinnes, 2007: 305; Raffe, 2012b: 265). Perceived chances at political success within the Scottish parliament also informed Country party members' decisions to oppose the Union, and Lockhart's memoirs for instance suggest that the feared loss in power resulting from incorporation was the Duke of Atholl's primary motive to oppose the treaty:

> he was very frank and chearful to enter into any, though the most desperate, measures [...] because, perhaps, he had but a small estate and could not expect to make so great an appearance after the Union as if the kingdom of Scotland remained. (Lockhart, 1995: 41, quoted in Young, 2004b)

Several Country commissioners even sought a closer union with England as a solution to the ongoing constitutional and economic difficulties, but wanted a federal rather than incorporating union, based on the loose confederacies of Early Modern Europe (Ferguson, 1964; Bowie, 2007; Jackson, 2008, 2012; Kidd, 2008; Whatley, 2008). In the wake of the Union passing a number of the Country party politicians were active in trying to bring about its repeal, or used their positions within the British parliament to fight for Scotland's best advantages in Westminster. Many of the Jacobite members of the party also remained committed to Jacobitism, either dabbling in Jacobite plotting or openly taking part in the risings of 1715 and 1745 (Wilkinson, 2002a; Macinnes, 2007: 256). Yet, though the loss of Scotland's parliament was felt keenly by many, their goals and concerns must be examined through the historic looking glass, in which economic liberty and dynastic aspirations influenced decisions alongside any sentimental attachment to the nation, and their composite and fluid nature must be acknowledged in any analysis of their variable behaviour.

The Squadrone Volante

The *Squadrone Volante* or *Neu Party* as they were initially known formed as a splinter group from the Country party, following irreconcilable divisions between its Presbyterian and Jacobite wings. Composed of various nobles of second rank who were closely tied by marriage or kinship, they shared familial ties but also a deep and long-standing commitment to Presbyterian church government and Protestant succession (Ferguson, 1977: 188, 216–218; Riley, 1978: 115–118; Macinnes, 2007: 264; Patrick and Whatley, 2007: 177). Fundamentally, a devotion to the long-term security of the Presbyterian Church government formed the centre-piece of their political platform, and they sought additional safeguards to guarantee the

Kirk's independence and freedom (Bowie, 2008: 44). Their separation was engineered by the creation of the new ministry in 1704, providing an opportunity for Country party affiliates to work with the Crown, rather than continuing in opposition. Given the fundamental mismatch between Squadrone ideals and those of the Episcopalian-Jacobite interest in the Country party, the opportunity appealed to a certain group within the fluid composition of the opposition, who would never be powerful enough in their own right to compete with the dominant Scottish magnates in the Court party (Scott, 1981: 278).

The party first emerged following the exposure of the *Queensberry Plot* in 1704 – in which the Duke of Queensberry sought to implicate some of his political rivals in a Jacobite plot. He was disgraced and removed from office, and John Hay, the second Marquess of Tweeddale was then approached to form a new parliament in 1704. A number of his associates from the Country party joined Tweeddale, forming the beginnings of the Squadrone, originally named the *Neu Party*.[9] Despite their earlier opposition stance, the chance for greater political power, their dedication to the Hanoverian Succession, and their realisation that the English would accept nothing short of an incorporating union, led the Squadrone to support the motion for incorporation (Whatley, 2006: 249). Their position continued until early 1705, when their involvement and poor handling of the *Worcester* affair discredited their leadership in parliament and called Tweeddale's conduct as chancellor into question (Macinnes, 2007: 271). Anne turned to the Court politician John Campbell, second Duke of Argyll, instead, who promptly expelled the Neu Party from office and formed a parliament under the Duke of Queensberry once more (Brown and Whatley, 2008: 89).

Yet Tweeddale and his men did not simply return to the ranks of the Country party. Rather, they formed the *Squadrone Volante* during 1705, which was accorded a supplementary presence in parliament, increasing the fluid nature of Scottish party positions. They continued to support incorporating Union and voted for its ratification in 1706–1707. Their

9 Prior to 1704, there had only been two interests in the Scottish parliament: Court and Country, thus the 'New Party' status of the Squadrone.

voting strength was vital to securing the Union, though they were notably compliant with the dictates of the English ministry (Macinnes, 2007: 264, 300). This change in voting behaviour was not, however, an unconditional embrace of Court party politics or desire to join the Court ranks. Rather it represented a changing perspective, spearheaded by the opportunities the new parliament of 1704 had opened up, the commitment to the 1689 Revolution they shared with the Court party, and a realisation that the current political system within the Scottish parliament would never be in their favour (Ferguson, 1964: 93). Many Squadrone members hoped that the transfer of the political stage to Westminster would enable them to ally with the English political groups, overturning Court party dominance in the process (Scott, 1981: 278, Wilkinson, 2002b, Patrick and Whatley, 2007).

However, concern for Scotland's future also played a prominent role in the Squadrone's decisions (Patrick and Whatley, 2007). Their agenda reflects a profound interest to ensure the continuation of certain Scottish liberties and institutions that were deemed particularly important on a national level, but within a specifically pan-Britannic context (Wilkinson, 2002b; Lang, 2004; Young, 2004a, 2006). The Squadrone recognised that an independent Scottish state was no longer viable, and incorporation offered better security than a partial or federal union, which could be abused by the English (Whatley, 2006: 249; Macinnes, 2007: 301; Jackson, 2012: 344). Unlike the Court and Country parties, which were rather fluid in their composition, the Squadrone was much more tight-knit and cohesive. They were firmly connected along both political and familial lines, and they continued to represent a relatively coherent body of politicians within the new British parliament following the Union (Simpson, 1970: 51, 60; Scott, 1981: 278–279; Macinnes, 2007). It is plausible therefore that Squadrone figures would demonstrate shared linguistic behaviour to a greater degree than commissioners from the other party interests within the Scottish parliament, particularly given the frequent political and personal correspondence that would have passed between them.

Scottishness and identity

The complex series of events characterising the lead-up to Union placed conflicting demands upon the political actors participating in its construction, continually informing their perspectives, concerns and ambitions. Alongside national interests, their personal and party allegiances were shaped by loyalty or adherence to religious, sociopolitical and pragmatic identities, exerting multidirectional pressures upon them. Yet largely these facets revolved around the nation whose future they were debating, and 'patriotism now wore a distinctively Scottish guise' (Macinnes, 2007: 260). Modern-day conceptions of identity and nationhood are perhaps slightly premature notions for early eighteenth-century Scotland (Finlay, 1999: 123; Wallace and Kidd, 2018: 194), but it would be simplistic to assume that there was no concept of a Scottish national past (Jackson, 2008: 62). That the principled considerations and shared sense of historical sovereignty unifying various groups and individuals did not leave their mark seems difficult to accept absolutely. Indeed, the competition over these conceptions may have even helped to strengthen the Scots' attachment to their national identity, and while parliamentary members from across the political spectrum were not necessarily bent on achieving a narrowly 'nationalistic' outcome, awareness of Scottish liberties and institutions suggest their central role shaping the debates as they took place.

It is conceivable that these ideological sentiments influenced language use, both across time and within individuals. Whether the use of Scots features in personal correspondence may have responded to the heightened tension and changing political dynamic outlined here, as part of a burgeoning sense of national identity, still remains to be discovered. First, however, a detailed understanding of why the use of Scots features was increasingly uncommon at this time, and concurrently how they may have become targets for identity marking, is outlined in the following chapter, which gives a brief history of Scots up to and including the early eighteenth century.

CHAPTER 2

'A small intermixture of provincial peculiarities may, perhaps, have an agreeable effect': Scots, its history and its status by 1700

Understanding the relation of Scots to English by the time of the Union debates, and the extent to which we can expect Scots features in correspondence from the eighteenth century, requires a discussion of its origins and evolution. Much of this has been discussed in detail in earlier scholarship, and as such, this chapter merely seeks to provide an overview of that narrative. The history of Scots and its development into what some characterise as a fully functioning national language by the sixteenth century (Romaine, 1982; Devitt, 1989; Pollner, 2000; Kirk, 2001), and others consider a language variety on the English dialectal spectrum (Aitken, 1984; Meurman-Solin, 1993; Görlach, 1996; Kniezsa, 1997; Kopaczyk, 2012), has been complex and diverse over the course of several centuries. The historical trajectory of Scots is in many ways one of fluctuations, juxtapositions and U-turns, with contrary developments involving both differentiation and convergence at various points in time, reflecting the multidirectionality of diachronic developments that influenced the language (Meurman-Solin, 2000: 158). The relationship between Scots and Standard English today is similar in many ways to that between the English dialects and the standard, though subtle differences are present (Millar, 2010: 249). Historically, the differences between the two were for a time more pronounced, but either side of their divergence much less distinct.

The thorny question of whether Scots was (and still is) a separate language or a highly discreet dialect of English remains without consensus within either the linguistic community or among its speakers. The idea that a language is a self-contained system of interdependent parts, wholly differentiated from every other language, would clearly exclude Scots from the language category. Yet there are many situations in which distinctions between languages are unclear and these situations are far from 'abnormal' (Millar, 2012: 572). Non-standardised languages often lack definable boundaries – as is the case with Scots, whose distinction from northern varieties of English is blurred and opaque in some senses, and yet categorical in others. A number of contemporary studies have attested to the sharp cross-border differences between Scotland and England, and the linguistic divergence taking place in apparent time (Glauser, 1974; Kay, 1986; Llamas, 2007; Llamas et al., 2009; Llamas, 2010; Watt et al., 2010), though this is matched with parallel change and even convergence in some locations (Maguire, 2015). Just because conventional language descriptions have no way to account for or explain such phenomena, does not automatically exclude these varieties from meriting language status in their own right (Millar, 2012: 577). Accordingly, Scots is referred to as a 'language' henceforth and the historical developments outlined in this chapter may lend support to this interpretation.

What is 'Scots'?

Scots is a West Germanic language derived from Anglian dialects spoken in the northern British kingdom of Northumbria, which spread into Lowland Scotland from the twelfth century. As a result, Scots and southern Standard English have the same origins in Old English and their cognate nature ensures considerable similarities between Scots and northern English varieties especially, both historically and today. Throughout their histories they have retained a large common core of lexical items, syntax and phonology, along with considerable overlap in orthographic practices (Romaine, 1982). Nonetheless, Scots is distinguishable from the southern English varieties that eventually formed the Standard on a number of levels. For instance, the Anglian dialects spoken in the north were considerably influenced by Old Norse during the Viking settlement of northern and eastern England (Corbett et al., 2003: 6), unlike the southern dialects. Moreover, Scots underwent significant growth in function and form in the twelfth century, aided by the burgh system established across lowland Scotland and northern England during this time (Maguire, 2012: 53), and the following centuries saw a flourishing in use across multiple textual mediums and all aspects of social, political and legal life.

Yet this story of exponential growth and linguistic divergence was matched by a subsequent, steady retreat from almost all spheres of written and lived communication in the face of increasing pressure to adopt southern English models and anglicised variants from the late sixteenth century onward. English became preferred in most formal and professional registers, while Scots was relegated to 'the domestic, the familiar, the sentimental, [and] the comic [...] in fact to the ambit of everyday life' (Murison, 1964: 37). Spoken Scots became heteronomous with English by the nineteenth century (Maguire, 2012: 53), giving rise to Scottish Standard English (SSE) – an L2 or 'D2' variety of English spoken in Scotland, especially by 'high' society (Corbett et al., 2003: 11–14; Johnston, 2007: 108–109).

The history of Scots is thus marked by processes of *divergence* and *convergence* to an English norm, whether this was the northern English dialect of the twelfth century or the emerging southern English standard in the seventeenth century (Meurman-Solin, 1997). The early eighteenth century is complex in itself – forming an interesting bridge between the period of intense anglicisation characterising the sixteenth and seventeenth centuries, and the Vernacular Revival which championed written Scots features from the middle of the eighteenth century onward. Scots and their changing fortunes are discussed in the following sections, beginning with their early Germanic origins.

The early beginnings of Scots, 500–1400

Scots has its original roots in the dialects of the Angles, who migrated from north-western Europe c.500–600, and settled from the Thames all the way up to the Forth (Corbett et al., 2003: 4). The founding of the kingdom of Bernicia in Northumberland, AD 547, was fundamental to the early origins of Scots (Murison, 1979), and the variety of English emerging here differed markedly from those in the middle and south of Britain. In the early seventh century, Anglo-Saxon speakers arrived in what is now southern Scotland, extending the reach of the Bernician lands and bringing Old English to South East Scotland in the process (Aitken, 1984). Gaelic dominated north of the Forth, the southwest and the Western Isles, and has left little trace in Scots bar a few vestiges in the lexis (Aitken, 1984: 517; Macafee and Ó Baoill, 1997: 256).

The fortunes of Gaelic were reversed in the aftermath of the Norman Conquest and the anglicising tendencies of Malcolm Canmore, Celtic king of the Scots, who married the English princess Margaret, and welcomed many noblemen fleeing the Normans following 1066 (Murison, 1979; Lass, 1987; Johnston, 1997a: 57). By the twelfth century extensive lands were being granted to Anglo-Norman families, who came largely from the North and East Midlands where the old Danelaw had been, and who brought considerable numbers of Anglo-Scandinavian-speaking retainers with them (Corbett et al., 2003: 7). This introduced the majority of Norse features present in Scots (Millar, 2007: 124–125), which tend to distinguish it most from southern English varieties, including the presence of velar consonants before front vowels where OE had the affricates /tʃ/ and /ʤ/, giving pairs such as *kirk*, 'church', *muckle*, 'much', *dike*, 'ditch' and *brig*, 'bridge' (Murison, 1979: 4; Corbett et al., 2003: 6–7; Maguire, 2012: 65).

Scots developed further through the introduction of the burgh system under King David I during the twelfth century. *Burghs* were fortified towns with trading privileges, and became a hub for tradesmen, artisans and merchants wishing to sell or trade goods, resulting in people from various parts of Scotland, England and overseas territories (notably the Flemish) mixing and interacting within the burghs (Maguire, 2012: 54). The result was an emerging northern Middle English variety, influenced by historical and ongoing contact, which spread throughout Lowland Scotland and became a kind of lingua franca, known originally as 'Inglis' (Templeton, 1973; Aitken, 1984). This would eventually be known as *Scottis* (or Scots), as it differentiated into several distinct dialects (Bugaj, 2004: 21) and developed written communicative functions. Gaelic consequently retreated to the Highland Line over the following centuries in the face of an arising prestige language that carried increasing economic weight (Murison, 1979: 8). The earliest attestation of *literary* Scots is John Barbour's *Bruce* in

1375, and the late fourteenth and early fifteenth centuries saw Scots expand into written domains that had previously been the preserve of Latin (and sometimes French), such as the Acts of Parliament, municipal records, court proceedings and chancery documents (Murison, 1979: 8; Corbett et al., 2003: 8).

During this time Scotland had gradually separated from the English lands south of the Tweed, and this political separation encouraged gradual linguistic divergence and expansion. While the Scottish-English border was permeable to change in both directions, given the areas were geographically contiguous, changes became more localised and certain bundles of features emerged along the border (Murison, 1979; Meurman-Solin, 1993, 1997; Williamson, 2002: 253–254; Maguire, 2012: 54). A major dialect boundary separating Scots and far northern dialects from southern and Midland English dialects developed and still exists today (Maguire, 2015), and such cases of phonological divergence came to be reflected in the spelling erstwhile, although many phonetic changes were only partially and imperfectly captured in the writing of the time. As a result, it was very seldom that a word had a single spelling in Scots – a situation which prevails today (Grant, 1931: xlv; Aitken, 1971: 178; Bann and Corbett, 2015: 18). Unique Scots features arose at multiple linguistic levels, including the morphology, in which derivational and inflectional variants – for example, the use of *-and* for the present participle '-ing' – distinguished the two varieties.

As a result, by the time of the fifteenth century, Scots had developed into a distinct written and spoken medium that was gradually beginning to show early signs of standardisation. The spoken and written variety was structurally and systematically different from southern English on many levels, and it continued towards standardisation in the following centuries.

The rise to standardisation, 1400–1600

Many of the diagnostic traits of Scots were in place by the end of the fifteenth century (Johnston, 1997a: 99), and up until the end of the sixteenth century Scots was the predominant variety of lowland Scotland. It formed the language of the church, Court, legal proceedings, administrative records and literature (McArthur, 1979; Devitt, 1989; Meurman-Solin, 1993; Görlach, 1996; Millar, 2005) and was used by speakers right across the social hierarchy, up to and including the king (Agutter, 1988: 22; Bugaj, 2004: 20). It was considered a suitable written medium for official and high-style literature intended for a wide audience, including legal texts, scientific and scholarly works, prose, poetry, personal writing, sermons and literary tracts, suggesting it was on its way towards standardisation (Romaine, 1982: 57; Bugaj, 2004: 50).

This period of time is considered the 'heyday' of the Scots language (Murison, 1979: 8); it was an all-purpose, fully functional national language, possessing an independent prose and verse tradition, and at this point fairly autonomous from southern English (Lass, 1987: 252). However, the march toward nationwide standardisation was interrupted by several historical events that generated a change in the sociopolitical climate between Scotland and England, leading to increasing convergence with English (Meurman-Solin, 1993: 41, 1997). The sixteenth century thus marked the flourishing of Scots but also its turning point in the direction of convergence, rather than divergence, with southern English.

The Anglicisation of Scots, 1560–1707

Developments from the fifteenth-sixteenth centuries suggest Scots was on its way to becoming a supra-regional and unrestricted means of communication. However, it was displaced at one of the final stages of standardisation – prescriptive codification – by the emergent southern English standard (Bugaj, 2004: 32). Scots concurrently diminished to the status of a regional vernacular, and instead a spoken and written variety dominated by anglicised features emerged. The nature of the two languages as close cousins enabled elements of originally English forms to enter Scots writings without appearing too incongruous (Aitken, 1971: 183–190,

1979: 89; Meurman-Solin, 2000: 166), especially as both were seen to be 'of ane language' (Aitken, 1997: 22). Consequently, the scope broadened to include various English options, akin to the sociolinguistic variation found in contemporary Scots studies (i.e. Macaulay, 1985, 2004; Stuart-Smith, 2004). The greatest impact was realised in the written domain, in which a shift took place from maximal differentiation to greater assimilation, as increasing numbers of English features were incorporated into the variety (Kopaczyk, 2013c: 253).

It was not just a shared linguistic heritage that encouraged this process; the steep reduction in use and applicability of Scots was rooted in the historical events that shaped, interwove and intersected with Scotland as a nation and Scots as a language variety from the mid-sixteenth century onward. The anglicisation of Scots was facilitated by power and prestige: those using English forms in writing and speech were often powerful and high status – whether politically, spiritually or socially (Meurman-Solin, 1997). Given the value of prestige norms is often built upon and increased by the perceived social status or importance of the speakers using it (Milroy, 2012: 572; Sairio and Palander-Collin, 2012: 626), the adoption of the incipient English standard by the Scottish royal family and Scottish elite inevitably bolstered its prestige at the expense of Scots. Four historical developments in particular are argued to be most significant in bringing about this change: the arrival of the printing press, the Reformation of 1560, the Union of the Crowns, and subsequently, the Union of the Parliaments. Each of these factors will be discussed in turn, providing the historical lead-up to the Union of the Parliaments and the state of written Scots by the time of 1700.

The arrival of the printing press

The printing press arrived relatively early in Scotland (c. 1508), but the prohibitive cost of printing and disseminating texts meant works had to reach the widest possible audience to ensure the process was profitable. This meant extending the target audience beyond Scotland's borders to the larger, English-speaking readership, making anglicisation increasingly necessary (Meurman-Solin, 1993: 137–148; Millar, 2012: 253). The original development of printing houses in England helped establish anglicised spelling as the norm, and Scottish-based printers shifted significantly towards English in their practices once the press arrived north of the Tweed (Aitken, 1971: 197; Corbett et al., 2003: 11; Bugaj, 2004: 29), anglicising work as early as 1560 (Robinson, 1983: 71). Printing came with highly restrictive codification practices (Tieken-Boon van Ostade, 1998, 2000: 297), and the practice of 'improving' the text in the direction of English norms became common by the seventeenth century (Meurman-Solin, 2000: 161), creating an industry standard that many adhered to (Templeton, 1973: 7). A general diffusion from public to private texts took place, and Scots orthographic variants were displaced intermittently at varying paces throughout the sixteenth and seventeenth centuries (Aitken, 1979; Bugaj, 2004; van Eyndhoven and Clark, 2019). Yet, even within the text-types favouring Scots, the mingling of Scots and English in texts became universal by the middle of the sixteenth century (Aitken, 1997). The story differed when it came to cheaper forms of print, which often contained works in Scots, especially those concerning local issues or current affairs, poetry and prose covering imaginative and informative subjects (Fox, 2020: 7; van Eyndhoven et al., forthcoming), and local newspapers continued to print extracts in Scots (Donaldson, 1989). Nonetheless, most printed works were anglicised, particularly when intended for the public (van Eyndhoven and Clark, 2019). Thus began the first stage of the retreat of written Scots, which operated in tandem with the religious upheavals characterising the mid-sixteenth century to further the anglicisation trend.

Religious upheavals

A number of dramatic upheavals to the religious landscape of both Scotland and England had the added effect of encouraging the anglicisation of Scots. England was the first to embrace Protestantism in the

British Isles (Bugaj, 2004) and Scotland soon followed suit with the Reformation of 1560, weakening the ties to Catholic France and strengthening the relationship with England religiously, dynastically and linguistically (Murison, 1979; Meurman-Solin, 1993: 45). Scottish reformers seeking to reach English audiences utilised the reach and power of the printing press, leading to their tracts being printed in English (Corbett et al., 2003: 10). In 1579 a law was passed that every Scottish household above a certain income had to possess a bible and psalms book in the vernacular (Templeton, 1973: 7), but translations required time and economic stability, something the Scottish reformers did not have (Millar, 2010: 253). Instead, an English reprint of the Geneva Bible of 1561 became the standard household bible in Lowland Scotland, while Scottish worshippers sang from an English Psalter (Grant, 1931; Templeton, 1973: 7). The net result was that the book that formed the blueprint for moral and spiritual life in Scotland – a cornerstone of most households – was in English, not Scots (Bugaj, 2004: 27).

Scots of all classes increasingly came to regard English as the most suitable medium for religious expression, and consequentially, English became associated with what was solemn, formal and dignified, while Scots slowly began to be associated with the day-to-day, domestic and homely (Murison, 1979: 9; Romaine, 1982: 24). The fact that English was the language of Christianity gave it considerable power and value, plausibly making anglicised variants worthy of imitation (c.f. Sandved, 1981). However, sermons were still usually extemporised in the spoken Scots dialect of the preacher (Murison, 1979; Robinson, 1983: 59) and over time the Kirk and ecclesiastical affairs actually became a site where Scots was preserved. This institution remained autonomous even after the Union of the Parliaments of 1707 took place, and specialised Scots lexis was retained within its field of practice. A similar pattern can be observed within educational institutions and Scots law, which also remained independent from their English counterparts (Dossena, 2005; Kopaczyk, 2013b), as these lexical variations signalled cultural differences that could not be straightforwardly translated into English.

Religious developments thus had the contradictory effect of encouraging anglicisation by increasing the value of English, whilst preserving specific Scots lexical items in the long run. Nonetheless, the anglicising tendency the 1560 Reformation engendered was strengthened considerably by the next large sociopolitical upheaval in Scottish society, the Union of 1603.

The Union of the Crowns, 1603

The Union of the Crowns that took place in 1603 was a personal dynastic union, in which King James VI of Scotland acquired the English throne, to become King James I of England. James VI's court and a number of Scottish gentry moved to London, and a major switch to southern English forms in the King's writings can be observed (Grant, 1931). These factors significantly exacerbated the difference in status between Scots and southern English (Millar, 2010: 253), as the Scottish aristocracy sought to follow the 'polite' conventions of courtly language by anglicising their poetry (Corbett et al., 2003: 11). Already in the late fifteenth and sixteenth centuries the correspondence and private writings of some Scottish writers was notably anglicised, particularly in authors who had connections with London, were resident in England, and/or were sympathisers with English political aims (Templeton, 1973: 7; Aitken, 1997: 1–5). They demonstrated a mixed dialect, in which both Older Scots and Tudor English equivalent forms were available as co-existing options (McClure, 1983: 131; Aitken, 1984: 519). Such tendencies were encouraged by the increase in face-to-face contact between the landed gentry of Scotland and England in the aftermath of the dynastic union (Bugaj, 2004: 30), and the upwardly mobile classes were pushed to imitate the lifestyle, manners and speech of their southern neighbours. Consequently, anglicisation became pertinent to these goals (Dossena, 2005: 56).

As the majority of its functions were ceded to southern English over the course of the seventeenth century, Scots occupied a dwindling literary register that no longer included most topics of intellectual matter or formal registers. Instead, it was increasingly confined to genres not directly intended for the public, including diaries, memoirs and household accounts (Templeton, 1973: 8), or to popular literature, such as ballads, folk tales and poems. By gradually losing status within 'high' domains, Scots acquired even closer associations with domestic, 'rustic' and jocular use (Johnston, 1997a), and some went further still, tarring Scots with the 'barbaric' brush, considering it not just a limit on social mobility but the 'relic of a backward society' (Jones, 1995: 1). Scots did, however, remain the majority spoken variety throughout 1600 (Aitken, 1979: 90), bar the uppermost classes who would come to speak Scottish Standard English (SSE) – a heavily anglicised speech variety that retained certain phonological and lexical items (Lass, 1987; J. Beal, 1997; Millar, 2020). The net result was a widespread change in linguistic tendencies, as anglicisation was taken to new heights by the dynastic union of 1603 (Lass, 1987: 254). The final 'nail in the coffin' was delivered at the turn of the eighteenth century, in the form of the Union of the Parliaments in 1707.

The eighteenth century and the Union of the Parliaments, 1707

By the time of the eighteenth century, the continued use of written Scots was identified largely with conservatives, eccentrics and 'the common people' (Aitken, 1979: 93). No longer seen as the medium for serious prose (Robinson, 1973; Lass, 1987), Scots was largely 'thrust sociolinguistically underground in written domains' (Millar, 2020: 100) after the Union of the Parliaments in 1707. With Scotland's political centre now dissolved into a single, pan-British institution based in Westminster, there was little keeping members of high society in Scotland. Political and economic power irrevocably and irreversibly moved south, and members of the ruling class followed suit. This created greater exposure to English norms, and the subsequent interpretation that the language variety of the English nobility was desirable and 'correct' (Conde-Silvestre and Hernández-Campoy, 2004: 138). The gap between prestige and context-suitability became dramatically wider as negative social perceptions found considerable reinforcement throughout 1700 (Dossena, 2011, 2012a), and certain members of

Scottish society increasingly looked to England as a model for social and intellectual improvement.

This was to take off dramatically during the Age of Politeness – the cultural movement that emerged out of eighteenth-century British society as the result of a rapidly rising middle class with increasing aspirations to social enhancement. This took off with considerable zeal from the middle of the eighteenth century and was marked by a fixation with 'politeness' and correct civic behaviour in everything from etiquette, language, literature, music, architecture and clothing. 'Polite' (i.e. standardised) language usage became a key concern, and saw zealous efforts by a highly organised and influential group of language commentators to establish linguistic conformity and uniformity (see Aitken, 1979; Murison, 1979; Jones, 1995, 1997b; Beal, 1997; Fitzmaurice, 1998 and Görlach, 2001 for further discussion). Scots diminished to a regional vernacular, having 'lost spiritual status at the Reformation, social status at the Union of the Crowns, and political status with the Parliamentary Union' (Murison, 1979: 9), while the functional flexibility of the burgeoning English standard, its high utilitarian value and the economic incentives involved in adopting the metropolitan norm were transparent to aspiring Scots (Millar, 2012: 576, Millar, 2020: 102). A number of influential individuals even overtly articulated their support for a common British language shared among its inhabitants (Dossena, 2005: 60), to facilitate major social, political and economic gain (Jones, 1995: 2).

Class, gender, age and educational background, rather than regional provenance, dictated variation between the two languages (Sorensen and Sorensen, 2000; Millar, 2020: 100), in which 'correct' spelling became associated with intellectual and cultural sophistication, while dialectal and idiosyncratic spellings saw increasing stigmatisation as characteristic of lower education and social standing (Görlach, 1999: 487; Tieken-Boon van Ostade, 2009: 47; Rutkowska and Rössler, 2012: 227). This anglicising tide eventually subsided around the turn of the following century, but left behind a lasting sense of cultural inferiority when it came to the Scots language.

Thus, by 1900 distinctive Scots syntax and graphemes had largely disappeared, although certain spelling practices and lexical items remained, especially in formal tracts tied to the Scottish institutions that remained independent beyond 1707 (Aitken, 1979: 95; Kopaczyk, 2012). Surviving written features that did remain were likely low-level and covert, not necessarily recognised as 'Scottish' within the anglicised variety (Millar, 2012: 75, 2020: 109–112), though there is evidence of several co-existing norms early in the eighteenth century (Millar, 2003: 318), and the continued use of Scots features for particular pragmatic or stylistic effect throughout 1700 and beyond (Templeton, 1973: 8–9; Beal, 1997: 335; Cruickshank, 2012, 2017). It appears lexis tied to a specifically Scots way of life was also difficult to anglicise entirely (Millar, 2013: 322).

There were some dissident voices who spoke against the anglicising trend throughout the eighteenth century (Robinson, 1973; Aitken, 1979; Dossena, 1997, 2005), such as James Buchanan (1716/17–1771) and James Boswell (1740–1795), who noted the desideratum of a 'small intermixture of provincial peculiarities' over attempts to ape 'High English' (Chapman, 1998: 469) and this reaction found outlets in the form of the antiquarian movement espousing the historical pedigree of Scots towards the latter half of the century (see Jones, 1995: 15; Dossena, 2011: 1003–1010). A similar movement took place in the literary world through the *Vernacular Revival* (see Grant, 1931; J. J. Smith, 1996a; Dossena, 1997, 2002, 2005) – a rejuvenation of Scots in popular literature that had its seeds in the Union of 1707, but gained considerable traction over the course of the eighteenth century (MacDonald, 2011: 1012–1021). This saw the rediscovery, reworking and championing of vernacular poetry, ballads and folklore, generating some of the great names of Scottish literature, including Allan Ramsay (1686–1758), Robert Fergusson (1750–1774), Robert Burns (1759–1796) and Sir Walter Scott (1771–1832).

Moreover, it was not the case that all traces of Scots had disappeared in writing by the conclusion of the Union, as a number of previous analyses have indicated (c.f. Millar, 2003, 2013; Cruickshank, 2012, 2017; Kopaczyk, 2012, and for nineteenth-century Scottish correspondence see Dossena, 2012b, 2013, 2019), while contemporary analyses of present-day Scots features also document the survival of many features as well as the formation of new innovations (e.g., Millar, 2018). Indeed, as the futures of the two nations were being debated and ideas around Scotland's position came under intense scrutiny, so too the importance of Scots as a cultural marker emerges very clearly during the years of 1705–1707, both in positive and negative senses (Kopaczyk, 2012: 99; Millar, 2013: 72; Dossena, 2011: 1011).

Scots today and the politicisation of language

Scots today is almost entirely limited to popular literature, whilst it continues to be spoken by comparatively high numbers of Scottish speakers, though for most this has become a situation of *diaglossia*, in which there is no 'Scots' – 'English' dichotomy, but rather a plane of variation with historical features of both varieties from which speakers can select variants (Maguire, 2012: 53; 2015). This diaglossic situation has been termed a 'Scots-SSE bi-polar continuum' (Stuart-Smith, 2004), in which Scots speakers can style-drift or dialect-switch depending on the situation, interlocutor, the level of formality required and their own role or positioning within those contexts, all encompassed within the multi-dimensional, sociolinguistic variation space in which they are operating (Dossena, 2002: 104, see also, in particular, Aitken, 1984; Maguire, 2012: 3). Reflecting back on the eighteenth century, it seems plausible that Scottish writers were similarly able to shift depending on audience, context and style. Drawing on the totality of linguistic resources available within their linguistic repertoire could enable them to fulfil particular goals, whilst recognising the constraints of the social and epistolary context. The specific time period under investigation (1689–1745) accordingly forms a bridge not only between Older and Modern Scots, but between its long period of anglicisation, and the bipolar linguistic continuum present today.

Concluding remarks

Reflecting on the complex, multi-directional diachronic developments characterising the history of Scots, it is fair to say Scots has seen dramatic changes in fortune, reach and usability within a window of slightly more than four hundred years. This extensive history makes a number of factors clear in particular. Firstly, Scots and English undoubtedly share various features as a result of their common origin, especially when it comes to northern English. Searching for 'Scots' in early eighteenth-century correspondence therefore must consider that many features cannot be clearly delineated from varieties across the border. Secondly, Scots clearly had a literary as well as spoken history within Lowland Scotland, and consequently our writers are likely to have been aware of and familiar with written Scots in some shape or form. Thirdly, given the long period of anglicisation prior to the eighteenth century, we can expect very low frequencies of Scots features restricted to certain graphemes and lexical items (c.f. Millar, 2012, 2020: 109–112). This is particularly likely considering we are investigating writings produced by the top layer of Scottish society – the group of language users most under pressure to anglicise their writing. Finally, the developments that took place during and beyond 1707 suggest that a connection between the use of Scots features and political identity-marking is feasible, at least for some members of society.

These assumptions can inform and guide perspectives into what written Scots usage may have looked like by this time, but a detailed examination has yet to take place. The early eighteenth century, in particular, falls into a curious gap in Scots research, perhaps because of the pervasive narrative of anglicisation characterising descriptive histories of Scots. Donaldson (1989: 9) noted the 'yawning gulf in the textbooks between James VI and Allan Ramsay', highlighting the dearth of work in the two centuries following the dynastic union of 1603, while Beal (1997) has suggested that the healthy amount of attention Older Scots has received is not matched by research into the modern Scots period. Indeed, Meurman-Solin's (1993: 47) call thirty years ago for research into the eighteenth century, has only been partially fulfilled. It has received comparatively less attention than earlier time periods, and while valuable contributions have been made (see for example MacQueen, 1957; Donaldson, 1989; J. J. Smith, 1996a; Beal, 1997; Corbett et al., 2003; Dossena, 2005; Cruickshank, 2012, 2017 and Corbett, 2013, and doubtless several others who would deserve mention here), most of their analyses focus upon descriptive accounts of the *Age of*

Politeness or the *Vernacular Revival*. This cannot tell us much about written Scots at the beginning of this time period, as the Scots produced during the Vernacular Revival for example looked back to Older Scots models – a time period no longer congruous with the eighteenth century.

Moreover, this time period has seen little in the way of quantitative work. While Cruickshank (2012, 2017) and Elder (2022) have undertaken valuable analyses involving a single individual, this approach has not yet been applied to a larger group of writers utilising the quantitative power of statistical modelling. Research has no doubt been limited by a lack of available corpus material, but as a result, where and how Scots persisted across multiple writers in the eighteenth century has not been investigated. Without attempting such an analysis, knowledge of the time period remains piecemeal and isolated. That Scots features could be indexical markers of sociopolitical identities in the lead-up to one of the most contentious political events in Scottish history is both intuitive and tantalising, and this book aims to explore this promising historical event, whilst shedding greater light on what written Scots did look like at the turn of the eighteenth century.

CHAPTER 3

'Using the present to explain the past?' Historical sociolinguistics, the Three Waves and political identity as tools for diachronic corpus investigation

As the previous chapter has made clear, written Scots during the early eighteenth century has the potential to demonstrate promising links to the political situation that was developing during the Union debates. It has also indicated the potential for Scots usage to have become highly individualised and sensitive to personally driven influences, such as the correspondent or stylistic desires. This suggests the value of exploring this time period through the lens of political identity and other extralinguistic factors and how they may have influenced variation observed within a corpus of politically active writers both collectively and individually. Such an approach connects theoretically and methodologically to the field and framework of *Historical Sociolinguistics*, and this chapter will elaborate upon its theoretical underpinnings to demonstrate their relevance to the research questions being explored.

The application of the sociolinguistic toolkit has been able to bring fresh insights into *diachronic* change, but the relationship between written and spoken data derived from diachronic and synchronic settings, respectively, is not uniform or parallel (Milroy and Gordon, 2003: 177). As one example, historically most writers do not write solely in dialect (except perhaps in some of the earliest surviving texts), but instead aim to meet certain imagined standards as being required by the text genre, a situation we still have today (Görlach, 1999: 149–150). There will be hidden constraints operating within letters for instance, such as acceptable forms of address and layout, formulaic constructions, politeness expressions and subscriptions, all of which impose upon the linguistic freedom of the text, and focus the mind of the writer. Consequently, the possible absence of Scots in political correspondence may have as much to do with politeness conventions as personal motivations. In addition, trying to map modern sociolinguistic concepts onto historical data, or 'using the present to explain the past' (Labov, 1994: 21–23) can be erroneous and misleading when applied in a blanket, one-to-one approach (Auer, Schreier and Watts, 2015: 285), and risks 'ideational anachronism' (Bergs, 2012: 84).

Yet correspondence and ego-documents in general can play a vital role in uncovering historical insights into socially constrained variation (Dossena, 2019: 80), and have often been seen as the most suitable material for historical sociolinguistic research, given the detailed personal information frequently available (Nevalainen and Raumolin-Brunberg, 1996: 39–54; Hernández-Campoy and Conde-Silvestre, 2005: 110, 2015: 17; Conde-Silvestre, 2007: 51–52; Palander-Collin et al., 2009). Analyses into the medium have demonstrated the validity of sociolinguistic 'universals' including prestige, changes from above and below, the s-curve of language change, and the importance of traditional sociolinguistic factors such as age, social status, gender and mobility over social, geographical and temporal spaces (e.g. Nevalainen and Raumolin-Brunberg, 1996, 2003; Conde-Silvestre, 2007; Hernández-Campoy and Schilling, 2012). Moreover, correspondence is well-placed for reconstructing participant relationships, plausibly accounting for individuals' stylistic choices. Letters are after all intended as exchanges of dialogue, albeit in written form, reflecting the personal, communicative style of an author and how they navigate social and contextual influences (Hernández-Campoy and Conde-Silvestre, 2015: 17–20).

Writers can utilise the variation available to them to infer or present particular personae, identities or desires, as a powerful means of self-representation, and this art of self-fashioning one's identity or identity performance (c.f. Greenblatt, 1980) is considered to be an inherent aspect of ego-documents (Dekker, 2002). Equally, pragmatic goals and intentions can shape variation within correspondence, for example by using modality or self-reference to influence recipients (Nurmi, 2013; Włodarczyk, 2013), yet writers also frequently recognise and converge to supraregional writing practices (Vandenbussche, 2002; Nordlund, 2007; Rutten and van der Wal, 2011). This suggests the hybrid nature of correspondence – while letters are likely to foster increased use of the vernacular (Biber, 1995), they will also show typical letter-writing characteristics, like epistolary formulae

(Martineau, 2013; van der Wal and Rutten, 2013: 4), which can severely circumscribe the freedom of linguistic choice and the variability available to the writer (Elspaß, 2012b: 158).

However, the complementary insights of corpus-related investigation utilising statistical approaches, and a qualitative approach informed by a pragmaphilological engagement with the historical ecology in which writers were operating (Millar, 2012: 58; Jucker and Kopaczyk, 2013: 22), whilst drawing on insights obtained from each successive 'wave' of sociolinguistic investigation, can generate research that is both data-driven and sensitive to the intricacies of the diachronic variation being explored. This is the approach taken here, and in the following section, a brief overview of the three major 'waves' in sociolinguistic research, and their application to historical data, will be discussed. This will introduce the multifaceted theoretical perspective as this applies to different components of the investigation. This is followed by case studies that link to specific methods, concepts and themes of this book, including eighteenth-century correspondence, Early Modern Scots, and both historical and contemporary studies looking at the relationship between politics and variation.

The 'Three Waves' of sociolinguistic research

Over the course of its development, three major approaches have developed successively within the field of sociolinguistics to analyse variation. These have been labelled by Eckert (2012) as the *First, Second* and *Third Wave*, sometimes renamed as the *Attention to Speech, Audience Design* and *Speaker Design* models, respectively. They have also been applied in various guises to numerous sociohistorical instances of diachronic change over the past forty years, underscoring the continuity between modern-day and historical occurrences of language variation and change. The latest development, the 'Third Wave' of sociolinguistic research, has seen growing attention within historical sociolinguistics as new, or previously unexplored resources have enabled fine-grained analyses on the level of the individual, through the lens of socially constructed meaning

(A. Auer, 2015; Conde-Silvestre, 2016; Hernández-Campoy, 2016) and persona or identity management (Hernández-Campoy and García-Vidal, 2018). Nonetheless, there are insights to be gained from each model, and all three can make valid contributions to historical variation. Eckert (2016: 11) suggests that rather than viewing each wave as a strictly separate, circumscribed theoretical structure, they should rather be seen as conceptual models that work in tandem, complementing one another and collectively contributing to a holistic understanding of the social processes behind language variation. Their main tenets are briefly summarised below.

The First Wave or attention to speech

The *First Wave* of sociolinguistic research grew out of a structuralist study of sound change and is primarily concerned with the influence of major macro-sociological categories in structuring social interaction. Categories of speakers are defined by the analyst, based on perceived groups thought to exist within the speech community and in the minds of the language users, such as class or gender. Such groups are recognised by speakers, influencing their language behaviour according to where they slot into the macro-social structure. It assumes that speech and stylistic repertoire are 'determined' by these categories, leading to linguistic diffusion and change over time which can be captured by quantitative methodologies (Hernández-Campoy and Conde-Silvestre, 2015: 14; Eckert, 2016: 68). Firmly associated with the original Labovian methodology (c.f. Labov, 1962, 1966b), the wealth of research that has since followed has found robust and repeated patterns of variation within aggregate data, correlating with socioeconomic class, gender, ethnicity and age, but also the formality and amount of attention required by the social setting (Wolfram, 1969; Trudgill, 1974; Labov, 2006).

While first wave research has proven very effective at documenting large-scale, population-wide sociolinguistic trends through quantitative methods, and continues to do so, it has also been criticised for viewing speakers as bundles of demographic characteristics, and passively placing them within a structure that determines their access to the standard language and their exposure to linguistic change. Within such a mechanically based framework, social agency is largely ignored or limited to self-correction which speakers can employ to greater or lesser degrees depending on their social background, rather than being the result of a choice between socially meaningful forms (Eckert, 2012: 89). The broad-based approach of such studies also comes at the expense of capturing the more nuanced and flexible kinds of identity relations that often arise in local and individual contexts. Quantitative approaches alone cannot provide the full picture, and sociolinguistic studies have increasingly recognised their inherent limitations (O'Connor et al., 2008: 121). Frequency is just one dimension of relevance to the study of social meaning (Moore and Podesva, 2009), and revealing insights can be gleaned from other aspects (Labov, 1966b; Sankoff, 1980: 51–52; Milroy and Gordon, 2003: 28–29).

Notwithstanding these shortcomings, insights from first wave studies have continued to be invaluable – in particular their coverage and replicability have allowed for many cross-linguistic, geographical and social comparisons within the field. Their use of statistical models to explore variable language behaviour has provided robust perspectives into the multiple factors capable of influencing speakers, enabling research to explain or capture the majority of the variation in the data. While detail is naturally lost in an approach that aggregates the linguistic behaviour of language users, first wave studies can provide an overview of the linguistic topography at large and can reflect important ideologies within the speech community.

Historical sociolinguistic research has also been able to apply the First Wave framework successfully to glean insights into diachronic language change (see for instance Nevalainen and Raumolin-Brunberg, 1994; Raumolin-Brunberg and Nevalainen, 1994; Raumolin-Brunberg, 1996b). Especially research on English in the eighteenth and nineteenth centuries has uncovered some of the prevalent social evaluations that arose in reaction to linguistic change and variable language norms, including notions of prestige and correctness (Jones, 1995, 2010; Tieken-Boon van Ostade, 1996; J. Beal, 2004; Fitzmaurice, 2004; Dossena, 2005; J. C. Beal and Sturiale, 2012). Research on Older Scots meanwhile has demonstrated cogent links between Scots or anglicised features and different social factors (Devitt,

1989; Meurman-Solin, 1993, 1994, 1995, 1997; van Eyndhoven and Clark, 2019), though eighteenth-century Scots has seen much less in the way of quantitative analyses (although see van Eyndhoven, 2018, 2021 and van Eyndhoven et al., forthcoming).

Accordingly, a First Wave approach is undertaken in the quantitative analysis presented in Chapter 6, exploring the possible role of political factors in conditioning variation across the political community at large. However, this only provides a 'top-down' perspective of the data. The complementary micro-social analysis will thus identify to what degree individuals fit into the wider picture cast by the quantitative analysis, and whether they demonstrate sensitivity to micro-social influencing factors, such as *Audience Design*.

The Second Wave or audience design

Second Wave analyses (e.g., Milroy, 1980, 1987; Bell, 1984; Rickford, 1986; Coupland and Giles, 1988; Giles et al., 1991; Meyerhoff, 2002; Purnell, 2009) identified and began to address the need for a micro-level focus in variationist study. These sought to unpick the broad social classifications characterising the First Wave, utilising ethnographic methods to focus on local categories and the social configurations of speaker networks. These configurations in turn accumulate into the social classifications and macro-social patterns of the First Wave through their repetition and consistency; in other words, social dynamics rooted in local practices and communities give rise to and model linguistic variation (Eckert, 2016: 69). Emphasis shifted onto day-to-day social interaction and the covert value of the vernacular, in which it was seen as an expression rather than product of local or class identity (Eckert, 2012: 91).

Often labelled 'Audience Design' (c.f. Bell, 1984), this developed from early social psychological work in *Speech Accommodation Theory* (Giles, 1973; Giles and Powesland, 1975), and demonstrated that speakers choose speech styles based on their orientation and attitude towards the interlocutor. Speakers can thus adapt or accommodate their speech in response to their interlocutors, to bring their usage patterns closer to the target variety when the speaker desires the interlocutor's social approval (Labov, 1990), or conversely to increase the difference between them (Giles, 1984; Giles et al., 1987, 1991; Coupland and Giles, 1988; Niedzielski and Giles, 1996), aligning themselves with a positive in-group identity that differs from the speaker (Thakerar et al., 1982; Auer and Hinskens, 2005; Purnell, 2009; Babel, 2010). This often occurs along dialect dimensions in which the use of the vernacular corresponds with in-group convergence or out-group divergence (Llamas et al., 2009: 385–386), but is also influenced by the speaker's pragmatic goals (Du Bois, 2007), and their ability to adapt, subject to their repertoire and a range of contextual factors.

Audience members do not necessarily have to be present – speakers are able to shift their variation in response to an imagined or expected audience in much the same way. This is particularly pertinent when we consider written correspondence, in which the interlocutor is presumably never physically present, but whom we might expect the writer to have in mind when constructing their letter. Within historical sociolinguistics, Audience Design has been shown to play a significant role: the level of politeness demonstrated by writers was often moderated by the relative power and social distance between the writer and receiver, and the need to reduce any imposition involved in performing a face-threatening act (Raumolin-Brunberg, 1996a: 14; Dossena, 2019: 71). Considering the accommodative patterns identified in previous historical Scots research (Meurman-Solin, 1993; Cruickshank, 2012, 2017), the role of the audience is promising, as are other, related Second Wave concepts such as *Social Identity Theory* [SIT] and *Communities of Practice* [CofP].

SIT posits that speakers are motivated to maintain a distinct and positive social identity. This identity is not fixed, as speakers' self-evaluation is often fluid and fluctuates across in-group and out-group categorisations negotiated during the interaction. This allows them to evoke, modify, define, challenge or support aspects of the persona they project, creating the desired self-image and maintain a positive appraisal of their in-group membership (Turner and Brown, 1978; Ting-Toomey, 1999: 40; Turner, 1999; Blackledge and Pavlenko, 2001: 244). Speakers may thus react to each other as representative members of different social groups rather than as individuals, and are perceived as such (Thakerar et al., 1982: 214).

Interpersonal relationships and individual characteristics play a role alongside these group memberships, creating an *interindividual-intergroup* continuum (Tajfel and Turner, 1979), in which each pole is not operating in isolation, but rather is correlated across the stratum of variation and salience.

Such individual considerations were likely pertinent to the politicians investigated here, given the need for alliances, influence and patronage, yet they also belonged to a particular group within the parliament and within the Scottish nation at large. In this respect, the commissioners may have even formed a *Community of Practice* or *CofP* (Kopaczyk and Jucker, 2013) within their institution. The 'community' is constituted through group membership embedded in complex social relations, which are enacted and reinforced through mutual engagement in an endeavour or jointly negotiated enterprise, shared activities, routines and feedback, a communal repertoire of resources, and collective practices which can include specific lexis or language use (Eckert and McConnell-Ginet, 1992: 464; Wenger, 1998: 72–85; Tieken-Boon van Ostade, 2000; Meyerhoff, 2002; Kopaczyk and Jucker, 2013: 6). Association is thus based around linguistic practice that is used to construct local social meanings (Milroy and Gordon, 2003: 19), facilitating variation and change in the process. Such communities do not have to be cohesive, for while individual members are known to each other, a CofP is 'neither a haven of togetherness nor an island of intimacy insulated from political and social relations. Disagreement, challenges and competition can all be forms of participation' (Wenger, 1998: 76), and it is this participation itself that engenders the emergence of shared linguistic behaviour.

Such attributes are central to the political community within the Scottish parliament – their jointly negotiated enterprise was the deliberating, debating and passing the Union agreement of 1707, and they were certainly no haven of togetherness, considering the opposing opinions that were often vocally aired. They may have sought to highlight or downplay their group and community membership depending on context, drawing on political, social and linguistic resources in the process, and the role of group and interpersonal identity relationships is central to both the top-down and close-up analyses of groups, individuals and their letters.

However, while the social relationships occurring in a particular time and place are central to understanding sociolinguistic change in society

(Millar, 2012: 45), they cannot always be full explanations in themselves. We must allow for other, unknown factors to play their role, such as motivations specific to the individual speaker themselves. Third Wave analyses have built upon this, viewing social categories as emergent through interaction rather than being pre-determined (Eckert, 2012, 2016: 69). Utilising insights from the Third Wave can thus add a final layer of nuance and perspective to variation in the data, and plays an important role in answering the main theoretical aims of this analysis, namely, the role of politico-national identity in determining variation in Scots.

The Third Wave and stylistic variation

The *Third Wave* (Agha, 2003; Moore, 2004; Schilling-Estes, 2004; Llamas, 2007; Podesva, 2007, 2011; Moore and Podesva, 2009) reflects a shift from the deterministic and system-oriented approaches characterising the First and Second Waves, in which focus was largely on inter-speaker variation and how it reflected collective social identities, towards a more constructivist and speaker-oriented one that views language as individual performance and practice, with a consequent emphasis on investigating intra-writer variation (Bucholtz and Hall, 2005, Bucholtz, 2010; Hernández-Campoy and Cutillas-Espinosa, 2012: 7, Hernández-Campoy and Conde-Silvestre, 2015: 14). At its core, this framework concentrates upon the creation and enactment of social personae, identities or meaning through interaction, which in turn accumulate into patterns of change over time and linguistic variation (Eckert and Rickford, 2001: 70; Schilling-Estes, 2002; Eckert, 2016: 70). Variability in language use is not just the result of external influences, but also the individuality, stance, performativity and agency of the speaker as they navigate communicative situations whilst negotiating and maintaining their personal and interpersonal social identity and authenticity (Johnstone, 2000: 72–73; Moore and Podesva, 2009; Eckert, 2012: 90; A. Auer, 2015: 134; Hernández-Campoy and Conde-Silvestre, 2015: 15). Variation is thus not the incidental fallout of forces based within the broad social categories of society, rather, it is dynamic, both constrained by, but also contributing to, macro-social patterns (Eckert, 2016: 68).

Linguistic variables are a resource, rather than a product or reaction, of social differentiation that individuals can exploit in a systematic way to add multiple layers of social meaning to their linguistic behaviour and shape their social identity (Mendoza-Denton, 1997: 75; Eckert, 2000, 2012: 93, 2016; Watts, 2015: 8). Through such behaviour they can enact dialect or social personae with sufficient uniformity within different social categories to create numerical patterns of stratification (Coupland, 2001: 198), accumulating into a recognisable style and social domain. Concurrently listeners and speakers recognise certain speech patterns as affiliated with certain groups of speakers on regional, social or individual terms (Purnell et al., 2009: 333), and they are able to align themselves with these recognised groups through indexing stereotypical social personae (Agha, 2005: 39–40). This creates a continual feedback loop, in which macrosocial patterns of variation are both the product of, and a constraint on, the complex system of meaning (Schilling-Estes, 2002: 389; Eckert, 2016: 68). Again, this suggests the value of recognising the inherent connections between the three frameworks, which are operating within the same boundaries.

Individuals are thus agents of their own stylistic behaviour, employing bundles of variation across multiple levels synergistically (Campbell-Kibler et al., 2006; Moore and Podesva, 2009: 448–449) to position themselves and others according to their macro-social relationships, as well as fashioning identities, and negotiating pragmatic and social meanings within interaction (Podesva, 2006; P. Auer, 2007; A. Auer, Schreier, and Watts, 2015: 278). Third Wave methodologies have been successfully transferred to grammatical variables in diachronic analyses, especially in personal writing (Conde-Silvestre and Hernández-Campoy, 2013; A. Auer, 2015; Hernández-Campoy and García-Vidal, 2018; Dossena, 2019). Historical identities were not homogenous after all, and when these collide with language in contested contexts, the nature and negotiation of sociolinguistic identities come to the fore, even within the realm of writing (Hill, 1999; Blackledge and Pavlenko, 2001). While the early eighteenth century may only be the beginnings of a contested situation for both Scots and Scottish identity, the political and linguistic situation was certainly heightened and complex by this time period as Chapters 1 and 2 have indicated, in which the linguistic negotiation or construction of sociolinguistic identities within the political sphere and variation space may be observed.

Identities are multifaceted, encompassing macro-level demographic categories, local, ethnographically derived cultural positions, and temporary, interactionally specific stances and participant roles (Bucholtz and Hall, 2005: 592), creating an inherent link between macro and micro-scale patterns of variation (Bucholtz and Hall, 2005: 22). Indeed, Blackledge and Pavlenko (2001: 244–245) note the fallacy of assuming that rigid categories exist in the minds of individuals, given the fluidity within which identity and group-membership can operate and change over time. Language users can be part of multiple communities and even these communities themselves are not necessarily homogeneous (Gal, 1979; Nicols, 1983). Rather, identity should be seen as an emanate, fluid, discursive phenomenon that emerges and is constructed in linguistic interaction (Gumperz, 1982; Le Page, 1985; Coupland, 2007; Moore and Podesva, 2009), and speakers can utilise features in ideological and indexical moves that characterise certain groups, to invoke ways of belonging to that population (Kiesling, 2001; Podesva, 2011; Eckert, 2012: 94), with such moves usually linked to a desire to assert group membership (Bucholtz and Hall, 2005: 18). This construction does not have to be overt – certain linguistic forms may point to social meanings without necessarily referring to them (Johnstone, 2010: 29), but this process highlights their synergistic relationship; as linguistic forms cannot exist outside of interactional contexts, the two need to work in tandem in order for identity to be performed and for linguistic features to index identity (Williams, 1992; Johnstone, 1996; Tabouret-Keller, 1997; Blackledge and Pavlenko, 2001: 244).

These considerations are particularly pertinent to the Scottish politicians being investigated here, given that they were part of multiple groups, played multiple roles and professed multiple identities simultaneously. They were sensitive both to local political and social machinations that could further their dominance at home, but also to the demands of the Court, Crown and English elite, recognising that favour and influence at Whitehall would aggrandise their positions in Scotland or indeed in London (Szechi, 2002: 46). Alongside this, they had their faith, potential

Jacobite loyalties and domestic affairs to consider as well. These demands could forge particular sociopolitical connections or identities that were not always congruous with one another. Linguistic groups are not necessarily isomorphous with culturally or socially conceived ethnic groups after all (Le Page, 1985; Giampapa, 2001), and it is plausible that these Scotsmen may similarly have felt part of different communities at different times, depending on a host of factors.

How different identity categories may have influenced variable Scots use, and conversely whether Scots had become indexical of these identities in the process, is yet to be explored. Its use may have already been indexed to 'Scottishness' or some other political or ideological agenda or construct, but 'agency does not equal awareness' and personae may not necessarily be entirely intentional (Eckert, 2016: 78–79). Yet contemporary research has shown that speakers' perceptions of the social meaning of variables can operate at a very unconscious level, even if they are stereotypes (Hay and Drager, 2010) or recent sound changes in progress (D'Onofrio, 2015). Scots was likely on the way to being *enregistered* (Agha, 2003) – considering the *Age of Politeness* and especially the *Vernacular Revival* movements characterising the later eighteenth century. Considering that material such as grammars and dictionaries, dialect literature and metalinguistic commentary was scarce at the beginning of the century, whether in historical, linguistic or literary research, it is likely that the enregisterment process was in its embryonic stages in 1707. Consequently, the influence of political identity remains unknown. A multi-dimensional approach that considers a range of plausible influences, derived from all the three waves of sociolinguistic investigation, is particularly beneficial in addressing this possibility therefore.

Combining the waves

To capture synchronic and diachronic variation holistically, we need to integrate practices and frameworks from across the methodological spectrum, recognising that the links between local stylistic practice and overarching social categories flow in both directions, causing variation within macro and micro-social scales (Eckert, 2016: 81–82). Correlating results taken from the population at large with more qualitative judgments of how individuals construct meanings in social practice enables both a 'bird's eye' and 'worm's eye' view of variation (Elspaß, 2007: 4). Ultimately, the combination of broad oversight with detailed micro-level analysis can allow us to identify community-based norms and how individual practice fits within, contributes to, and shapes these norms (Podesva et al., 2008: 82; Moore and Podesva, 2009; Dossena, 2019: 67–69), and previous studies have already done so successfully (Milroy and Milroy, 1992; Chambers, 1995; Raumolin-Brunberg, 1996a; Hernández-Campoy and Conde-Silvestre, 1999, 2005; Hernández-Campoy and Conde-Silvestre, 2015; Conde-Silvestre and Hernández-Campoy, 2004).

Accordingly, I utilise this multifaceted approach, firstly by drawing from the First Wave paradigm to aggregate results across the pool of Scottish politicians in examining the influence of extralinguistic factors on Scots frequencies, in Chapters 5 and 6, respectively.

Secondly, Chapter 7 applies both a Second and Third Wave methodology in observing intra-writer variation in selected individuals, considering audience and accommodative practices, as well as stylistic influences, on observed variation. Overarchingly, however, these analyses are also informed by the interaction between political identity and variation in the eighteenth century. The following sections will thus briefly examine previous research and their insights in these areas, respectively.

Variation and politics in the eighteenth century

In terms of sociolinguistic research on eighteenth-century Scottish correspondence, detailed investigations have been fairly thin on the ground. There are a few notable exceptions, including Cruickshank's (2011, 2012, 2013, 2017) analyses of the letters of Lord Fife, and Elder's (2022) investigations of correspondence produced by the Countess of Mar and her family. Late Modern English has seen comparatively more attention, and the interaction between historical correspondence and politics has been explored in detail by Fitzmaurice (1998, 2000, 2007). Comparing English letter-writing practices across elite writers on different social levels, Fitzmaurice (2015) found that variation very much depended on the power relations between the correspondents in question. While most members did observe 'standard' grammatical practices, particularly concerning conventional epistolary patterns, all of them utilised variable language norms to maintain a relationship with their interlocutor, as well as to perform a particular persona and identity. In doing so, they reflected their belonging to the English aristocratic community, their stylistic variation conveying information about their self-positioning within the complex political and social hierarchies structuring the network (Fitzmaurice, 2015: 179).

In several aspects, the political figures being investigated here share similarities with these English aristocrats, although as a sociopolitical layer of Scottish society they are not as defined as the English networks. In general, however, the influence of political identity on language behaviour has received comparatively less attention in historical sociolinguistic analyses. For this, we must turn to contemporary research, which may provide additional scaffolding through which to explore variable Scots use.

Politics, identity and variation

Studies examining the interaction between politics and language have identified tangible links between the overt and covert language choices of political individuals and their specific goals. Such research has often focused on the ways in which the discourse of politicians creates a recognisable communicative style to accomplish certain types of governance (e.g. Wodak, 1989; O'Connor et al., 2008). This is an obvious target for audience-design, accommodative desires and style shifting, given that a positive evaluation is a necessity for political success (Beebe and Giles, 1984; Moosmüller, 1989). Political performances accordingly become sites for the construction and emergence of particular public identities within parties or individuals, utilising discourse features and their associations. Features are used as a means of indexing collectivity and connectivity (Wales, 1996: 62; Kirkham and Moore, 2016: 102–103), or to index politicians' stake within the party they represent, thereby expressing solidarity, group identity and leadership of that sociopolitical group (Fetzer and Bull, 2012: 132). Indeed, the identity of the political party has come to play a major role in investigations of sociophonetic variation among politicians, with previous research (Pearce, 2001, 2005; Hall-Lew et al., 2010, 2012, 2017; Kirkham and Moore, 2016) highlighting the potentially rich social information that it can convey. Party identity is after all generally more central to a politician's public image and the composition of their social networks than the average individual (McGraw, 2003), and identity can be negotiated and mediated in response to audience design through both phonological and lexical indexes.

Such behaviour can be deliberate – politicians may seek to use vernacular variants to index solidarity or familiarity (Giles and Powesland, 1975; Dittmar et al., 1986; Schlobinski, 1987; Hall-Lew et al., 2012), or standard variants which are most often associated with intelligence, competence and status-related traits (Moosmüller, 1989; Purnell et al., 2009; Hall-Lew et al., 2010; Podesva et al., 2015). This underscores the performative aspect of political speech – regional or supra-regional features do not necessarily have to be interpreted as characteristic of the speaker's language; politicians may be choosing variants in the hope of 'satisfying' their audience, a characteristic that has been found in correspondence too (Rutkowska and Rössler, 2012: 217). Similarly, the dichotomy between indexing familiarity with close recipients, and the prestige (and ergo politeness) of the arising southern English standard was a plausible negotiation being faced by politicians within elite Scottish society.

Several studies have looked specifically at Scottish members of the UK parliament or political broadcasters working in the Westminster Village (Carr and Brulard, 2006; Hall-Lew et al., 2017), where Received Pronunciation (RP) is still a normative accent. Earlier work has often noted that Scottish politicians, lawyers and broadcasters frequently have anglicised speech, plausibly influenced by convergence to southern English norms (Romaine, 1980; Scobbie et al., 1999). Carr and Brulard (2006, 2013), for instance, examined political speeches and interviews of Scottish politicians and journalists, and found a range of accent modifications among speakers; some were consistently SSE, whereas others were near-RP in speech style. Hall-Lew et al.'s (2017) findings suggested that accommodation observed by Scottish MPs was not the *direct* result of national identity, but rather was indirectly indexed through political party identity. MPs in each respective party converged to a party baseline value, which may be correlated with either a middle-class, conservative persona or conversely a rejection of this institutionalised identity (Johnston, 1984; Romaine, 1985). This situation mirrors in some ways the linguistic environment of the Scottish politicians in 1700 – while they all had exposure and familiarity with southern Standard English norms as a result of their position and mobility within society, their motivations to anglicise their writing could also be dependent upon the conception of their role as representatives of those particular groups.

Finally, links between Scottish political identity and *written* Scots were explored by Shoemark et al. (2017) and Shoemark, Kirby and Goldwater (2017). They examined the use of Scots words and spellings on Twitter during the Scottish Independence Referendum of 2014, given political surveys have indicated a relationship between a sense of Scottish identity and voting decisions in the 2014 Referendum. Moreover, research by Llamas et al. (2009) on Scottish and English interlocutors within the linguistically fluid border region of Scotland and England has indicated the strong and persistent speaker awareness of both the Scots-English divide, and of salient Scots or SSE variants as indexical of national identity. The well-established orthographic standards operating in most of today's languages mean the use of non-standard variants is marked, often deliberate (de Beaugrande, 2006: 43), and constitutes a 'powerful expressive resource' (Jaffe, 2000: 498). Shoemark et al. (2017) investigated the intuitive hypothesis that those who support independence would be more likely to use Scots features than opponents. Looking at pro and anti-independence users on Twitter, their first study confirmed this relationship, though the audience added a further layer of influence.

In their follow-up study, Shoemark et al. (2017) found this was largely dependent on the topic being tweeted about. topic has been found to influence levels of Scots usage on Twitter (Tatman, 2015), and drawing on explanations by Pavalanathan and Eisenstein (2015), Shoemark et al. (2017: 66) suggest that these users may use Scots to stake claims to local authenticity, using features associated with Scottish identity for a topic salient to Scotland, with an audience for which this has strong currency. These findings have clear parallels with the political situation in the early eighteenth century, though considering the fluid and amorphous nature of the Scottish parliament as Chapter 1 has made clear, it is plausible that Scots use was more narrowly confined to certain sub-groups of writers, who utilised Scots features to achieve particular pragmatic or ideological ends.

Extrapolating from the insights these contemporary analyses offer, the question is thus whether political factors similarly act as an informative and valuable social category in the Scottish historical setting. Of course, political parties and their platforms were still in the process of emerging during the eighteenth century, and thus their 'identity' might be more strongly linked to the familial connections and shared ambitions characterising each party rather than the collective label of the party itself. Nonetheless, these studies suggest its importance in creating shared values and membership, and similar concerns may have been active, in which it was beneficial for politicians to foreground certain identities depending on their recipient or personal goals. Accordingly, by applying the frameworks of all three waves of sociolinguistic enquiry, and recognising the inherent links between political identities and linguistic variation repeatedly found in sociolinguistic research, the previously unexplored and complex situation characterising Scotland during the Union debates can be examined through the lens of political change.

CHAPTER 4

From documents to database: The identification, digitisation and compilation of archival material into a text-searchable novel corpus

Before we can examine the results and the analytical findings, a brief overview of the methodological pathway to constructing a novel corpus, and searching it for Scots language features, is required. The written medium used, political figures and their writings, the semi-automatic digitisation of their letters, corpus building process, and the creation of a Scots feature list are all discussed, providing context to what follows, as well as suggesting a plausible route for navigating eighteenth-century Scottish correspondence as well as historical manuscript material more generally.

Correspondence: The text type

The benefits of using correspondence for sociolinguistic investigation have already been touched upon in the previous chapter, and in addition, Chapter 2 has indicated the anglicised nature of printed texts (though even by the mid-eighteenth century the language of print was not fixed, see Tieken-Boon van Ostade, 2000, 2006 and Donaldson, 1989 for examples). Correspondence, and ego-documents more generally, provide a first-person perspective from the writer, whose personal and social information can be traced, allowing us to come closer to understanding the actual linguistic choices of the individual themselves. This investigation furthermore rests upon exploring a large body of written work that is as 'reactive' and reflective of personal linguistic behaviour as possible, rather than conforming to the codified norms of particular text-types or being subject to multiple editing processes that reduce the scope and possibility of variation. Work that is the direct product of the writer committing thoughts to paper can bring us closer to assessing whether Scottish political figures may have been sensitive to political and ideological factors in their language choices. Written language by nature tends to be more conservative and constructed than oral language (Conde-Silvestre and Hernández-Campoy, 1998: 109–110), but correspondence has been argued to be closer to speech than other text-types, forming perhaps the most 'natural' of written texts (Nevalainen, 1991; Raumolin-Brunberg, 1991; Biber, 1995: 283–300; Romaine, 1998: 18; Elspaß, 2012b; van der Wal and Rutten, 2013: 1; A. Auer et al., 2015: 7). Personal letters are among the most involved and therefore the more oral of written genres, as letters imply interaction and therefore participation (Biber and Finegan, 1989). While the addressee cannot immediately hear the information that needs to be conveyed, the writer 'commits potential utterances to the text for want of a recipient, thus the writer remains in near-speech mode' (Schneider, 2002: 72). This speech-like quality thus encourages the probability of variation, at higher rates than other conventional genres of written work.

Correspondence is also more 'immediate' than many texts types – letters tend to be more informal and unplanned relative to 'distant' text types such as legal contracts (Meurman-Solin, 2000: 158; van der Wal and Rutten, 2013: 2), thereby encouraging language variation and change along the vector of formality (Elspaß, 2012b: 160). This formality is conditioned upon the relationship with the recipient, which can be created, affirmed and reaffirmed through the process of letter-writing itself (Auer, Schreier and Watts, 2015: 282). In the process, letter-writers often fluctuate at various points along the standard-dialect continuum, within certain sociocultural contexts (Görlach, 1999). To that end, studies examining correspondence have frequently found increased innovation and variation, a reduced unidirectionality in patterns reflecting standardisation, and a more tolerant attitude towards forms that are geographically marked than the stringent standards of print culture (see Görlach, 1999; Meurman-Solin, 2000: 155; Dossena, 2002: 106; Nevalainen and Raumolin-Brunberg, 2003; Elspaß, 2005).

Additionally, a whole system of social, cultural and linguistic mores was integrated into the act of letter writing, thus correspondence practices in England and Scotland were not necessarily mirror images of each other. This is promising for eighteenth-century Scotland, given the severe reduction in written Scots variation by this time. Any factors encouraging its use can enable us to make more informed observations of when, how and why it was patterning, and to this end correspondence is an ideal medium. Relevant historical actors and their letters were thus sourced and compiled to construct a specialised corpus, the process of which is outlined in the next section.

The political players

Deciding which politicians to include in the corpus was determined through a two-fold approach that considered who was present in each of the three Scottish political parties, and who was represented by appropriate manuscript material or transcriptions in archive holdings or online publications (see the following two sections for more detail). This led ultimately to the inclusion of some of the more minor players in the parliament thanks to the preservation of their personal records, and the exclusion of a few major politicians as the unfortunate consequence of their lack of (preserved) correspondence, or lack of access to their records. Thankfully, almost all the most important and politically dominant commissioners were included in the analysis, as most came from powerful ducal families whose records have been well preserved within comprehensive archival records. Background research, and the online *Records of the Parliament of Scotland to 1707* [RPS] (RPS, 2022), assisted with identifying and locating relevant correspondence material. RPS contains minutes and attendance lists for all the historical sittings of the Scottish parliament up until 1707, including how ministers voted on any motions tabled or passed. Targeted research utilising the *Oxford Dictionary of National Biography* (ODNB, 2023) and the volumes of the *Scots Peerage* (Paul, 1904) then identified important contributing factors such as their political leanings and role within the Scottish parliament, their religious loyalties and possible Jacobite sympathies. It is of course desirable to locate as much information about the writers as possible (Elspaß, 2012b: 165), yet our knowledge and understanding of past sociocultural situations can only be reconstructed rather than directly observed or experienced by the researcher, and will remain incomplete and usually non-representative (Hernández-Campoy and Schilling, 2012: 63). Nonetheless, we are fortunate in that there is comparatively more information available on the gentry and members of the elite, rather than lower- and middle-class writers who have simply faded into obscurity (Fitzmaurice, 2002; Tieken-Boon van Ostade, 2003; Dossena, 2019). Additionally, their texts have been better preserved, and they have been historically literate far longer, with the time, resources and need to write in greater quantities than the middling and working classes, even when literacy became more widespread (Elspaß, 2012b: 159). These factors are promising benefits when it comes to the examination of Scottish politicians, given they were often nobility or gentry and hence fit the above characteristics.

Alongside the politicians, the correspondence of a clergyman who was outspoken against Union and achieved national prominence – Robert Wodrow – was also included in the qualitative analysis. This enabled a comparison of the writing practices between the commissioners in parliament and a politically active but non-parliamentary figure, and the extent to which the former represented a community of practice bound by common interests, goals, beliefs, and a shared repertoire (Jucker and Kopaczyk, 2013). This provided another perspective through which to view the political-linguistic interaction.[1] The significance of these potential effects will become clear in the inter/intra-writer analysis in Chapter 7. A prime motivation to include this correspondence, in particular, comes from the large volume of online, digitised letters

1 The original corpus contained the writings of several politically active and influential political figures operating outside of parliament. For the purposes of improved homogeneity, their letters were ignored for the analyses in this book. Only the letters of Wodrow were kept, though his letters were excluded from the statistical analysis in Chapter 6 to create a more coherent dataset.

produced by Wodrow (all of Wodrow MSS. Octavo i.),[2] which offered a historically appropriate online resource at a time when manuscript access was unavailable.

Wodrow was outspoken in his rejection of incorporation, arguing that the treaty provided insufficient security to the Presbyterian Church of Scotland. He wrote both privately and publicly on the matter, and his *History of the Sufferings of the Church of Scotland, 2 vols* can be considered his greatest literary contribution to the debate (Yeoman, 2004). Although not a member of the elite, Wodrow was well-educated, undertaking divinity studies at Glasgow University and becoming fluent in Latin and French, before pursuing further intellectual interests upon ordination. It is not the case that he represents a lesser-schooled, monolingual writer with no experience of the world beyond Scotland's borders, despite not coming from Scotland's top social layer. While his motivations for opposing the Union were derived from a profoundly theological and doctrinal basis, we can expect his literary and linguistic education to have been similar to the other political figures in the corpus.

A summary of how these writers is spread across the political factors investigated is given in Table 4.1.

Table 4.1: Counts for number of writers across political factors.

Factor	Levels	Count
Political	Pro	18
Affiliation	Anti	9
Party	Court	11
	Country	8
	Squadrone	7
Religious	Presbyterian	18
Affiliation	Episcopalian	9
	Yes	5
Jacobite	No	16
	Tactical	5

2 Wodrow arranged his own correspondence in four Octavo series, which contained copies of his own letters, and his letters in this corpus are taken chiefly from the first Octavo (Sharp, 1937: xv).

Whilst not entirely balanced, this reflects broader issues around historical research, in which resources may be limited or missing, and what has been preserved is subject to random chance and interests that are not transparent. Nonetheless, these numbers also reflect the historical reality quite accurately – there simply were less Episcopalians and Jacobites in parliament in general, and there was a pro-Union majority overall. The final list of political figures included in the corpus and their group membership are summarised in Table 4.2 below.

Table 4.2: The writers included in the corpus according to party or group.

Political Group	Author
Court	David Boyle, Earl of Glasgow Archibald Campbell, Earl of Ilay Hugh Campbell, Earl of Loudoun John Campbell, Duke of Argyll Hew Dalrymple, First Baronet John Dalrymple, Earl of Stair John Erskine, Earl of Mar Thomas Hay, Earl of Kinnoull David Melville, Earl of Leven James Ogilvie, Lord Seafield Sir John Clerk of Penicuik, Second Baronet
Country	William Cochrane of Kilmaronock Andrew Fletcher of Saltoun Alexander Forbes, Lord Pitsligo James Hamilton, Duke of Hamilton Charles Hay, 13th Earl of Erroll William Johnstone, Marquess of Annandale George Lockhart of Carnwath John Murray, Duke of Atholl
Squadrone Volante	John Cockburn of Ormistoun John Haldane of Gleneagles John Hay, Marquess of Tweeddale Patrick Hume, Earl of Marchmont John Ker, Duke of Roxburghe John Leslie, Earl of Rothes George Mackenzie, Earl of Cromartie
Minister	Robert Wodrow

In total twenty-seven authors were included in the corpus. Each political group was largely characterised by similar considerations and backgrounds, given the Scottish political parties were made up of landowners who often shared social or family connections, as well as religious convictions, alongside their political persuasion, as has been discussed in detail in Chapter 1. The four individuals that are analysed for the micro-analysis will be discussed in more detail in Chapter 7.

The source material

There is currently no single repository or corpus of political Scottish correspondence covering the period of the Union debates, either as an online corpus or as digitised manuscript material made available by national archives or libraries. While the *Helsinki Corpus of Scottish Correspondence* (CSC) has been available since 2016, it is not specifically focused on political correspondence from the Union debates. To locate appropriate data, the self-sourcing of relevant documents was required. Original unedited autograph documents, as opposed to reprints or copies of later editions were desirable, given that copies can be problematic for sociolinguistic analysis. It is often unclear to what extent the editing practices of the later eighteenth and nineteenth centuries would have interfered with the output of the original texts, but we can assume that in cases where editing did take place, this was most likely in the direction of anglicisation (Bugaj, 2004: 29; Macafee and †Aitken, 2015b: 6). Two main sources were identified for this research: original manuscripts from archive holdings, and digitised material from the *Scottish History Society* volumes.

The Scottish History Society publications

Several eligible online collections of digitised correspondence were identified within the digitised Scottish History Society publications (SHS), available through the National Library of Scotland (NLS) website. The

SHS produce yearly volumes, in which they publish tracts from various Scottish figures across a wide-ranging time-frame including, but not limited to, the eighteenth century. Although the focus of the volumes is arguably literary and historical rather than linguistic, the transcription notes preceding the collections suggested that fairly conservative and rigorous transcriptions practices were followed. Wherever possible original spellings were kept, as well as misspellings, repetitions, and sometimes abbreviations as well. This kind of attention to detail is paramount to ensuring any plausible Scots features are maintained, rather than being quietly altered to modern day English out of a desire to improve 'comprehension' for the reader.

Of the collections included, all maintained original spellings and orthographic practices, with the exception of the Wodrow correspondence, in which the highly frequent <quh-> abbreviations were expanded. Thus, words such as *quhat, quhen* and *quhere* (what, when and where) were written as such, instead of qt, qn and qr. The editor does note that all other misspellings or idiosyncrasies are kept, sometimes with an accompanying footnote suggesting the intended word or spelling. In the remaining collections of correspondence abbreviations, including <quh-> and <y-> (<th->) contractions have been retained. A number of the SHS correspondence collections were able to be checked against the manuscript originals, including the Wodrow, Lockhart and Seafield letters. This verified that the transcription practices of the editors were sufficiently rigorous enough for linguistic analysis, with original spellings and lexical items retained.

From the SHS volumes, the correspondence of the following authors was identified: George Lockhart of Carnwath, James Ogilvie the Earl of Seafield, John Cockburn of Ormistoun and Robert Wodrow. Lockhart and Wodrow produce the fullest form of correspondence – sending out large numbers of letters to multiple recipients over the course of several years. However, all the letters in the Seafield collection are written to Sidney Godolphin, the Lord High Treasurer of England. This naturally limits possible intra-writer variation, but fortunately, Seafield's correspondence was later supplemented with material from the archives. Cockburn similarly wrote to a single recipient, and his letters date to the decade after the Union had taken place, again limiting the scope of possible variation. The uneven composition of these online sources aptly demonstrates the difficulty in utilising pre-digitised material, even when seemingly valid source material is identified. Nonetheless, despite their shortcomings, these online works provide a baseline of linguistic material that may shed interesting light on these authors' language use, as long as caution is exercised in interpreting their results.

The online SHS publications contain digital transcriptions of each page in the volume, thus each letter could be directly copied and pasted into a text (.txt) file. Any important information that accompanied the collections (i.e. date, location, addressee, etc.) was added to metalinguistic tags included in the text file. Each transcription was checked carefully for character errors, as abbreviations and currency symbols in particular were not rendered correctly in the online transcription, and had to be corrected. This provided a valuable baseline of material to the corpus, supplementing the original manuscript material taken from the Scottish archives.

The archives

Manuscript catalogues at the National Library of Scotland (NLS), National Records of Scotland (NRS), and Blair Castle archives were searched for correspondence produced by the target authors, and relevant records were photographed. Correspondence between political members was of particular interest, but letters to their household and acquaintances were also included. The majority of the material was sourced from family collections within the NRS, and a number of the collections, such as GD45 (Papers of the Maule Family, Earls of Dalhousie) and GD124 (Papers of the Erskine Family, Earls of Mar and Kellie) were freely accessible to view and photograph by advanced request. Other collections had restricted access only and written permission had to be obtained from the current collection holder to photograph these letters. In almost all cases this was granted and I am grateful to these holders for their generosity and co-operation (see Appendix A.1 for details).

The National Library of Scotland contains several important collections such as the Tweeddale Correspondence and Wodrow Quarto, while the Blair Castle archives contain correspondence produced by the Atholl family, including John Murray, Duke of Atholl. An advance appointment to visit and photograph relevant material was requested and kindly granted by the archivist at the Estate, and I am thankful for their co-operation and assistance. For a full list of collections consulted, see Appendix A.2.

Only autograph letters were included – the archival notes accompanying the collections, as well as sudden changes in writing style, and the opening or closing salutations of the letters (which tended to contain apologies if the letter was not self-written) were carefully checked to ensure letters were the original product of the author themselves. Letter-writers could on occasion employ scribes to write on their behalf, particularly when they were short on time (Hernández-Campoy and Schilling, 2012: 68; Fairman, 2015: 64). This removes their direct involvement in the construction of the letter, inhibiting the analysis of personal variability. This practice, however, tends to be more common in early historical time periods (Hernández-Campoy and Conde-Silvestre, 1999; Hernández-Campoy and Schilling, 2012: 68–69), and amongst the elite it was generally considered a mark of respect to send autograph letters. Any anonymous letters or unknown recipients were ignored, as being able to establish a one-to-one relationship between linguistic output and the communicators in question is crucial to answering the research questions being investigated here, and indeed is central to historical sociolinguistic research in general (Raumolin-Brunberg, 1996b: 43). Once photographed, the next stage was to convert the manuscripts into text-searchable documents by digitising the output.

Digitisation

In order to successfully digitise handwritten text, photographs ideally have to be correctly positioned, clear and well-lit, while the document must possess minimal damage causing any disruption to the text. In reality, historical documents come in various degrees of wear and tear, often characterised by damaged or faded characters, half-formed words or letters, thin, fragile or degraded paper, discolouration, blotches, rips and bleed-through from the other side, and are frequently bound in tight volumes that do not allow for flat, even photographs of the letter in question (Bukhari et al., 2017). While the quality of most letters collected for this corpus was sufficient, to assist with their digital transcription as far as possible, photographs were loaded into a simple photo editor (*Microsoft Photo Editor*, Windows 10) and manipulated with some basic filters to improve the quality of the text. This included adjusting light percentage, clarity and angle of the document, as well as cropping out unwanted bits of text (for example, from neighbouring pages). Photographs were then tagged by archival shelf mark and sorted into collections according to the author, ready to be transcribed using the online transcription software *Transkribus*.

Transkribus

To transcribe even a relatively small volume of letters by hand involves many hours of work, especially given the occurrence of unfamiliar spellings and words, archaic sentence structures and unusual place-names, not to mention poor image quality or illegible writing styles. However, the transcription software Transkribus (Kahle et al., 2017), developed at the University of Innsbruck, is able to handle moderately challenging images with a fair degree of accuracy, enabling seamless transcription of several hundred photographs at a time. Using a neural network approach, the software is able to 'learn' the script of an author and identify characters and words within the written text under investigation. This approach can in theory be applied to any language, alphabet, time-frame or script. As a result, users are able to semi-automatically transcribe photographs or scans of handwritten or printed texts, using Handwritten Text Recognition (HTR) or Optical Character Recognition (OCR). This is achieved either by creating a custom-built HTR model or using a pre-existing model appropriate to the language and timeframe. To build a model from scratch, around 15,000 words of handwritten text, which equates to roughly 100 pages of manually transcribed training data, is needed as input data.

The transcribed pages are then split into a 'training' set and a 'test' set at a ratio of 4:1, which are fed into a model-building algorithm. This learns to recognise the individual characters of a particular script, by matching its predictions, taken from the training set, against the true values in the test set, which are subsequently used to assess the performance and accuracy of the algorithm. This process undergoes several iterations, by random sampling with replacement, and more training data can be added to improve the recognition rate. The model is usable once it achieves a comparatively small Character Error Rate (CER) – the percentage of characters the model fails to recognise correctly. The smaller the value, the more accurate the model will be. The HTR model can then be applied to previously unseen material, as well as other scribes, provided they are writing in a similar language, similar time-period, and with a similar script. The CER can be improved by feeding a small number of manually transcribed pages from other hands into the baseline model and retraining it, using the original training data plus the new material. Unlike the initial set-up, only around 10–20 pages of the new material are needed in each case. Once this has been run on the remaining images, the output requires manual correction, as there will be occasional errors, particularly if the image is compromised or text is missing. Despite the errors, the time investment is considerably smaller than manual transcription and still produces comparatively accurate transcriptions.

To manually transcribe documents, text regions and individual lines are automatically identified within each image, though these can be manually corrected as required, and these correspond to lines in the transcription panel below, enabling simple, easy transcription.[3] Once each page has been transcribed, the transcription is saved and the process repeats for the following photograph. An example image is shown on the following page (Figure 4.1).

3 For more detailed information on the various functions of Transkribus, managed by the READ COOP, see <https://readcoop.eu/transkribus>.

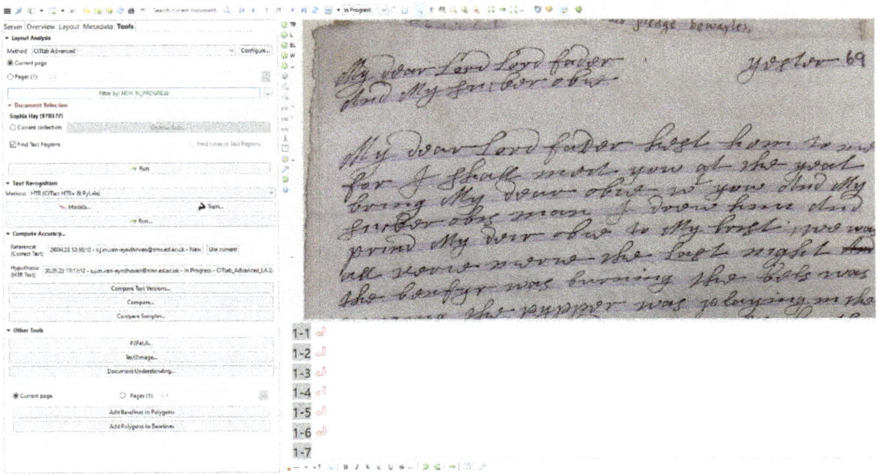

Figure 4.1: Example image of transcription pane following line segmentation.

Transkribus offers a viable means to transcribe archival material, and was used for the bulk of the manuscript material.[4] Accordingly, the first 100 pages of letters from the second Marquess of Tweeddale were manually transcribed in Transkribus and used to build an early eighteenth-century Scottish handwriting model using PyLaia (Mocholí Calvo, 2018), a deep, neural-network learning toolkit for handwritten document analysis. The resulting model achieved a CER of 3.4 per cent – a very good rate by historical text standards. This indicates only 3.4 per cent of characters were incorrectly transcribed by the model. For each subsequent author in the corpus, twenty pages of their manually transcribed correspondence were added to the baseline model, split into fifteen for training data and five as test data. The model was retrained, and checked for the CER, which achieved a rate of 4.1 per cent. The increase in CER is not surprising, given the higher level of variability introduced into the training data, but 4.1 per cent is still acceptable, especially for historical documents.

4 I am grateful to the READ COOP team for granting me free Transkribus credits, which enabled me to transcribe these photographs free of charge.

Once the same iterative training and evaluative process outlined in the previous subsection was complete, the HTR model could then be applied to the remaining letters awaiting transcription. Transcribing original manuscript material requires transparent and linguistically rigorous editing standards and principles that ideally recognise the material nature of the documents themselves (Woesler, 1998: 946; A. Auer, 2008; Fairman, 2008, 2015: 60; Elspaß, 2012a: 164). Accordingly, repetitions, abbreviations and crossed out words were included when possible, and long dash (—) at the end of a line of text was also kept, though superscript letters and long <S>, commonly used at this time, were converted to regular letters, to prevent an error code in the corpus software. Unknown words were marked as [ ], and comments in the margins or above the lines of running text were transcribed separately. Recognition of unusual characters and difficult hands was aided by letter-finders of Scottish handwriting from the seventeenth and eighteenth centuries, produced by the NRS.[5]

The finished transcriptions were exported in txt. format from Transkribus and uploaded to the corpus-building software *LaBB-CAT* (Fromont and Hay, 2008) – the platform used to store and search all the transcripts.

Metadata

Ideally, the metalinguistic information accompanying letters is as complete as possible, given that many 'unknowns' in the dataset can significantly undermine the value and interpretation of patterns of variation (Nevalainen and Raumolin-Brunberg, 1989, 1994; Nevalainen, 1991; Raumolin-Brunberg, 1991; Raumolin-Brunberg and Nevalainen, 1994; Milroy and

5 These guides were acquired through online resources provided by the Scottish Records Association (<https://www.scottishrecordsassociation.org/publications>) and their sister organisation, Scottish Handwriting.com (see <https://www.scottishhandwriting.com> for basic guides and tutorials). Script recognition was facilitated by participation in the Scottish Handwriting short course offered by the NRS, which also provided additional palaeography resources.

Gordon, 2003), and inhibit successful reconstruction of the sociohistorical setting (Raumolin-Brunberg, 1996a: 18). However, information was sometimes unavoidably unidentifiable, though thankfully 'unknowns' represent only a small amount of the total extralinguistic information characterising the dataset. The factors that were included in each letter and their different values (or examples thereof) are presented briefly in Table 4.3 (for a list of political factor levels and their counts, see Table 4.1.).

Table 4.3: Main extralinguistic factors.

Factor	Levels
Political Affiliation	Pro, Anti, Unknown
Party	Court, Country, Squadrone Volante
Religious Affiliation	Presbyterian, Episcopalian
Jacobite	Yes, No, Tactical
Recipient	Various
Recipient position	e.g. Family, Duke, Scholar, Tenant
Relationship	Close, Distant
Address	e.g. North East, England, Europe
Location	e.g. East Central Belt, South, Highlands
Birthplace	e.g. West Central Belt, Central
Date	Various
Year	1689–1745

The geographic labels consisted of three parameters: *Address, Location* and *Birthplace. Location* specifies where the letter was written from, *Address* concerns where the letter was sent to, and *Birthplace* reflects where the author was born. The factor levels for these predictors were simplified to 'England', 'Europe', and the counties of Scotland in the dataset, as too many levels complicate statistical analysis and interpretation of the data. Some factors demanded greater methodological consideration, such as *Political Affiliation* in the case of the Squadrone members, who shifted from an opposition stance to supporting the Union. Ultimately, their pro-Union stance after 1704 was taken as indicative of their leaning. *Jacobite* was initially a binary category of 'Yes' or 'No', but some authors professed hidden sympathies, or dabbled with Jacobite plotting as and when it suited them, thus the third category, 'Tactical' was created.

Relationship was more complex, as determining the level of amicability, respect and alignment between two writers were based largely upon the availability and interpretation of the background information available. Familial connections, marriage and landowning aspirations as well as religious denomination, ideological concerns and social ranking were key informants in determining how 'close' and 'distant' two figures were. While this binary distinction lacks nuance, this is not the main focus, nor is a fine-grained distinction feasible within the scope of this book. The micro-analysis in Chapter 7 explores the relationship between select individuals and their recipients, providing some insight into how this factor might pattern in more complex terms. This suggests possible avenues for further investigation into recipient relationship.

Which factors are included in the final sociolinguistic analysis is naturally limited by the amount of information available, and accordingly, educational background could not be included. While we know most of these writers attended university, very little is known about their early experiences when they were acquiring literacy. We might expect that the model for Scottish grammar by the eighteenth century was largely English (and Latin), and it seems likely that pupils might have adopted at least some of the spelling and writing practices of their writing teachers (Macafee and †Aitken, 2015b: 186). Yet variable options may still have been available even within the strict confines of the classroom (Fitzmaurice, 2015), and even more so through private tutoring, which was often the norm at the beginning of the century (A. Auer, 2015: 136). It is, moreover, just as possible that the tradition of free choice and variation in written language overruled the tendency for a writer to adopt the preferred choices of the written models around them (Aitken, 1971: 186). Idiosyncrasy and local background likely played their role as well as register and educational experiences in conditioning variable choices (Macafee and †Aitken, 2015b: 34). Rather, the final set of factors included aims not to explain all the variation present, but merely to suggest possible contributing factors to any patterns observed.

The extralinguistic factors were added as labels to the transcribed text files exported from Transkribus, as well as the digitised SHS records. LaBB-CAT is able to recognise this information and add it to the appropriate fields in the corpus matrix. Each complete text file was then given a unique identifier and uploaded to the pre-existing, custom-built corpus *POLITECS* – (**P**olitical **O**pposition, **L**oyalty or **I**ndifference in **T**exts of **E**ighteenth **C**entury **S**cotland), built previously by the author (see van Eyndhoven, 2021 for details), which is stored within LaBB-CAT. A new subcorpus was created within POLITECS for the specific writers in question here. Table 4.4 on the following page gives a summary of the final corpus counts once this process was complete.

Table 4.4: Counts for POLITECS subcorpus used in these analyses.[6]

POLITECS	Count
Word Count	401,087
Number of Letters	900
Number of authors	27

An overview of the software used to store these transcriptions (LABB-CAT) along with its specific features is discussed in the following section, before the final section of this chapter (Section 4.6) describes how 'Scots' was defined and categorised, to enable searches for appropriate features within POLITECS.

POLITECS

LaBB-CAT

The browser-based, freely accessible software LaBB-CAT (Fromont and Hay, 2008), developed at the University of Canterbury, New Zealand, was used to compile and search the transcripts of these letters. LaBB-CAT can store audio, video and text files, and enables users to conduct

6 These numbers are for the letters used in the analyses presented here only (all politicians and Wodrow). For full corpus counts used in the original analyses, see van Eyndhoven (2023a).

detailed and multilayered investigations of the data in question, utilising various filters to highlight features of interest. Searches within the corpus can be undertaken across whole (sub-)corpora simultaneously, or be filtered according to the transcript or author(s) if required. LaBB-CAT comes with a number of pre-defined annotation layers (which include orthographic, syntactic or phonological layers) and specialised word filters, which can be selected to extract precise linguistic data while filtering out unwanted results. This can assist greatly in searching a corpus containing two languages, such as Scots and English. The researcher can also manually add extra, searchable layers as required by the phenomenon under investigation to extract more specific results. These operate across different linguistic layers, such as orthography or phonology, and act as an overarching organisational function into which specialised word-search filters can be incorporated. An example of the search matrix is shown on the following page, in which the 'Orthography' layer has been checked, and the search term (in this case *auld*) is specified in the search box below (Figure 4.2).

Extra word-filters added for this investigation are also visible in Figure 4.2, such as 'Scots_English', whose relevance will be discussed in more detail in the following subsections. Results are exported to a comma separated values (csv) file, along with accompanying information derived from participant or transcript attributes (Fromont and Hay, 2008). While LaBB-CAT contains a number of 'default' categories such as *Gender*, further attributes can be added manually by the researcher, such as *Party* and *Jacobite*, for instance.

A word-search layer was also implemented to enable corpus searches for multiple linguistic features simultaneously, so that a range of Scots features can be identified in tandem, rather than focusing on an individual spelling or lexical item. Chapter 2 has highlighted the likely dearth of Scots in elite correspondence by this time, suggesting the desirability of holistically capturing as many features indicative of Scots as feasible within the corpus. Yet, to conduct a sociolinguistic analysis of Scots and southern English usage, we need to define a binary variable. In this case, the variable is 'language', with multiple Scots features composing the one variant, and their anglicised equivalents the other. However, LaBB-CAT's

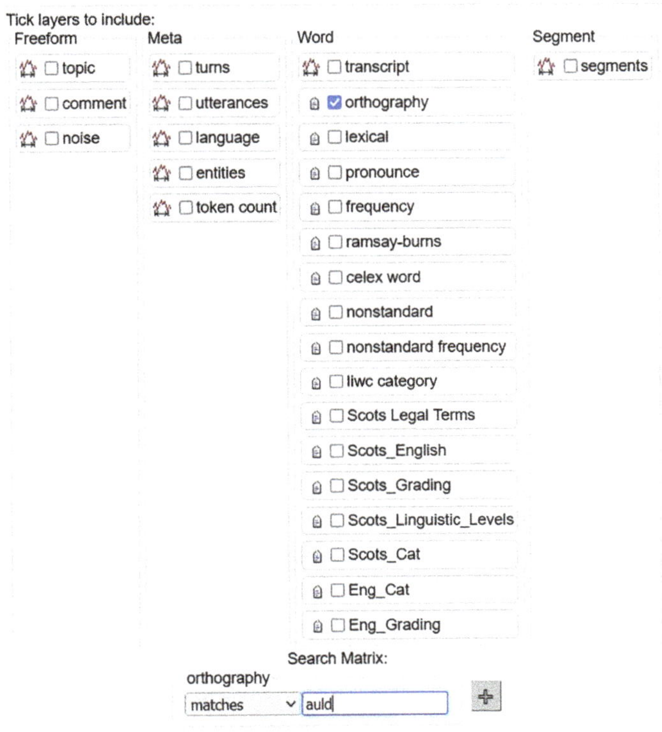

Figure 4.2: Example image of the search matrix in the POLITECS corpus.

default parameters are based upon extracting an individual phonological or orthographic feature, and this necessitated the implementation of a *Linguistic Inquiry and Word Count* [LIWC] (Tausczik and Pennebaker, 2010) layer manager.

LIWC

Traditionally, LIWC is a text-analysis model used to identify aspects of a writer's personality, by assigning target words to psychologically meaningful categories or 'dictionaries', which are then identified and extracted from the text (Tausczik and Pennebaker, 2010: 24–27). Multiple dictionaries can be created and run through LIWC to determine which categories have the highest frequency of occurrence in an individual's text, providing some insight into their cognitive behaviour. In this instance, we can determine how Scots or Anglicised the writers are, using LIWC to measure the frequency of representative features in their correspondence. The 'dictionary' uploaded to the LIWC layer thus consists of a list of words containing Scots orthographic or lexical features (detailed in Section 5.6), and a second list with their southern English equivalent, giving a 'Scots' and an 'English' category. This essentially gives a long list of individual words containing target features, a sample of which is shown below (Table 4.5).

Table 4.5: Sample wordlist uploaded to LIWC manager.

affer	Scots	offer	English
drapt	Scots	dropped	English
fermer	Scots	farmer	English
enuch	Scots	enough	English

LIWC thus enables an untold number of Scots lexemes to be compiled under a single category, before scanning through the corpus and tagging every instance of a target Scots or English token where it occurs. This is the 'Scots_English' word-layer within the search matrix, enabling the researcher to extract *all* relevant tokens at once, across the corpus or within an individual transcript. The target features incorporated within the Scots-English dictionary, however, rest upon accurately and objectively identifying eighteenth-century Scots in the first place. This last part of the methodological process is detailed below.

Identifying Scots

Searching for Scots in correspondence at the turn of the eighteenth century is challenging on a number of fronts. Recall from Chapter 2 that written

Scots had largely retreated from most text-types by 1700, as the transition to anglicised features was well underway. Searching for an individual feature or lexical item thus provides a limited insight into the frequencies and forms of written Scots surviving at this time, as it seems likely usage was becoming increasingly variable and subject to subtle differences that cannot be captured by a single variant. Such a focus denies us a broad picture of what was happening to *Scots* overall. Moreover, comparatively little is known about which features were still present in elite correspondence dating to this time, making it unclear which features should be focused on. Instead, the first step was simply to identify Scots features as they cropped up during transcription and compile these into a dataset.

However, labelling something as purely 'Scots' is of course problematic in its own right, as linguistic varieties do not recognise national borders as definitively as cartographers might. Frequently, lexical items or spellings identified as Scots were shared with northern dialects. Their common origins have already been discussed in Chapter 2 so will not be repeated here. However, given the target variety for anglicising authors would have been southern English, variants were labelled Scots if they were localised within Scotland and the far north, whilst being scarce or non-existent in the metropolitan variety emerging from the southern capital. Each identified Scots token was matched with their southern English equivalent, for instance, the word *deen* with the double <ee> spelling in Scots corresponds to 'done' in southern English.

Choosing the Standard English equivalent is a necessary process in order to circumscribe the variable under investigation, yet the English standard itself was not static, and there is evidence of changes occurring throughout the eighteenth and nineteenth centuries, during which a number of variants could co-exist as acceptable norms (Allen, 2015: 203; Fairman, 2015: 53).[7] There is no straightforward way to solve this issue, but care was taken to check the time-frames and regional provenance of spellings within the Oxford English Dictionary, to determine which were

7 Occasionally, there was potential to include more than one of the prevalent English variants when same Scots word occurred with two different spellings. Thus, *deuty* and *diutie* in Scots could be represented as 'duty' and 'dewty' in Southern Standard English (SStE), and both were included to account for more possible variation in the texts.

current at the time of writing. This provided a broad overview of the Scots features still present in correspondence at this time, which could then be sorted into categories of spelling features that unambiguously represent a feature of Scots (rather than English) phonology. This ensures future replicability which is central to rigorous sociolinguistic investigation (Bailey and Tillery, 2004: 1).

Classifying Scots

Many Scots spelling variants represent phonological changes or regular sound changes that took place historically in northern varieties but not in southern English, or vice-versa, and they occur systematically enough to be considered defining differences between Scots and southern English varieties. Aitken (1971: 186) suggests that it may prove convenient and revealing in comparative investigations to group together words which share the same variant sets, or used different members of that set in varying proportions. In this way, a system of orthographic variant and member sets with a lexical inventory can be created, which can then be related to a phonemic system, or other reconstructed systems. He also notes that we can treat Scots spellings simply as phenomena in their own right, independent of whatever spoken forms they might be thought to represent, and the approach taken here partially adopts Aitken's proposed methodological approach.

Thus, while orthographic variants have been organised into sets with lexical inventories, the classifications used here do not necessarily suggest that such words were still *pronounced* differently. A feature may have become fossilised as part of Scots' 'tendency to retain established orthographic arrangements after the phonemic arrangements which they formerly reflected had ceased to exist' (Aitken, 1971: 187). Once such spellings were established, they may have become merely orthographic rather than phonemic for some writers over time (Macafee and †Aitken, 2015b: 12, 16). The point is that they provide a quantifiable difference that can be analysed from a sociolinguistic perspective, and previous work on Scots (i.e.

Aitken, 1971; Kopaczyk, 2012) has already suggested the value in approaching orthographic variation through the lens of phonological distinctions, even if we analyse their distributions and patterns of incidence as spellings rather than pronunciations.

Accordingly, the following categories were identified from the original list of Scots words. These are briefly discussed following Table 4.6. For more detailed explanations, see van Eyndhoven (2023a).

Table 4.6: Scots categories included in analysis, including example Scots spellings with their southern English equivalent.

Scots Category	Example
MATE	*debait* – debate
PART	*cairt* – cart
OEa	*clath* – cloth
a-o	*aff* – off
Front Vowel Merger	*greit* – great
er-ar	*ffermers* – farmers
i-e	*blist* – blessed
ie-y	*manie* – many
Northern Fronting	*dae* – do
u-w	*niu* – new
MOUTH	*fluor* – flower
ch-gh	*enuch* – enough
dg-g	*bagedg* – baggage
qu(h)-wh	*quhich* – which
ng~n	*cleang* – clean
s~s(c)h	*pouss* – push
Consonant Deletion	*hae* – have

MATE

This refers to the spelling of words which had the Older Scots (OSc) /a:/ (MATE) vowel. Scots appears to have preferred <ai> spellings for non-final developments of OSc /a:/, compared to southern English <a(C)e> spellings. /a:/ underwent raising in each variety, but southern English tended to represent this with <a(C)e> spellings, while Scots preferred <ai>, giving rise to the distinction between *debait, caise, haist* and 'debate', 'case', 'haste'.

PART

The PART set also involves <ai> spellings, though this affected a different set of words, and happened in Scots early on. This resulted from Early Middle English lengthening of original short /ar/ followed by certain consonants in northern varieties, including Scots, giving OSc /a:r/. The lengthening of short /a/ in PART was particularly common before /rt/ and /rd/ clusters, including variants such as *cairt, caird, gairden* and *pairt*, 'cart', 'card', 'garden' and 'part'. There were also some instances of short /ar/ lengthening without an <rt> or <rd> spelling in the final consonant cluster, as in *airm* and *airch*, 'arm', 'arch' (Macafee and †Aitken, 2003: 148).

OEa – Old English ā

Lass (1992: 46) labels the reflex of OE ā, present historically in 'bone', 'stone', 'home' < OE bān, stān, hām etc, as 'one striking difference between modern northern and southern dialects'. This concerns words which had [ɑ:], which developed differently in far-northern English varieties and Scots, than in Midland and southern dialects. The vowel fronted in the north, especially in traditional dialects and conservative rural vernaculars, initially giving [a:], which then raised through the Great Vowel Shift (GVS). This typically gives spellings with <a> (though <ai> is also common), i.e. *hame, stane* (Aitken, 1977: 3; Aitken, 2003: 143–148). In the south, the vowel rounded and raised to [ɔ:], usually represented by spellings involving <o>, such as <oCe>, <oa> and <o>, as in 'home' and 'stone'. This developed into one of the fundamental north/south isoglosses (Lass, 1992: 47) and is a major distinguishing characteristic between Scots and southern English. Writers and text-types were variable in their adoption of the change, and this switch to <o> was never completed in written Scots.

'Regular' cases of this distinction include the examples given above, but there are several smaller subsets which have their origin in the same change, including the KNOW subset (giving *blaw, knaw, snaw, thraw* vs. 'blow', 'know', 'snow', 'throw'), the LONG subset, consisting of words with Old English -ang, (giving *amang, lang, strang* and *wrang* for 'among', 'long', 'strong' and 'wrong', see Alcorn et al., 2017: 20) and the OLD subset (*cald, hald, ald/auld* for 'cold', 'hold', 'old'). The MORE subset also falls within this change, in which words with OE [ɑ:] before /r/ typically have <a> or <ai> spellings, compared to southern English <o> spellings, as in *mair, sair* – 'more', 'sore'.

a-o

This category describes instances in which Scots has <a> spellings where southern English would have <o>. This superficially looks like OE [ā] given it seems to reflect the same patterning; however, this represents a different vowel set and different process. In Older Scots, originally short /o/ (which can also be symbolised as /ɔ/), became /a/ in labial environments, especially before /p/ and /f/ (Macafee and †Aitken, 2015a: 34), giving *aff, drap* and *tapp* for 'off', 'drop' and 'top' (Aitken, 1977: 10).

Front vowel merger

This describes a long front vowel shift and merger that affected both Middle English and Older Scots, but manifested in slightly different ways in each variety. This corresponded to spelling differences, specifically for the MATE and BEAT classes which overlapped and were sometimes confused (Aitken, 1977: 8). Note that the processes discussed for MATE in this section differ from the /ai/ spellings outlined above, which were indicative of lengthening or a MATE-BAIT merger, rather than the BEAT-MATE merger discussed here.

Both Middle English and Older Scots originally had the same long front vowels and these all rose in the GVS (Aitken, 1977: 2; Aitken, 2003: 143). /a:/ and /ɛ:/ ultimately rose two steps (to /e:/ and /i:/, respectively). However, the raising of /ɛ:/ was relatively late, and there is plenty of evidence in the Early and Late Modern periods that the /ɛ:/ – /i:/ merger was not complete in all areas of Scotland, and failed to take place in some dialects (see Curtis, 1894: 34; Heuser, 1897: 339–341, 406–407; Craigie, 1940: lvi and Aitken, 1977: 8, as cited in Macafee and †Aitken, 2015a: 10). There was thus potential for an overlap or merger of /a:/ (MATE) and /ɛ:/ (BEAT), if the MATE set rose to /ɛ:/ or /e:/ before the BEAT set rose to /i:/. This seems to have occurred in certain varieties of English and Scots, but appears not to have taken place in southern Standard English and central Scots dialects, or perhaps disappeared early on in the ancestor of these varieties (Anderson, 1987: 69, 83; Johnston, 1997b: 456–463).

Within certain Scots dialects therefore there is evidence of merger of /a:/ and /ɛ:/ (the 'BEAT-MATE Merger'), and this is usually reflected in historical spellings of the BEAT set with <a> or <aCe> – spellings originally used to represent MATE. Thus we get the spellings *dale, dath, lave* for 'deal', 'death', 'leave'. Sometimes there are also <ai> spellings for BEAT words, which probably derive from the previously merged MATE class. As a result, we get examples such as *dail,* 'deal' in the corpus. In English, the BEAT class was usually represented with <ea> or <ee>, reflecting its merger with /i:/ by this time period (Johnston, 1997a: 73). In Scots by contrast, <ee> remains rare until much later in the period. There are also some reverse spellings in the corpus, in which MATE and BAIT words are spelled with <ea> and <ei>. Spellings previously used to represent BEAT applied to words of the MATE class, giving *streit,* 'straight' and *ordean,* 'ordain' (Macafee and †Aitken, 2015b). There is thus evidence of both patterns in the corpus and they have been categorised as Scots, whilst acknowledging that they may have been possible for some writers of English too.

er-ar

This spelling feature represents Old English and Old French short /ɛr/, which commonly became short /ar/ in southern English varieties by the mid-sixteenth century, but often remained /ɛr/ or became /er/ in Scots instead. This is reflected by a spelling preference for <er> where we would expect <ar> or <ear> in Standard English, for example *fermers,* 'farmers', *hert,* 'heart' and *merket*, 'market' (Aitken, 2003: 148).

The reverse is also possible, in which we have <ar> spellings instead of <e(a)r>. These usually occur in words which were borrowed later (from Latin or French for example). In southern English the pronunciation became /ɜr/ > /ɜ:/, giving the regular <er> or <ear> spellings in use today. However, Scots and some English varieties typically retained the original pronunciation /er/ (later / ɛr/) or lengthened to /e:r/) in these words, represented with <ar> spellings, as in *larn*, 'learn'.

i-e

The use of <i> for <e> reflects a common, non-standard historical phonological change, also found in Scots, for /ɛ/ to rise to /ɪ/. This is usually represented in the spelling with an <i> rather than <e> especially before /t/, next to palatal consonants, before <-ver> as in *cliver,* 'clever' and sometimes before /s/ as in *blist*, 'blessed' (Zai, 1942: 126; Dobson, 1968; Aitken, 1971: 202; Lass, 1992). While this change is not unique to Scots alone, these spellings were transitioning out of the emerging standard variety and were becoming restricted to non-standard and regional varieties.

ie-y

This refers to the preference of Scots to spell word-final [i] in the CITY word-class as <ie> rather than the more usual <y> in Early Modern

English. In Scots, <ie> and <ye> became the digraphs used in open syllables (Macafee and †Aitken, 2015b: 182–183), thus we get *anie, carie, certanlie* in Scots, whereas 'any', 'carry' and 'certainly' were the more usual spellings found in southern English. This preference for <ie>, while not unique to Scots alone, does differentiate it from southern English practice and preference, and accordingly was included as a category.

Northern fronting

This change was complex phonologically and in terms of spellings, but is an essential far north/Scots – Midlands/South distinction, in which Early Middle English /o:/ fronted in the far north to [ø:], a change which did not take place in the south. In the south these words remained /ʊ/ or /u/ (Lass, 1992: 56). This forms a key distinguishing feature of Scots and northern English varieties (Lass, 1992: 56). Typically Northern Fronting is represented either by a front vowel spelling (including <i> or <e>), or by <uCe> or <ui>, depending on its individual developments, rather than by spellings containing <o> which was generally used in English to represent /o:/. Various spelling features can represent this process – there are a number of 'regular' cases, such as 'soon' and 'moon', commonly represented as *sune* or *muin*, while before velars, /o:/ was regularly fronted and there was some early diphthongisation to /iu/ (Johnston, 1997a: 69), represented by spellings such as <eu>, as in *teugh,* 'tough', *eneugh*, 'enough' (given the final <gh> was pronounced /x/), as well as <ui> as in *buik*, 'book' (Aitken, 2003: 149).

Northern Fronting also took place in pre-rhotic position, giving *muir, puir*, 'moor', 'poor', though in many dialects there was later unrounding and lowering to [e:], often spelled <air>, i.e. *mair*, 'moor'. There are word-final cases as in 'do' and 'to(o)', giving variants such as *dae* and *tae*. These spellings stem from a very widespread change for the resulting [ø:] from Northern Fronting to become [e:], which was often represented in the spelling as <ae> in morpheme-final position. In North-East Scots the outcome of this fronting was sometimes even further forward, giving /i(:)/

as the output. This could be represented in the spelling with <ee>, as in *sekeered,* 'secured'. In environments preceding <-ther>, Northern Fronting can also manifest in the spelling as <i> or <a>, as in *brither, mither, ather* – 'brother', 'mother', 'other' (Aitken, 1977: 10; Macafee and †Aitken, 2003: 149). Finally, in some cases, words with Old French /y/ ended up as part of this spelling variation, as /y/ merged with the resulting /ø:/ (or /y:/), giving <a> spellings, as in *refase*, 'refuse'.

u-w

In Older Scots it was established practice to use <u> in non-final position where southern Standard English would have <w>, as in *neus*, 'news', *rau*, 'raw' and *hollou*, 'hollow', though the two could be in free variation (Aitken, 1971: 182). This is not unique to Scots, commonly occurring in northern English areas as well, and reflects a general tendency of Scots to preserve and generalise Middle English spelling practices from northern areas (Kniezsa, 1997: 35–36).

MOUTH

The MOUTH set refers to words with Middle English and Older Scots [u:], which diphthongised to the [aʊ] diphthong in the South as a result of the GVS, but remained a monophthong in the north. The usual spellings for /u:/ had been <ow, ou> and these continued in both Scots and English (Lass, 2000: 79), although Scots seems to have preferred <ou>. Some words could also shorten with <uC> spellings from the sixteenth century onward, possibly suggesting the retention of the historically short vowel, such as *clud, muntan, pultrie*, 'cloud', 'mountain', 'poultry' (Johnston, 1997a: 83). In the corpus, most of the words in this set have the vowel proceeding an alveolar consonant, such as *boued, doun, flouer* and *pouer* – 'bowed', 'down', 'flower' and 'power', respectively. MOUTH was kept separate from the u-w variation in the thesis to explore whether MOUTH words behave differently in the feature analysis (not included here, see van Eyndhoven, 2023a for more details).

ch-gh

The use of the <ch> digraph in Older Scots represented Old English and Old Norse /x/. In Old English this sound was originally represented by <h> in non-initial position, including before /t/, changing first to <x>, before <gh> became the standard spelling by late Middle English. <gh> also entered the Scots spelling system in the second half of the sixteenth century (Macafee and †Aitken, 2015b: 184), thus <ch> came to vary with <gh>, though the preferred grapheme was <ch> in Older Scots (Bann and Corbett, 2015: 25). This gives *dochter*, 'daughter' and *licht*, 'light', for example. Spelling variants could also include <Ø>, as in *hy*, 'high', given that /x/ could be deleted, especially after front vowels, or <f>, as [x] became [f] in word-final position after back vowels, as in *enuff*, 'enough'. Occasionally <ch> was inserted in words with no etymological justification, such as *delicht* for 'delight', which is still common in modern dialects of Scots. Both words with a preceding front vowel, i.e. *eicht, nicht*, and a preceding back vowel, as in *enuch*, are attested in the corpus.

dg-g

In Early Modern English the digraph <dg> replaced the Old English <gg> digraph in medial or final position for words pronounced /ʤ/, as in Middle English *hegg*, 'hedge'. Conversely, in French borrowings ending in <-age>, the original French spelling was preserved. In Older Scots these words were more variable, giving *hege* or *hedge*, and this variability similarly applied to French borrowings, thus both *baggage* and *baggadg* are possible.

qu(h)-wh

The representation of Old English [hw] as <q(u)h>, in contrast to southern English <wh>, is a ubiquitous feature of Older Scots. Three main spellings emerged: <qu(h)>, <qwh> and <qw>, but by the seventeenth century the feature had largely narrowed down to <qu(h)> forms only. This feature was not restricted to Scotland; it was also used extensively in the far north of England from the end of the thirteenth century onwards (McIntosh et al., 1986: vol 2, 177; Kniezsa, 1997: 31), but it is a key distinguishing feature between southern English varieties and the far north. There is evidence of hybrid Scots-English spellings combining <quh> with the southern vowel or consonantal ending, such as *quhom* instead of *quhaim, quhich* instead of *quhilk* from the sixteenth century onward (Aitken, 1971: 190; Kniezsa, 1997: 45), and most <q(u)h>/ words in the POLITECS corpus show evidence of this hybridisation.

ng~n

This refers to two different phonological processes affecting the spelling of Scots nasals. The first refers to the Scots spelling <ng> where southern English would have <n>. Final historical /n/ in Scots is normally represented by <n>, whilst final /ng/ is normally represented by <ng>. In some cases, however, Scots uses the spelling <ng> where we might expect <n>. This is found in French loanwords (and occasionally in Gaelic, mostly placenames, see Macafee and Ó Baoill, 1997: 261) which had the palatal nasal [ɲ], as in *reing, sing, aling,* 'reign', 'sign', 'align'. What the <n> spelling indicates is not certain, but this spelling was used across all of Scotland for much of the Older Scots period, and spellings with <n> are only attested after anglicisation was well underway (Murray, 1873: 124; Johnston, 1997a: 106).

The converse alternation involves spellings in which <ng> spellings in southern English occur as <n> in Scots, when followed by <th> as in *lenth*, 'length' and *strenth*, 'strength'. Kniezsa (1997: 43) notes its regular occurrence throughout the fifteenth century, though it became more variable later on. The loss of /g/ is likely the result of assimilation to the following dental fricative, concurrently leading to the deletion of <g> in <ngth> clusters.

s~sh

s~sh captures the variable phonological and orthographic realisations regarding the Scots sibilants, focussing on two particular variants. The first relates to the traditional Scots spelling <sch> which represents /ʃ/, as in *scho*, 'shoe'. In southern English varieties the regular spelling was <sh>. This is not a phonological feature as such, but rather an orthographic difference between Scots and English for representing the same sound. The second feature relates to /s/~/ʃ/ interchange, which consists of two subtypes. The first is the presence of /s/ where one would expect /ʃ/, represented in the spelling with <s> and affecting a small number of words, such as *sall*, 'shall'. The second is the reverse process, reflected in the spelling with <sch> or <sh> where English would have <s>, as in *veshell*, 'vessel'. This is one of the more salient features of Older Scots phonology and is not tied to any one dialect area (Johnston, 1997a: 105).

Consonant deletion

Consonant deletion refers to the absence of certain consonants, particularly <v> and <l>, from the spelling, as the result of their phonological omission. These deletions derived from various sound changes that took place in Older Scots (Aitken, 1971: 195) and occurred early on, attested already in fourteenth-century Scots manuscripts (Robinson, 1985: 260). In Older Scots /l/ was vocalised or deleted in coda position after the back or low short vowels /a/, /o/ and /u/, in morpheme-final and pre-consonantal position (Johnston, 1997a: 108; Macafee and †Aitken, 2002: 101–105; 2015a: 33; Maguire, 2012: 58). Scots spellings reflect this accordingly, i.e. *gau*, 'gall', *cauf*, 'calf' and *bok*, 'bolk' – 'belch' (Bann and Corbett, 2015: 27). However /l/ did not generally delete after /a/ (derived from /au/) before /d/, giving *auld*, 'old' and *cauld*, 'cold' rather than 'aud' and 'caud'. Occasionally it did delete in some of these words, such as *had*, 'hold', perhaps because they were frequently unstressed.

There are also other consonant deletions in Scots, such as /t/ in the clusters /pt/ and /kt/ in final position, and /d/ in /nd/ in both final and medial positions (Aitken, 1971: 182). Examples include *distink*, 'distinct', *contrak*, 'contract', *excep*, 'except' and *accep*, 'accept', all of which are attested by the mid-fifteenth century (Robinson, 1985: 181). The process of /nd/ simplification had taken hold in coda position by the fourteenth century, giving *lan*, 'land', while medial /n/ is attested from the fifteenth century onward in *winnow*, 'window' (Robinson, 1985: 355). These stop deletions are, however, rare in the corpus, with most deletions involving <l> and <v>. These changes were not unique to Scots alone; the absence of medial /v/ in words such as *deil* 'devil' defines all of North Britain from the north Midlands up (McIntosh et al., 1986; Johnston, 1997a: 104), although they were never common in southern English varieties.

Lexical and 'Other' items

Alongside the phonemic/graphemic variables listed above, a further two categories were created. Items could also differ on the *Lexical* level. These are words that were frequently tied to a uniquely Scottish way of life or specific institutions, such as the Kirk or the Scottish legal and education systems. For example, the Scots word *haining* refers to an 'enclosure', whilst to *homologate* is to 'countenance'. Lexical items can be problematic in variationist study, given that there is not always a straightforward equivalent between two languages. In these cases, either the closest equivalent was given, or the 'English' column was left blank. While this does not fulfil the requirements of a 'Scots-English' variable, the existence of Scots lexis within the corpus can still provide insights into their importance or function. Its use among highly educated elite writers might suggest the integral role lexical items played in certain contexts for instance, enabling their continuation despite the anglicising trends of the previous centuries.

There was also an *Other* category. These were words containing phonological and orthographic distinctions between Scots and English, but were frequently single examples of a phenomenon. This did not warrant placing them in separate categories. For example, the Scots spelling *weel,* 'well' is one such type. This was the only example of the use of [iː] corresponding to southern English [ɛː] represented in the corpus, yet it is a well-known Scots feature. This belongs to the HEAD/DEAD group, in which Scots retained the historical long vowel /iː/, whereas English had sporadic shortening, giving modern /ɛ/. This does not, however, suggest there was only a single count of *weel* in the corpus, indeed it occurs multiple times across various writers. For a full list of features included in the Lexical and Other categories, see Appendix A.3.

Following classification, each category was populated with applicable words and examples in both Scots and English, and these were then added to their corresponding LIWC dictionaries (remaining words with no clear category or ambiguous origins were discarded). Through this approach, this analysis seeks to follow Conde-Silvestre and Hernandez-Campoy (2004) in utilising a select number of graphemic variables to give an average outlook on the traits of a writer, in this case how Scotticised or anglicised they are. Once complete, the final methodological step was to extract the results from the corpus.

Data analysis

The LIWC dictionaries were uploaded to POLITECS as a word layer, enabling searches to extract overall frequencies in the corpus. The subcorpus of Union politicians was selected, along with the 'Scots_English' word layer, and 'Scots' and 'English' were specified in turn in the search matrix. Their output was extracted along with the metalinguistic information into csv files and combined into a singular dataset. This was uploaded to R (R Core Team, 2020) for macro-social statistical analysis, utilising modelling techniques including Variability-based Neighbour Clustering [VNC] (Gries and Hilpert, 2008), Bayesian regression modelling (Bürkner, 2017) and Multiple Correspondence Analysis [MCA] (Kassambara, 2017). These will be discussed in more detail, in the following two chapters. For the micro-analysis, four writers were selected in the search matrix, and their frequencies of Scots features were extracted from the corpus. Their individual letters were also examined in LaBB-CAT, running the 'Scots_English' layer through each text, which highlights the features as they occur in their letters.

Thus, by focusing on the Scottish correspondence of key political players active during the Union debates, locating their writings in online and archival repositories, digitising the manuscript documents and tagging them for factors of interest, uploading these to a novel, purpose-built corpus, identifying a selection of written Scots features to be searched for, and finally extracting these features from the corpus in aggregate and within individuals, a combined macro and micro-analysis could now take place to answer the research questions. These analyses are presented in the following three chapters, to explore how written Scots patterns across time, across authors, and across recipients within individuals, considering the role of the turbulent political situation and the extent to which writers show sensitivity to stylistic and social influences.

CHAPTER 5

'We can never expect a more favourable juncture for completing this Union, than at present': Frequencies of Scots during and beyond the Union debates

The time period of the Union debates was tense, complex and prone to sudden change, but also a time when ardent proclamations of national spirit were frequent in parliament and the popular press. Whether this had a measurable influence on the use of features indicative of written Scots is as yet unknown, demanding a temporal analysis into the patterning of written Scots over the time period to shed light on this specific window of time. This analysis seeks to identify firstly whether Scots occurs in measurable quantities at all, and secondly, whether the particular years of the Union debates behave differently to the preceding or following decades. Partially for this reason, correspondence dating outside the crucial years of the Union debates (1701–1707), was included in the corpus. This enables a direct comparison between the key Union years with those on either side, whilst keeping the genre and most writers constant. Furthermore, ongoing discussion prior to and in the aftermath of the Union suggests the value of including such years, especially in light of the Jacobite risings of 1715 and 1745 which renewed hostilities and debate, generating a distinctly nationalistic discourse. Such correspondence was produced by the same writers involved in the debates themselves, ensuring a degree of continuity was maintained, and may speak to the persistence of Scots during the early eighteenth century.

Table 5.1 indicates the word-counts and the counts of Scots and anglicised variants for the four main time-periods within the corpus, providing an overview of how well-represented they are (for individual year counts, see Appendix A.4).

Examining Table 5.1, it is clear that the key union years between 1700 and 1710 are much better represented than the remaining year groups.

Table 5.1: Raw word counts and variant counts for year groups in POLITECS.

Year	Word count	Scots	English
1689–1699	64,005	709	4,702
1700–1709	289,433	4667	17,045
1710–1719	62,667	339	17,145
1720–1729	82,283	232	17,245
1730–1739	24,677	74	12,138
1740–1745	20,901	30	5,223

Naturally, this is to be expected, given the central aim of exploring written use Scots during the Union debates, but may cause concern for representativeness. However, as written Scots is explored as a variable, in which Scots variants are matched by anglicised equivalents, we are examining *relative* frequencies of Scots, in relation to their English alternatives. The temporal analysis will therefore seek to explore the proportions of Scots features over time, rather than their raw counts, using VNC or *Variability-Based Neighbour Clustering* (Gries and Hilpert, 2008). The theory and application of this model is explained in the following sections.

VNC

The theory

VNC represents a bottom-up, data-driven clustering technique that identifies meaningful time periods within the data. Rather than imposing set time-frames on a historical corpus, structured in interval-scaled years spanning ten-, fifty- or hundred-year periods, VNC works by allowing the variable data to determine the best temporal arrangement and visualisation of meaningful changes over time. Diachronic corpus data by nature tends to be heterogeneous, which becomes problematic when traditional approaches toward historical data are used, basing partitions on theoretical accounts or simply using convenient divisions that match the time-frame being covered (Gries and Hilpert, 2012: 137). Partitioning data into time slices may give considerably different interpretations regarding the presence or absence of trends, the slope of trends, and turning points in the data (Gries and Hilpert, 2010: 295–296). Particularly when studying many different linguistic phenomena operating simultaneously (as is the case here, where not one, but several different features were included in the category of 'Scots'), partitioning data into even chunks by design is unlikely to provide the optimal temporal classification.

Such issues are also exacerbated when dealing with trends and developments that are not long-lasting or linear in their expression, as there may be 'extended periods of stasis followed by short spurts, and these divergent developments will be more fruitfully analysed as separate periods, even if they fall within the same seventy-year span' (Gries and Hilpert, 2010: 302). Diachronic developments can be dynamic and anaerobic in their nature, often through their complex nonlinear relationships or interactions with other contributing factors (Gries and Hilpert, 2010: 297). Arbitrarily splicing the corpus data into neat time slots might, as a result, identify the overall trend of ongoing anglicisation for example, but could fail to identify any short-term changes, U-turns or peaks in Scots usage in consequence.

One option could be to simply look at the raw data across each individual year, especially in light of the small time-frame under investigation. However, approaching the use of written Scots features on a year-by-year basis is likely to incorporate a lot of noise, considering that values for individual years may be driven by particular constellations of writers, and that written Scots was much reduced in scope and breadth by this point in time. This can also cause issues in analysis, as this leaves individual time points too scarcely populated, or heavily skewed due to the presence of an outlier. Additionally, this can only really provide a descriptive account rather than diving deeper into exploring a phenomenon and possible forces at work. Partitioning diachronic data into successive stages through the appropriate conflation of data points, on the other hand, enables us to make meaningful generalisations even within a small window of change (Gries and Hilpert, 2012: 135). VNC offers a viable alternative, providing the researcher with an empirical and objective analytical approach to exploring change and stability over time. This allows for a temporal exploration that is more sensitive to the phenomenon under investigation, and more reliable than intuition alone (Hilpert, 2013: 32–34), meriting its use.

The model

To perform a VNC analysis a script is run in R (R Core Team, 2020), which takes as input a simple frequency table of variant counts, and the total variable count, per year (in this case number of Scots and anglicised variants). The model then computes a percentage value for the target variant, for each of the years included in the timeline. The data points that are represented in the model are thus relative rather than raw frequencies. The algorithm also measures the standard deviation – a measure of the difference between percentage values for each adjacent time-point – creating a measure of their similarity. From this, the algorithm is able to determine which of all the standard deviations is smallest, forming the two most similar year values, whose variant frequencies are summed. This process continues in a stepwise process, as the algorithm amalgamates data points on the basis of mutual similarity between neighbouring year values into successively larger groups, starting from the smallest standard deviations and gradually increasing, until all datapoints are merged into a single cluster. Once complete, the standard deviations are plotted in reverse order onto a scree plot. This enables the researcher to determine how many temporal stages to assume on the basis of how much variation is captured within each successive standard deviation, starting from the largest to the smallest (Gries and Hilpert, 2010: 301). The favoured solution is a compromise between capturing as much dissimilarity between periods as possible, and positing as few clusters as necessary (Gries and Hilpert, 2012: 140).

The temporal stages subsequently identified in the data are based on the behaviour of the clusters, which are characterised by a high degree of within-group similarity (the extent to which the variant percentages contained within the cluster were the same or similar in value) and a low degree of between-group similarity (the frequencies occurring within one group and the next are sufficiently different from one another to be considered two separate clusters). Each cluster is thus likely to constitute a relatively homogeneous period of interest (Gries and Hilpert, 2012: 135). This utilises the same methodology as other commonly used, hierarchical, agglomerate clustering approaches such as similarity matrixes, but unlike the latter, VNC is sensitive to the temporal ordering of the variants. It recognises that clusters must be arranged chronologically, preventing it from grouping together data points into nonsensical clusters that span hundreds or thousands of years (Gries and Hilpert, 2008, 2012). VNC is as a result restricted to identifying and merging clusters within temporally adjacent files and datapoints.

Meaningful time partitions are thus derived directly from the data itself, which may not necessarily align with traditional divisions of the language variety. Indeed, much of the previous discussion of historical Scots has tended to distinguish a singular cut-off point between 'pre-1700 Older Scots' and 'post-1700 Modern Scots' (i.e. Aitken, 1985: xiii, although see Templeton, 1973, Murison, 1979 and Meurman-Solin, 1989 for more nuanced subdivisions of the timeline, and see Kopaczyk, 2013c for a detailed discussion on the problematic nature of previous Scots periodisation). Yet, while 1700 is chosen as the division between Older and Modern Scots, Older Scots did not disappear overnight, nor did Modern Scots arise out of the well-spring of Union to take on a new, Anglocentric identity. Rather, 1700 marks a point in the ongoing transition from majority Scots options to majority English or anglicised options, which had been at work over the past 150 years.

While reliance on pre-defined, global corpus divisions will not necessarily obscure or distort such trends, they are more likely to do so, and as will become clear, this approach would fail to capture the intricate patterning and detail that was occurring precisely around this pivotal moment in time, both historically, politically and linguistically. Instead, VNC recognises that historical periods should not be treated as discreet entities with abrupt boundaries and clearly defined beginning and end points, since they often begin as reactions against preceding stages (Hernández-Campoy and Schilling, 2012: 64). Instead, VNC can be much more fine-tuned to

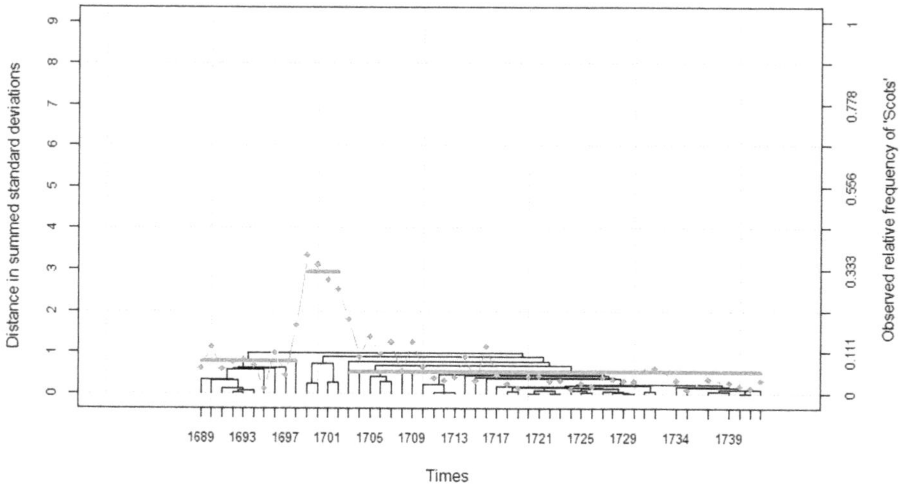

Figure 5.1: VNC dendrogram showing proportions of Scots variants over time.

small changes in the data and to the particular phenomenon and context under investigation.

The VNC algorithm is available as an R script, which was kindly sent by Stephan Gries (p.c.). The defaults for similarity measure and amalgamation rule were used, and the frequency table containing raw and summed counts of Scots and English variants across each year, was fed into the script. Once run, the resultant scree plot indicated that three clusters were optimal for capturing the variation over time. This produced the dendrogram shown in Figure 5.1.

The dendrogram contains three different pieces of information. The timeline is represented on the x-axis, this stretches from 1689 (the date of the Revolution, and the beginning of the Union debates) to 1745, the date of the last Jacobite rising. The observed relative frequency of Scots is shown on the right y-axis, in which the scale is from 0 (no Scots recorded for that year) to 1 (100 per cent Scots recorded for that year), represented by the datapoints on the graph. Recall that the frequency is relative – values for Scots are relative to the overall count of Scots and anglicised variants combined. On the left-hand y-axis, the 'Distance in summed standard deviations' is given – this is represented by the boxes in the graph itself. The taller the boxes, the greater the difference between one cluster of data points and the next, suggesting a higher degree of variability for that time period. The width of the boxes indicates how many data points are contained within the summed standard deviation, suggesting a wider time-frame. The yellow lines on the graph indicate the temporal clusters identified in the scree plot; accordingly, we can see three clusters depicted in Figure 5.1.

The difference between the first and third cluster is very small, and suggests a highly anglicised corpus of writers, and the small and flat standard deviations in the graph imply they were also relatively homogeneous in their writing choices. Leaving aside the second cluster for a moment, the overall picture presented here indicates that written Scots had largely retreated from elite correspondence by the time of 1689, and this process continued throughout the opening decades of the eighteenth century. Examining the relative frequencies, the initial years see slightly elevated levels of Scots, but this tails off fairly quickly after 1715, the year of a major Jacobite rising and a time of renewed hostilities and heightened tensions. The dendrogram does reflect several small spikes in Scots use and continuing variability following the Union until about 1716. This offers a tempting link between post-Union grievances, Jacobite intrigue, and heightened levels of Scots usage, though frequencies are nowhere near the levels of the pre-1704 period. By 1720, the relative frequency of Scots has fallen to minute levels and variability is similarly reduced, while the last years barely register any Scots at all. This is not surprising – written Scots had already been anglicising for over a century prior to 1700, and this process was encouraged by the Union of the Parliaments and the movement of Scotland's political elite to the metropolitan English capital, to take part in the new political order.

There is however, a notable exception to the general trend outlined above. The second cluster identifies a considerably higher relative frequency of Scots, driven by a few years in particular. These years fall roughly around the key years of the Union debates in the Scottish parliament. From 1699 until 1704 there is an observable clustering of Scots frequencies, which is noticeably higher than the values to either side. This small period is also marked by a slightly higher level of variability, indicated by the minor increase in the height of the boxes (the standard deviations). This effect is not being driven by the fact that more correspondence covering these exact years is contained within the corpus, as all frequencies are *relative*. Thus, in an anglicising scenario, we would expect any increase in Scots-indicative features to be matched by an increase in anglicised variants. Moreover, smaller wordcounts are more likely to produce 'outliers', given the presence of single writer behaving unusually cannot be moderated as easily by the remaining data (though VNC can handle such behaviour better than descriptive statistics). Instead, the second cluster suggests that this small window of time was unique in some sense, encouraging an increase in written Scots features. This highlights the value of VNC, given that the rough corpus divisions shown earlier in Table 5.1 reflected an increase across 1700–1709, yet here it is clear that it was the first half of this ten-year time period that was responsible in particular for the heightened Scots frequencies.

This suggests the events around the debates, and perhaps the debates themselves, did have a measurable influence on the occurrence of Scots features, and furthermore generated an increase in their use. Given that the same body of writers produced the written material covering this timeline, with the majority of the politicians represented not just during the critical Union years, but either side of the debates, the result is all the more striking. The patterning reflected in the VNC analysis suggests that these writers *changed* their behaviour during this critical moment. This lends support to the possibility that written Scots features may have been used to index political identity, Scottishness or related ideological concepts and in-group identities.

Examining this particular window of variation more closely, it is curious to note that Scots frequencies begin to decline around 1704/5, two years before the Union agreement was ratified and completed. In the first instance this might seem counter-intuitive, given the key role the last two years played in the debating, finalising and ratifying of the Union agreement. However, this might be a reflection of the build-up of tension between England and Scotland leading up to 1705, especially in the wake of the Darien failure, during which relations between the two nations were at their nadir. Following 1705, there was a noticeable decline in hostilities, and this might be echoed in the percentages indicated on the plot. Equally, this observed reversal could reflect the consolidation of the Squadrone

Volante, following the formation of the new ministry under Tweeddale during the session of 1704. This formation was not uncoupled from the rise in tensions – indeed elements of each are closely related, plausibly leading to their twin influence on the observed rise and fall in written Scots. Both of these aspects will briefly be considered in turn to identify how they may have contributed to the change in written Scots usage observed during the course of the first seven years of the century.

The rise in tensions to 1705

Friction between Scotland and England was exacerbated by several events that took place in the opening years of the eighteenth century, some of these have already been touched upon in Chapter 1. That chapter highlighted the fractured and tumultuous time period in which consideration of an incorporating union took place: a time of heightened social, political, religious and economic tensions, against a backdrop of parliamentary and monarchical absolutism exercised by the English Court and Crown. Such issues were increasingly untenable for the Scottish elite, and these tensions became palpable in the opening years of the eighteenth century, as a series of contentious and volatile events contributed to hostilities on both sides.

Among the first of these was the failed Darien scheme (1698–1700) – the project by the Company of Scotland to build a Scottish colony on the Isthmus of Panama. King William and his English parliamentarians were blamed for its failure, and William's refusal to send aid to the colony once it came under attack was particularly egregious (Bowie, 2007: 28; Stephen, 2007: 17). The failure of the scheme caused widespread shock, resentment and an outpouring of despair couched in overly patriotic terms. This included members of the Scottish elite, many of whom had invested considerable sums of money into it, and the fallout naturally contributed to a rise in discussion and debate around Scotland's future and sovereign status. It is not implausible to assume that such discourse, infused as it was with a simmering animosity towards the English Court, might have induced higher levels of written Scots. The salience of the discussion itself, as well as perhaps a tightening of allegiances and political or ideological identities arising in response to the event, could have had tangible influences on language use, especially within correspondence between political members.

Darien was followed by a series of tit-for-tat Acts issued by the English and Scottish parliaments which added fuel to the fire. This included the *Act of Settlement* passed by the English parliament in 1701, which claimed that any future heir to the throne must be Protestant, followed by the Scottish *Act of Security* in 1704, which asserted Scotland's right to choose a Protestant successor. Finally, the English *Alien Act* in 1705 essentially declared Scottish merchants in England to be aliens, leaving them unable to trade. These three Acts chart an increasingly strained, divisive and uncompromising constitutional relationship between the two nations, but they also had serious consequences wrapped up within their stipulations. In each case they threatened the security, harmony and prosperity of the countries involved, stoking an increasingly intense fire of discord that left them teetering on a volatile political brink. Scotland's *Act of Security* in 1704 for instance was seen an act of open defiance, intensifying the dynastic crisis further but also harbouring the potential threat of war (Whatley, 2008: 3). Indeed, it came close to imploding the tense relations between Scotland and England in 1704–1705 (Stephen, 2007: 23, 35).

Between 1701 and 1705 a mounting hostility and enmity between the two nations is clearly observable, and these events had an immediate connection to the political sphere. They would have directly involved and influenced the politicians within the Scottish parliament, and a connection between their occurrence and increased vernacular language use is fathomable, in light of the discussion around Scottish interests, liberties and sovereignty they inspired. As such Acts also touched upon the key concerns of politicians, including not just economic security and political power, but also their Presbyterian, Episcopalian or Jacobite designs, they may have contributed to a strengthening of politico-religious identities within the parliament, leading indirectly to heightened patterns of Scots use along these lines. The following chapter (Chapter 6) will explore this potential further, examining Scots use specifically in relation to such contributing factors, but it is worth bearing in mind how such identities may have become more salient, leading to this observed increase in Scots for a small window of time.

The climax to these hostile events came with the hanging in 1705 of Thomas Green, captain of the English ship the *Worcester*, along with two of his men, on trumped up charges of piracy. The level of anger, both among the public and many of the politicians in parliament, was palpable by this point, and Anglo-Scottish tensions peaked at an all-time high (Macinnes, 2007: 272; Patrick and Whatley, 2007: 173). Reverend Robert Wylie wrote to the Duke of Hamilton on the 19th of March 1705, disparaging 'this English insolence insulting us upon our coasts' (NRS, GD 406/1/5297, quoted in Whatley, 2006: 201), and a crowd numbering as many as 80,000 congregated to watch the hanging (Graham, 2005). Relationships between the two nations had reached their lowest ebb, yet paradoxically, this also had the effect of bringing union back to the debating table. During this process, the Squadrone consolidated into a separate political interest, and their formation may have contributed to a shift in political identities and concurrently, language use. The hanging of the Worcester crew could thus form the 'tipping point', reflected in frequencies of Scots within the VNC analysis, which drop off quite suddenly from their previous level after 1704.

It is not inconceivable that these events and the rising sense of anger and animosity directed towards England may have had a tangible influence on language choices. Particularly in letters penned between fellow Scots of a similar political ilk, the use of Scots features may have been encouraged by their concordance over these issues, which were playing out in real time as the correspondence was being produced. Chapter 6 considers this backdrop in assessing the role of different social, political and religious factors (or not) in influencing probabilities of Scots use, while Chapter 7 will explore these possible links in more detail through a micro-analysis of individual authors within the corpus and their recipients. The possibilities outlined here have to remain hypothetical, but the VNC analysis has still been able to illuminate an increase in Scots frequencies during the opening years of the eighteenth century that match a rise in Anglo-Scottish tensions within the same time period. Following this rise however, is a rather sudden decline in Scots frequencies after 1704, which aligns with the consolidation of the

Squadrone Volante in the wake of the hanging, as previously mentioned. To this possibility we must now turn and discuss in more detail.

The development of the Squadrone Volante

Alongside the diffusion in tensions, another factor plausibly influencing the post-1705 drop in relative frequencies of Scots might be the consolidation of the *Squadrone Volante*, following their formation in 1704. Their history has been detailed in Chapter 1, but to quickly recap their development, John Hay the second Marquess Tweeddale was asked to form a new ministry in 1704 following the discovery and subsequent failure of the *Queensberry Plot*. A group of political contemporaries assembled around Tweeddale, composed of former members of the Country party who had been gradually forming into an alliance since 1702, based on a Presbyterian, pro-Hanoverian political platform (Whatley, 2008: 105). The group however failed to condemn the Worcester affair in 1705, leaving them disgraced, and they were dismissed in favour of the Duke of Argyll. Rather than returning to the Country party, they instead formed the Squadrone Volante and chose to support an incorporating union.

The close-knit alliance between the Squadrone members, driven by their religious and ideological adherence but also their kinship ties, may have encouraged similar language use among them and their network of recipients. If they did form a community of practice, sharing social practices and ties but also linguistic resources (Meyerhoff, 2002; Kopaczyk and Jucker, 2013: 6), then perhaps, as a coherent body of commissioners breaking away from the Country party and coming to vote along Court party lines, their variable language use subtly changed in the process. This change in linguistic behaviour, however slight, can be captured by the VNC analysis, especially if it was consistent across multiple members.

The drop in Scots frequencies observed in Figure 5.1 would suggest that, post-1705, the Squadrone adopted an increasingly anglicised register. This could point to their changing allegiances as they moved toward a position more closely aligned with incorporation. Prior to 1704, they were still part of a Country party opposition and may have used more vernacular variants during this time, especially if the opposition was associated with elevated levels of Scots as we might hypothesise. In light of the tense Anglo-Scottish relations ongoing at the time, higher levels of Scots among Country party supporters, including the pre-1704 Squadrone members, may have been the result. Following their splintering off however, the Squadrone's adherence to the Court party line may have been matched by a change in linguistic behaviour, not only signalling their changing alliances, but perhaps also their increased correspondence with Court party figures. As leading members of powerful Scottish families, the Court magnates wielded significant socio-political power, and their status could have encouraged Squadrone members to shift toward 'polite' (and therefore anglicised) language use when corresponding with them. It is not yet clear whether the Court figures demonstrated a more anglicised writing style, nor whether political party influenced variable language use, and this will be explored in detail in the following chapter. Nonetheless the possibility that these political constellations, with their intertwined ideological, religious and familial connections, influenced linguistic choices, is tangible.

What this temporal analysis has indicated, nonetheless, is that there was a small but discernible rise in the relative frequencies of written Scots during the opening years of the Union debates, suggesting this time period was indeed unique in influencing the linguistic behaviour of this particular group of writers. It is the years immediately proceeding the breaking-away of the Squadrone Volante, during which the greatest deterioration of Anglo-Scottish relations took place, that see the greatest increase in Scots use, presenting a palpable link between these events and language use. Naturally, any instance of language variation and change is likely to have been conditioned by multiple contributing factors interacting with individual writers, letters and features in a complex cross-road of influences. Nonetheless, given what we already know about the political and linguistic situation of the Union debates, such patterns strongly imply this cannot be mere coincidence. Additional support or rejection of these possibilities will be uncovered in the following chapters, and any patterns observed can feed back into the clustering observed here.

CHAPTER 6

MCA and brms: A two-fold statistical approach to multifactor regression analysis of historical written Scots use and the role of political identity

Most previous research into eighteenth-century Scots has not yet taken a quantitative approach to exploring variation (though see van Eyndhoven, 2021, 2023b for two pilot studies), given their inherently qualitative and descriptive nature (see for instance Jones, 1995; J. J. Smith, 1996a; Dossena, 2005; Cruickshank, 2012; Corbett, 2013 and Elder, 2022 for examples). Whilst these methodologies are appropriate for investigating the language behaviour of individuals, they become impractical when analysing and summarising across multiple authors and predictors. Furthermore, insights gleaned from quantitative analysis can feed forward into qualitative analyses, providing a scaffolding that enables stylistic behaviour to be situated within its broader macrosocial context. Accordingly, this calls for an empirical analysis, utilising statistical methodologies to analyse the language behaviour of authors in aggregate through the prism of larger, macro-social factors. This offers a broad-based view of the linguistic landscape in which variation is operating, while statistical tools provide greater explanatory power than descriptive statistics alone, which fail to take into account the multifaceted nature of the phenomena and extralinguistic constraints operating on it (Gries and Hilpert, 2010: 297).

However, statistical methodologies can become complicated or even unworkable when applied to historical linguistic data. A quick check of the dataset indicated that only 12 per cent of the variable tokens were Scots. This is comparatively high considering the status of written Scots by the eighteenth century and the nature of these writers, but as the minority variant the data is inherently imbalanced, and there is still considerable risk that statistical analysis might produce weakly informative or insubstantial results. To address these issues, two multi-factorial statistical models were used – Bayesian regression modelling and Multiple Correspondence Analysis or MCA (Kassambara, 2017). In combination, they illuminate multiple extralinguistic influences contributing to the sudden rise of Scots during this politically volatile time, as observed in Chapter 5. The theory behind these two models will be discussed in turn, prior to their application to the data, highlighting the strength of each to navigate the challenges of historical data towards an outcome encompassing greater interpretative power.

Bayesian modelling

GLMER vs BRMS

An intuitive starting point would be to use frequentist statistics and build a generalised, linear, mixed-effects regression (glmer) model. Glmer models offer a robust methodology that can assess both the strength of multiple predictors simultaneously, and the importance of individual predictor levels, and these are already commonplace in contemporary sociolinguistic research (e.g. Bates, 2005; Baayen, 2008; Baayen et al., 2008; Jaeger, 2008; Johnson, 2009). They have also seen increasing recognition in historical sociolinguistic investigations (e.g. Gries and Hilpert, 2010; De Cuypere, 2015; Fonteyn and van de Pol, 2016; Zimmermann, 2017; Petré and van de Velde, 2018; van Eyndhoven and Clark, 2019). Mixed-effects regression models recognise that an observed phenomenon may arise from several causes operating in concert, and can account for multiple and complex causation whilst identifying predictors that are highly correlated or in interaction at the same time (McElreath, 2020: 123). Their inclusion of *random effects* also recognises that there is always 'random' variation present in a data set, often stemming from individual language users or variants which might behave in unexpected ways. Incorporating random effects enables the model to recognise where a potential source of the variation comes from, thereby reducing the chance that the significance of certain predictors is inflated (Baayen et al., 2008; Johnson, 2009; Baayen, 2010; Tagliamonte and Baayen, 2012). This makes them a valuable tool in sociolinguistic and diachronic research, enabling the researcher to obtain a more nuanced picture of the patterning of variation.

However, Bayesian regression modelling offers a viable alternative to glmer models. Bayesian models can also statistically assess the influence of multiple factors and their levels, producing robust results, but do not rely on the significance values of mixed effects models, which may be too arbitrary for data of this kind.[1] The **brms** package (Bürkner, 2017) in R enables regression modelling within a Bayesian, rather than frequentist, framework. This provides the same benefits as glmer, but with the added benefit that the model will always converge. While relatively simple models will return similar estimates for both kinds of statistics, more complex models often won't fit if they are run within frequentist packages such as lme4 (Bates et al., 2014), given glmer's sensitivity to small sample sizes. Bayesian models will successfully converge regardless, simply returning estimates with greater uncertainty, which is a more conservative approach (Coretta et al., 2021). This is an unequivocally practical reason for choosing Bayesian modelling to analyse this data, but there are a number of other theoretical reasons why working within the Bayesian framework is desirable. While a thorough discussion of Bayesian methods would be beyond the scope of this book, a basic overview of the theoretical basis of Bayesian modelling, as well as the methodology underpinning the model outputs, is necessary to interpret the results, especially as these methods are less-well known or used in historical sociolinguistics.[2] This will also help to explicate the differences between the Bayesian and frequentist framework, and why this approach may in fact be preferred.

1 Initially, several attempts were made to build a glmer model, using the **lme4** package (Bates et al., 2014) in R v3.5.3 (R Core Team, 2020), but none of the models reached convergence.

2 For a general introduction to Bayesian statistics see Kruschke (2015), Etz et al. (2018), McElreath (2020) and references therein. For more specific uses of Bayesian statistics in phonetics, see Nicenboim et al. (2018) and Vasishth et al. (2018).

The theory

The Bayesian framework is based upon *priors* and *posteriors*. The posterior is what we are trying to determine – in this case the effect of a certain predictor on the choice to use Scots or English. Effect values are all the possible values for a factor, which can either be numerical in the case of continuous predictors, or categorical, as is the case here. These values are usually referred to as a *parameter*. The model output reports *posterior distributions* – the distribution of relative probabilities, for each combination of the dependent variable and an effect value (or *parameter*). For example, it will consider the probability of a Scots or English variant in combination with 'Yes', 'No' and 'Tactical' for the predictor *Jacobite* and suggest the range of probabilities for each (at varying levels of credibility). A distribution can include positive or negative values, or both, depending on the direction of the effect (in this case suggesting an increase or decrease in Scots use relative to the global baseline level in the corpus).

The posterior distributions are reported through several different values, to provide particular types of information on the distribution. This includes the *estimate* (β), which is the mean probability. This has the highest probability density within the spread of the distribution – most of the probability is based around this value. The *standard deviation* (SD) of the distribution is also reported, along with the 95 per cent *Credibility Interval* (CrI), which has two bounds. These indicate the upper and lower bounds of the probability range – in other words, there is a 95 per cent probability that the true value is within that interval range. For example, if the predictor level 'Party – Court' had a 95 per cent CrI between 20 and 40 per cent (once converted from log-odds), there is a 95 per cent probability that the true probability value is between these figures, with extreme values being less likely than values in the centre of the interval (Coretta, 2020). In other words, it suggests that there is a 20–40 per cent increase in Scots use when the writer was a Court figure, at 95 per cent probability. A wide distribution suggests a weaker effect, as the probability is spread across a wider range of values (Dobreva, 2023), and when the spread of the interval is around 0 it is unlikely that there is a reliable effect, as this suggests that a proportion of the probability is distributed at or near the value of 0 per cent probability.

Taken together, these reported values (the *posterior*) provide not just a summary of the mean probabilities, but a more detailed picture of how probability patterns across different parameter values. We are able for instance to see the absolute, rather than the relative, magnitude of a relationship between the outcome and a predictor, as well as the level of uncertainty surrounding an average relationship (McElreath, 2020: 14). The *posterior distribution* is thus an approximation of the *parameter* distribution, but it also takes into account probabilities taken from the data itself, and the specified *prior* for that parameter. Priors are both engineering assumptions – chosen to help the machine algorithm learn – and scientific assumptions – chosen to reflect what we know about a phenomenon. They capture the initial degree of belief about the likelihood of an event, by defining the distributional limits for the parameters through allocating credibility over this to suggest a feasible range.

In the case of the data being worked with here, applying specific priors beforehand would be rather fruitless, given there is no prior distributional information available about the predictors, and none of the predictors are continuous (in which we could specify a realistic range). Rather, when unable to propose a prior that is intuitive and reasonable, we can use *non-informative priors* (or *uninformative priors*) instead. This may at first glance seem meaningless within a framework predicated on pre-existing information, yet the name is a bit of a misnomer. Their main function is to express vague or general information about a variable, and they can provide an appearance of objectivity, for example by assigning all possibilities equal probabilities, rather than those that are subjectively elicited. This can prevent the biasing of results, and non-informative priors are becoming increasingly popular in Bayesian analysis (Dobreva, 2023). Moreover, while they allow some impossibly strong relationships in the parameter range, non-informative priors generally tend to bind the distribution to the possible ranges of variables (McElreath, 2020: 154). Their use typically yields results not too different from conventional frequentist analysis, but with the added benefit that the model will always converge, as well as a number of other benefits which are outlined below.

Bayesian vs frequentist modelling

There are various motivations for choosing Bayesian modelling over frequentist alternatives, both in historical sociolinguistics and statistical analysis more generally. Fundamentally, Bayesian and Frequentist statistics are driven by different assumptions, offering two different methods to answer different questions. Unlike the frequentist framework, which is based on a series of hypothetical experimental replications that are never actually carried out (Wagenmakers, 2007), Bayesian inference is centred around a reallocation of credibility (Kruschke, 2015). The output is thus *probability distributions* of parameters rather than *point estimates*, and so there is no arbitrary cut-off between 'significant' and 'non-significant' as in frequentist modelling. The Bayesian framework thus allows us to ascertain the *tendencies* and *directions* in which the data is patterning, acquiring an overview of the dataset and how different predictor levels are behaving with respect to the dependent variable. This is a promising approach for historical data that may not neatly align with one predictor or another, and whose patterning may be too vague or scattered to be captured by the $p < 0.05$ cut-off point in a traditional frequentist model.

There are also a number of practical reasons for choosing Bayesian over frequentist models. In particular, Bayesian models will always converge towards the true value in the long run, thanks to their iterative process (Coretta et al., 2021) using Markov chain Monte Carlo (MCMC) methods. These comprise of an ensemble of iterative probability chains that sample from the data and converge towards the highest probability region. This makes it possible to compute large hierarchical models without becoming destabilised like traditional linear models (Banerjee et al., 2015). Bayesian models also dodge the problems associated with the reliance on p-values in statistical inference. Frequentist models are liable to report non-conservative p-values, giving increased false positive (or Type I error) rates, in which there is no underlying effect but significant values are still reported (Wagenmakers, 2007; Munafò et al., 2017; Kirby and Sonderegger, 2018; Roettger, 2019; Coretta et al., 2021). This does not deem p-values irrelevant, but they are easily tweaked through questionable research practices (i.e.

'p-hacking'), and uncritical acceptance of their value can be problematic. These various strengths do not mean that no other approach is justified (McElreath, 2020: 24), but there are a number of practical and conceptual benefits to Bayesian modelling that merits its use alongside offering a viable alternative pathway to frequentist regression models, and thus formed the natural choice to analyse this dataset.

However, when a brms model was run on the data, it was characterised by a lot of uncertainty, indicated by very wide distributions for most parameters and a large number of predictor levels that showed negligible effect in conditioning the probability of written Scots (see Appendix A.5 for log odds of all effects in the model output).[3] This suggests the general difficulty of finding robust patterns of variation within historical, imbalanced data. Yet it also highlights the more conservative approach of Bayesian modelling, which returns results with greater uncertainty, reflecting the scattered and unclear nature of the data. These results suggested the high dimensionality of the data, which is not surprising given the presence of multiple predictors, several of which were highly correlated. While MCMC methods can handle multi-dimensional datasets better than glmer models, when the number of dimensions (predictor levels) rise, they too can suffer the 'curse of dimensionality': regions of higher probability tend to stretch and get lost in an increasing volume of space that contributes little to the integral (Rebeschini and van Handel, 2015: 2814). A solution that works in tandem with Bayesian modelling, without losing its predictive power, is to use *Multiple Correspondence Analysis*, or MCA.

Multiple correspondence analysis (MCA)

The theory

Multiple Correspondence Analysis or MCA is an extension of the Principle Components Analysis (PCA) framework. Whereas PCA is designed for analysing a data set containing continuous variables, MCA

3 For the posterior distribution plots and visualisations, see van Eyndhoven (2023a).

works with multiple categorical variables (Abdi and Williams, 2010). In this instance, these variables are the predictors or independent effects – they form the extralinguistic factors in the regression model. MCA analyses the association between various categorical variables included in the model across the authors in the dataset, searching for global patterns in the data without being given any prior information or limits. Once these are identified, MCA summarises and visualises these associations, presenting the values in a matrix before mapping the data points onto a multidimensional space. This provides a basic picture of the possible interactions between two variables, for example, the frequency of authors who are both 'Pro-Union' and 'Court' politicians.

MCA replaces the original variables with a much smaller set of 'dimensions' that capture similarly behaving predictors, depicted visually on a multi-dimensional plot. Usually, this is a biplot[4] – a two-dimensional space with an x and y axis ranging from -1 to 1, each of which captures some of the associations present in the data. Usually, individual predictors will be strongly associated with a specific dimension; being positioned closer to −1 or 1 suggests they are well represented by that dimension. Some however will not be captured by either dimension, and data points that contribute very little are close to the origin of the biplot and are relatively unimportant to the interpretation of variation. MCA thus removes the high dimensionality of a complex, multifactorial data-frame by incorporating multiple predictors into a much smaller set of dimensions. Each dimension captures a certain percentage of variation within the dataset, independently of the next. Ideally, the first dimension will capture the most variation, and this will decrease for each subsequent dimension (Jolliffe, 2002: 1). The higher the retention of variation in each dimension, the more subtlety from the original data is retained in the low dimension solution (Bendixen, 2003).

Interpretation of the MCA biplot is based on the proximity between points in the low-dimensional map, and proximities are only meaningful between points of the same set – i.e. between authors (suggesting certain

4 Normally the first two dimensions (which contain the most variation) are chosen, although, in theory, all the dimensions identified by MCA could be plotted. However, this produces decreasing returns in capturing variation and would prove visually challenging to interpret.

authors cluster together and thus have a similar extralinguistic profile), and between factors (suggesting they may be correlated or in interaction). Negatively correlated row points are positioned on opposite sides of the plot origin (in opposing quadrants), indicating a high level of dissimilarity between those authors or factors. Alongside proximity of the independent variables, the predictor levels themselves can also be plotted within this space, indicating whether they cluster or diverge. The distance between their points gives a measure of their similarity, for example, we might expect 'Episcopalian' and 'Jacobite (Yes)' to be situated close together, given that the former almost always begets the latter.

Methods like MCA or PCA often reveal meaningful and intuitive structures in the data, depicting underlying relational arrangements including associations and similarities within each plane of variation (Jolliffe, 2002: 63). This forms an unbiased, objective method for grouping together multiple variables, but also multiple observations, within an original dataset (Kassambara, 2017), making MCA a very useful tool for the investigation of structural variation in sociolinguistic variables. We are able to see whether particular groups of writers are clustering in obvious or unpredictable ways across these factors, as well as whether particular factors behave in similar ways. In this instance, the dimensions capture the association between the authors and their extralinguistic features, such as *Birthplace* or *Political Affiliation*. Their language choice (Scots or English) is not included in the MCA, as this forms the dependent variable in the Bayesian model, with the MCA dimensions as independent predictors.

There is of course some danger to blindly adopting the methodology of Correspondence Analysis without exploring alternative pathways, given it is based upon exploratory data analysis with more or less arbitrary choices of parameters and procedures. Methods such as MCA can consequently produce results even in situations in which there is no underlying structure (Jolliffe, 2002: 278), and care must be taken to avoid interpreting dimensions which are merely the result of random features in the dataset. This is where the combined power of MCA with Bayesian modelling can help to mitigate this issue. By reducing the extralinguistic dimensionality of the data to just two dimensions, and applying these dimensions as independent variables in a Bayesian regression model, which controls for random effects and takes an inherently comparative methodological approach to examining variation in data, the weaknesses of any singular model are somewhat circumvented by their combination.

The MCA model

To run the MCA, the dataset was first subset to include only active variables, which included *Party, Political Affiliation, Jacobite, Address, Birthplace, Location* and *Relationship*. These were treated as factors and sum-coded. 'Unknowns' were removed from the dataset and, to further reduce dimensionality, the minister Robert Wodrow was removed as well. His datapoints may be introducing extra 'noise' and variation into the dataset, especially if the politicians form a language community of their own. Once the data had been filtered and sorted, the MCA analysis was run on the dataset using the MCA() function of the **FactoMineR** package (Lê et al., 2008). The output of this analysis is illustrated in the biplot below, produced using **factoextra** (Kassambara and Mundt, 2020) which provides MCA data visualisation (based within the **ggplot2** (Wickham, 2016) package).

Figure 6.1 depicts the MCA factor map – this indicates the amount of variation captured by the dimensions (16.32 per cent and 9.5 per cent for Dimensions 1 and 2 respectively). These percentages are very low overall, only capturing 25.8 per cent of the variation in the data. This might point to the scattered and disharmonious nature of the factors conditioning the writers. Politicians were motivated by a complex combination of interests and ideals that intersected in varying and diverse ways. Many writers aligned with particular identity combinations, but some fall outside of this or fluctuate across extralinguistic constraints, which may complicate the MCA's ability to identify global patterns in the data. However, the first two dimensions will be able to suggest relationships that hold for the largest, *consistent* proportion of the data.[5] Whilst recognising their limitations,

5 One possibility could be to include more dimensions, but checking the subsequent dimensions revealed that they captured increasingly smaller percentages, complicating interpretation and feasibility.

statistical methods like MCA can still shed light on undercurrents and common threads woven into the data, however faint they might be, particularly when used in combination with other models like bmrs.

To return to Figure 6.1, alongside the percentage of variation captured, it also depicts the patterning of predictor levels relative to one another, across the multidimensional variation space. The distance between different predictor levels gives a measure of their similarity (or dissimilarity), in relation to the dimensions. For instance, examining the map, we can see a possible clustering for the factor levels 'Squadrone_Volante', 'Presbyterian' and 'No' (non-Jacobite) toward the bottom-left corner. This is an intuitive correlation, given that Squadrone members were a highly coherent group

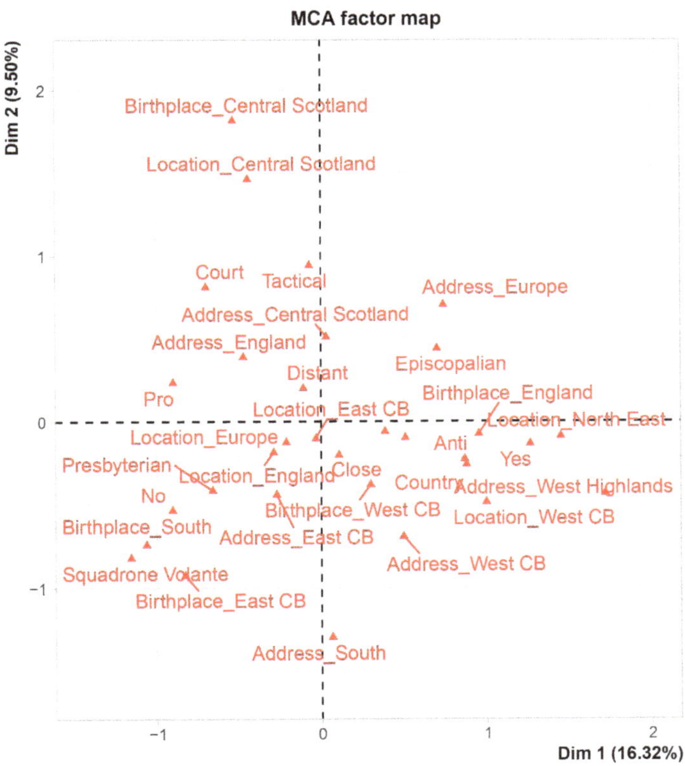

Figure 6.1: MCA plot showing similarity distances between predictor levels.

of politicians primarily motivated by their staunch Presbyterianism, making them naturally antagonistic to Jacobitism. The birthplaces 'South' and 'East CB' also cluster here, which matches what we know about the party members – there was a collection of Squadrone family estates within the Borders and around East Lothian (Macinnes, 2007: 264). In the opposite quadrant 'Episcopalian' is located, suggesting it is negatively correlated with Squadrone Volante and these birthplaces. Again, this is not surprising, given the Presbyterianism of the Squadrone Volante and the concentration of Episcopalians in the North East and Highlands. This also indicates the reliability and validity of the analysis. The model is performing as expected, recognising individuals who share similar characteristics.

While visualising the connections between social factors in the data does not tell us anything about language use, understanding the associations between predictor levels is important in acquiring an overview of how they interact. This tells us for example the extent to which factor levels might work in tandem to influence language use, or how they might at times exercise contradictory or conflicting influences upon members of specific groups. For instance, 'Court' is considerably further away from the Presbyterian and non-Jacobite values than the 'Squadrone' data-point. This indicates 'Court' is not immediately associated with these values, likely because not all Court politicians fit these exact characteristics (for instance the Earls of Kinnoull and Mar were Episcopalian). Accordingly, the factor map recognises this, and places 'Court' further away from the cluster. Thus, if the subsequent brms model suggests higher probabilities of Scots are associated with 'Episcopalian' – then we might expect a strong negative probability of Scots for Squadrone members, but a weaker effect for Court politicians, reducing the internal linguistic consistency within the party.

We can also examine the independent variables themselves in Figure 6.2 below, in which the interactions between the different factors and the dimensions become particularly clear.

Party, Jacobite and *Political Affiliation* reflect a strong association with Dimension 1 – they are all located close to the value 1 which suggests they are captured particularly well by this dimension. *Party* and *Jacobite* cluster very close together, which is logical given party lines were largely (though not entirely) split along Jacobite associations after 1704, with

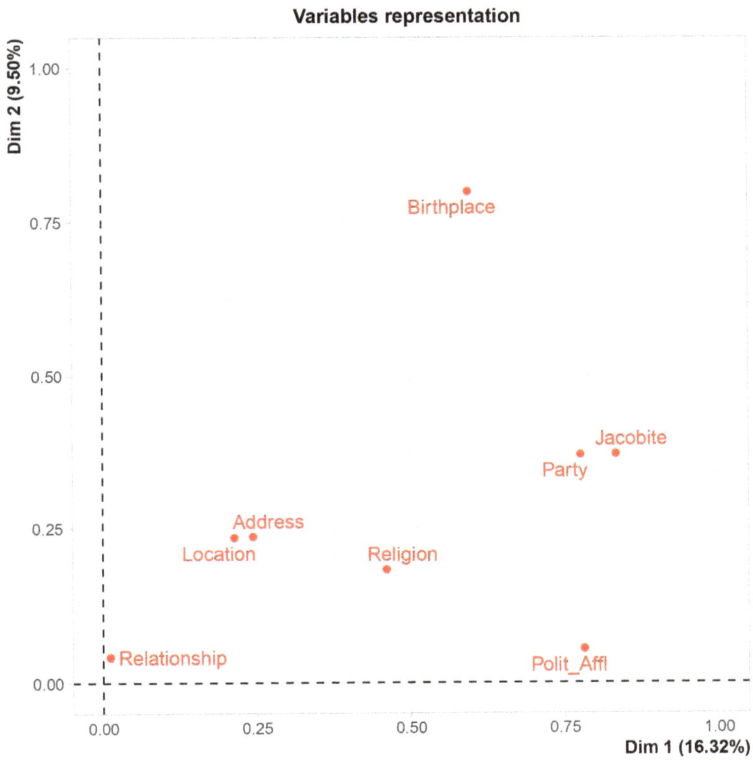

Figure 6.2: MCA plot showing similarity distances between predictors.

the breakaway of the Squadrone members. *Address* and *Location* are also highly correlated, but are not captured particularly well by either dimension, given their weak relationship to both, while *Birthplace* has a moderate relationship with both dimensions, especially Dimension 2. *Relationship* meanwhile is located very close to the origin, suggesting it is not captured well by either Dimension 1 or 2, likely because it would be better captured in a different dimension. Nonetheless, the MCA has clearly identified logical and intuitive correlations suggesting the dimensions are a good fit to the data. Having identified the dimensions, these were then applied as independent factors in a brms model.

Combining MCA and brms

Combining the dimensions of MCA with a Bayesian regression model enables us to identify whether there are possible correlations between Scots-English use and the particular MCA dimensions that have been identified. Another Bayesian regression model was fit to the dataset using **brms** (Bürkner, 2017) in R v3.5.3 (R Core Team, 2020), with Dimensions 1 and 2 as continuous independent predictors. These were extracted from the MCA analysis and merged with the existing dataset, using left_join() in **dplyr**. This identifies which datapoint in the MCA corresponds to which author in the dataset, and adds a column that contains their dimension value (a set of coordinates). The independent variables included *Dimension 1, Dimension 2* and an interaction between them, and *Scots_English* was the dependent variable. *Author* was included as a random effect. The model was run with four MCMC chains[6] and 3,000 iterations per chain, of which 1,500 were for warm-up.[7] A Bernoulli (binomial) distribution was used in the model as the response distribution. Figure 6.3 below gives the output, including posterior mean, standard deviation, and the 2.5 and 97.5 quantiles for the second model.

The numbers reported in Figure 6.3 are the log-odds of each parameter, and the combination of the Estimate (mean), Est. Error (Standard Deviation) and lower and upper bounds of the 95 per cent Credible Interval together constitute the posterior. The output suggests that both dimensions and their interaction do affect the probability of using Scots, as none of the parameters are spread around zero. A quick check of model performance indicated this was behaving as expected (see Appendix A.6). Both dimensions lead to a decrease in log-odds of Scots usage, i.e. the ratio of the odds of producing Scots, to the odds of producing English, for each incremental increase in the dimension. Predicted probabilities for Scots use is lower when Dimension 2 is positive than Dimension 1. A negative distribution is also observed when the dimensions are in interaction (β = -2.64, CrI: [-3.07, -2.21]). This suggests an inverse correlation: an increase

6 This refers to the sampling of the data - see description of MCMC above.

7 This provides the model with an initial sample for probability distribution, before further sampling takes place.

```
 Family: bernoulli
  Links: mu = logit
Formula: Scots_English ~ dim_1 * dim_2 + (1 | Author)
   Data: Scots_mca (Number of observations: 34636)
  Draws: 4 chains, each with iter = 3000; warmup = 1500; thin = 5;
         total post-warmup draws = 1200

Group-Level Effects:
~Author (Number of levels: 31)
              Estimate Est.Error l-95% CI u-95% CI Rhat Bulk_ESS Tail_ESS
sd(Intercept)     1.14      0.21     0.80     1.59 1.01      841     1134

Population-Level Effects:
            Estimate Est.Error l-95% CI u-95% CI Rhat Bulk_ESS Tail_ESS
Intercept      -2.64      0.22    -3.09    -2.22 1.00      939     1054
dim_1          -0.85      0.24    -1.33    -0.40 1.00      860      817
dim_2          -1.39      0.17    -1.73    -1.06 1.00     1187      912
dim_1:dim_2    -2.64      0.22    -3.07    -2.21 1.00     1130     1013

Draws were sampled using sampling(NUTS). For each parameter, Bulk_ESS
and Tail_ESS are effective sample size measures, and Rhat is the potential
scale reduction factor on split chains (at convergence, Rhat = 1).
```

Figure 6.3: Output of brms model with MCA dimensions.

in probability of Scots use is observed when Dimension 1 increases and Dimension 2 decreases, and inversely the same is observed when Dimension 2 increases and Dimension 1 decreases. Overall, the interaction between the two dimensions has the largest effect, and we can examine the posterior distributions to get a quick overview of these relationships, in Figure 6.4 below.

Examining the distributions, the credible intervals and spread are relatively small, indicating the validity and benefit of using the MCA dimensions as opposed to all the individual predictors. The plot also clearly indicates the respective distances of the posterior distributions from zero, in which the interaction between the dimensions is distributed furthest from zero and thus has the strongest relationship to the probability of using Scots. This suggests the value of examining the bi-dimensional MCA space to investigate probabilities of using Scots, as it is the dimensions in interaction that shows the most robust probability.

Plotting the conditional effects acquired from the brms output within the MCA bidimensional space enables us to visualise the relationship

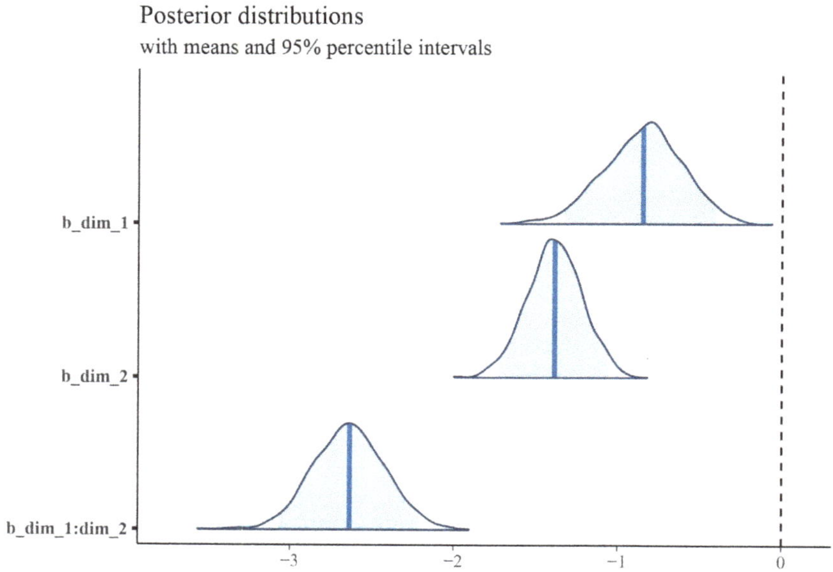

Figure 6.4: Posterior distributions for brms model run using MCA dimensions.

between probabilities of Scots and the dimensions in interaction. This indicates where higher and lower probabilities of Scots pattern across the variation space. To plot this relationship, the output was visualised using a raster plot from the **ggplot2** package. Figure 6.5 puts the relationship between the two dimensions into perspective.

The Dimensions 1 and 2 are not superimposed on the bi-dimensional space here but run through the 0.0 value of the x and y-axis accordingly. Probabilities of Scots are indicated by the shading: yellow indicates higher probabilities of Scots and dark blue very low probabilities. Figure 6.5 suggests higher probabilities of Scots usage occur where the model predicts: a slight concentration can be observed when Dimension 1 is negative and Dimension 2 positive, but the probability of Scots is highest when Dimension 2 is negative, and Dimension 1 positive. As Dimension 2 has a stronger effect than Dimension 1, this reverses the negative relationship of Dimension 1 with Scots usage, when the two dimensions are in interaction, as evidenced by the yellow shading in the bottom right-hand corner.

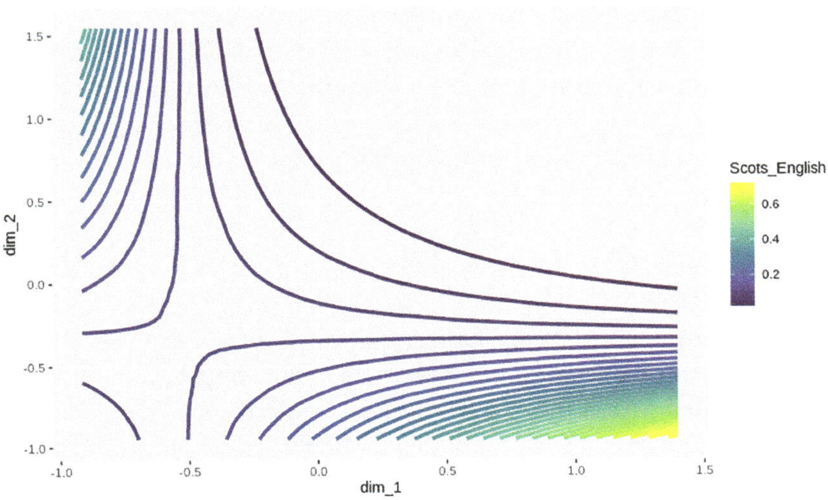

Figure 6.5: Conditional Effects for interaction between Dimensions 1 and 2.

The next step is to examine the writers within the corpus according to each extralinguistic factor in turn, and how they cluster within the same dimensional space. This enables us to map the Scots probabilities found by the brms model onto these writers in a one-to-one relationship, within the same bi-dimensional space. It is visually easier and more insightful to examine each factor on a case-by-case basis. This allows us to build up a picture of Scots use by factor, as the same writer will be in the same location each time. It is unlikely that a single factor will account for all variation in the dataset, but by examining each in turn, we can layer the associations between higher probabilities of Scots and certain predictor levels. This enables each factor to contribute to the story, rather than getting lost in the 'noise' of a combined dataset.

The Scots probabilities will not exactly match the factor data points on MCA biplots, given brms produces *predicted* probabilities, rather than real-time values. Figure 6.5 merely suggests where Scots would be *likely* to occur with greater probability within the variation space – in this case, the bottom right-hand corner of the biplot. By matching this space with the individuals located closest to it, we get an idea of which groups are more *likely* to use Scots in their writings. Accordingly, the different factors will now be examined in turn, keeping in mind that the **bottom-right** of the dimensional space is where the highest probabilities of Scots are found, with a slight concentration in the **top-left** corner.

Factor biplots

Starting with *Political Affiliation*, an individual factor map was plotted using **factoextra.** The output indicates where the politicians in the dataset are located within the two dimensions, and how *Political Affiliation* patterns across them. Each point is a particular politician, writing to a particular recipient and address, in a specific location. Their clustering is indicated in Figure 6.6 below.

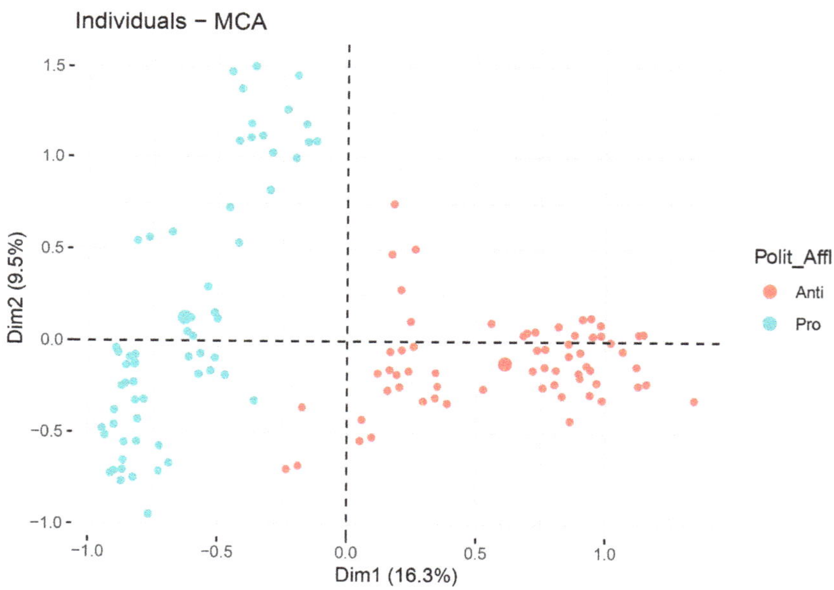

Figure 6.6: MCA individuals plot for predictor 'Political Affiliation'.

Examining the plot, there are two distinct groups for 'Pro' and 'Anti', and the clusters are fairly well defined, with Anti to the right, and Pro to the left, although there are a few outliers within the former. Figure 6.5 indicated that the highest probability of Scots usage was located in the bottom right-hand corner and comparing these plots, this higher probability is located near the Anti-Union side of the biplot, suggesting that an increase in Scots is associated with an Anti-Union agenda. This relationship is particularly strong, given that there are no Pro-Union datapoints nearby, nor is a higher probability of Scots located more centrally within the dimensional space, which would suggest both groups laid equal claim to use of Scots in their writings. This finding indicates that the intuitive hypothesis – writers who opposed the Union would use more features indicative of Scots in their writings – is indeed borne out by the data presented here. Perhaps these writers were subconsciously reflecting a nationalist agenda within their correspondence, heightened by the tense debate and increased awareness of Scotland's sovereign status, particularly during those volatile opening years identified in the temporal analysis. Equally, this might suggest the formation of a shared political identity in response to the religious and ideological discord characterising the opposition. The fluid and amorphous nature of the Country party has previously been highlighted, in which it became clear one of the few facets keeping them together was their collective rejection of incorporation.

This might have stimulated the emergence of a constitutional political identity, realised partially through linguistic choices. This shares interesting parallels with the results found by Shoemark et al.'s (2017) and Shoemark, Kirby and Goldwater's (2017) Twitter analyses on the use of Scots during the 2014 independence referendum, which found pro-independence tweeters (with their intuitive links to Scottish national identity) to use more Scots. Other studies have found accent to be utilised by speakers to support a national identity claim (Kiely et al., 2000), even when their perceptions of the social meaning of variables can operate at a very unconscious level (Hay and Drager, 2010; Hall-Lew et al., 2017). It is plausible that Scots use was subconsciously tied to a certain national agenda that encompassed a rejection of political amalgamation, much like the pro-independence Twitter users. This might indicate that written Scots was becoming available as a vital identity marker in the early eighteenth century, especially given correspondence does not just reflect social groupings, but assists in constructing and maintaining them. Anti-Unionist writers may thus have conceived of themselves as an in-group and marked this through use of particular, locally rooted variants.

Yet, as has already been discussed previously, it is by no means guaranteed that a straightforward interaction between language choice and political ideologies can be identified, particularly when distilled down to a simple 'yes-no' split between the writers in the corpus. While national and linguistic identity often coincide, they don't necessarily need to (Brulard and Carr, 2013), and given we are only observing a particular snapshot of the data in this plot, it is too simplistic to attribute the probabilities of choosing Scots to mere voting choices alone. It is likely that underlyingly, those who were 'Anti' Union comprised a host of related and intertwined characteristics, which operated their own subtle influences on language choice and social identity. What can be observed here is possibly the amalgamation of these influences, producing a broadly defined pattern of linguistic preferences across the 'divide' over incorporation. Being Anti-Union was most likely a part, rather than the sum total, of the identity which these writers aspired to or were affiliated with. Language users can be part of multiple communities linguistically, politically and socially, and even these communities themselves are not necessarily homogeneous (Blackledge and Pavlenko, 2001: 245). Such characteristics could equally apply to a diachronic setting, especially as these two voting groups encompassed a whole range of religious, political and personal views within their scope.

Furthermore, Figure 6.5 also indicated a very slight concentration of probabilities of Scots towards the top left corner, and examining Figure 6.6, this space is matched most closely by a group of Pro-Union writers, who seem to be behaving differently from the rest of the Pro cluster. Political affiliation alone cannot explain this, suggesting it cannot be the full story. Examining other variables can help to build up a possible picture of the groups underpinning higher probabilities of Scots and provide further nuance. The next logical variable to explore is *Party*, shown in Figure 6.7 below.

Examining the plot, the three main parties are largely distinct from one another within the dimensional space. Members of the Country Party are associated closest to the bottom, right-hand corner, the space with the

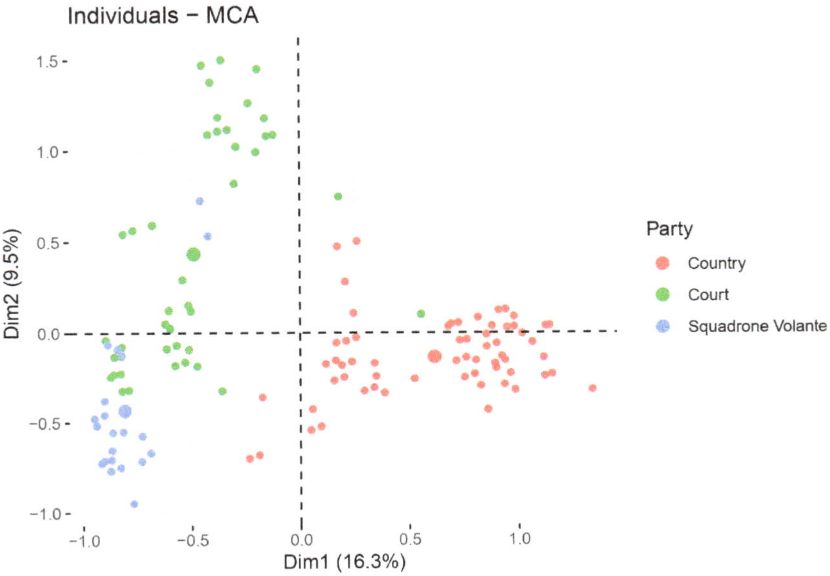

Figure 6.7: MCA individuals plot for predictor 'Party'.

highest probabilities of Scots. This is hardly surprising, given the previous plot indicated that Anti-Unionists also correspond to these data points. Nonetheless, this verifies the reliability of the MCA output, and suggests that members of the Country party were more likely to use Scots variants in their letters than Court or Squadrone members. The Squadrone Volante meanwhile clusters particularly concisely, bar one or two outliers, an interesting observation given the party was made up of a tight-knit, politically congruous group of Scottish families. It remained largely intact even after the Union agreement had passed, and continued to command a presence in the new British parliament for several years following incorporation (Simpson, 1970; Scott, 1981). The plot here confirms they were socially homogeneous, and they are associated with a more anglicised register in the biplot, as their position in Figure 6.7 matches a space of very low Scots probabilities.

These are two important observations, given their harmonious social composition may have led to linguistic congruence, thus a collective change in their linguistic behaviour might indeed be responsible for the post-1705 reduction in Scots observed in the VNC analysis of Chapter 5. Moreover, the Court party is also associated with lower probabilities of Scots, given the Court and Squadrone parties are both associated with the negative values of Dimension 1, mirroring their Pro-Union clustering depicted in the first plot. The Squadrone and Court parties behave similarly when it comes to predicted Scots use, strengthening the possibility that Squadrone members writing to Court politicians may have been influenced by their anglicised style, particularly after 1704 when they sought to associate more with the Court. The tentative explanations offered for the rise and fall of Scots during the key Union years, can therefore become tangible in a statistical analysis.

Political party does appear to influence the choice to use Scots variants, an interesting finding given it is by no means guaranteed that the clear party-line distinctions found in several contemporary studies examining politically motivated variation (c.f. Fairclough, 2000; Hall-Lew et al., 2010, 2012, 2017; Kirkham and Moore, 2016) would have been present in Early Modern times. Party structures were still in the process of emerging during the eighteenth century, and it would be anachronistic to assume a one-to-one association between political party in its present-day sense and the groups involved in the last Scottish parliament. Yet these findings do suggest a relationship between party and language choice. The reduced Scots probabilities among the Court and Squadrone parties, and increased likelihood among the Country party, has interesting parallels with Hall-Lew et al.'s (2017) examination of Scottish MPs in the UK parliament, which suggested that observed accommodation was indirectly indexed through political party identity. This indeed seems to be playing out in the patterns observed here – the political groups most closely aligned with the English Court and incorporationist ideology demonstrate lower probabilities for Scots (and conversely, higher probabilities for the anglicised variants), while Country party members are least likely to anglicise their writings, which aligns with their grievances with the English terms of the Union agreement, and their Jacobite sympathies. The party identity of these Scottish political groups does appear to resonate with the linguistic data.

Yet whether *Party* is the sole or primary factor driving usage is far from certain, especially considering the other Scots concentration (the top-left) maps to a group of Court party members located nearby. That they are not behaving similarly to their fellow members might again reflect the influence of other underlying factors, such as religious denomination, and this is the next factor to be examined in Figure 6.8.

The Presbyterians and Episcopalians are relatively differentiated within the dimensional space, although this factor is less distinct than *Political Affiliation* or *Party*. The Presbyterians are mostly located on the left of Dimension 1, though a small group are positively associated with this dimension. The Episcopalians are mostly clustered where the Anti-Union and Country party members were located, on the right of Dimension 1. This is not surprising given many members of the Country party, particularly after 1704, were Jacobite Episcopalians who rejected the Union agreement. They are also, again, located closest to the highest probabilities of Scots within the dimensional space, indicating that it was this group within the Country party in particular who were more likely to use written Scots features.

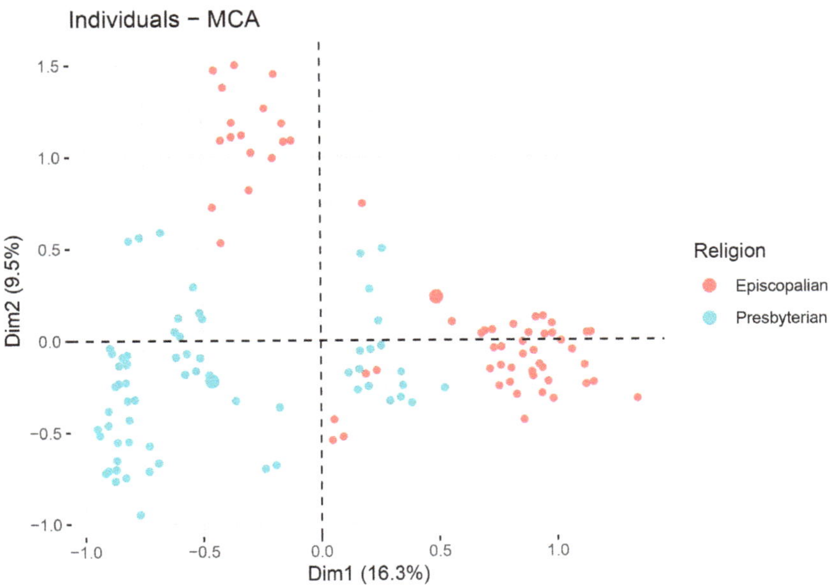

Figure 6.8: MCA individuals plot for predictor 'Religion'.

However, there is a small group of Episcopalians behaving differently from the rest, in the upper-left quadrant. This location maps onto the secondary, weaker concentration of Scots probabilities identified earlier. It seems a greater probability of Scots usage is thus associated with Episcopalians in general, though a particular subgroup of them do not express as strong a likelihood of using Scots variants as their Anti-Union contemporaries. They are Episcopalians who were members of the Court party and supported the Union. Perhaps their Scots use was moderated by their political stance and party membership, therefore.

This highlights the complexities at play in the early eighteenth century – politicians were members of several groups split along familial, political and religious lines, among others. Each of their associations may have exercised some influence on their stylistic choices. Certainly, the fact that Court party Episcopalians were less likely to use Scots than their fellow, Anti-Union contemporaries suggests that their political allegiances may have moderated their linguistic behaviour. Equally, the fact that they are not clustering quite so neatly with the remainder of the Court party, using slightly elevated levels of Scots in comparison, suggests that their religious ideology also contributed to the output, creating contending influences or pressures.

The addition of *Religion* thus adds another layer to the story, suggesting underlying influences feeding into, but not necessarily dominating, the overall patterns of Scots use across these writers. Their linguistic behaviour represents in many ways a microcosm of eighteenth-century political Scottish society, which was amorphous and dynamic, with positions much less tightly defined than contemporary perspectives might assume. To pigeonhole writers into one category or another thus creates the false illusion that such rigid categories exist in the minds of individuals, without considering the fluidity within which identity and group-membership can operate (Blackledge and Pavlenko, 2001: 244).

While the first three factors have already built up a convincing picture of the extralinguistic influences at work on variation, more factors need to be considered. The next to be analysed is *Jacobite*, in Figure 6.9 below.

Examining the plot, Figure 6.9 suggests this clusters quite neatly into three distinct groups, largely associated with the values in Dimension 1. 'No' is to the far left, and demonstrates a mostly negative relationship with

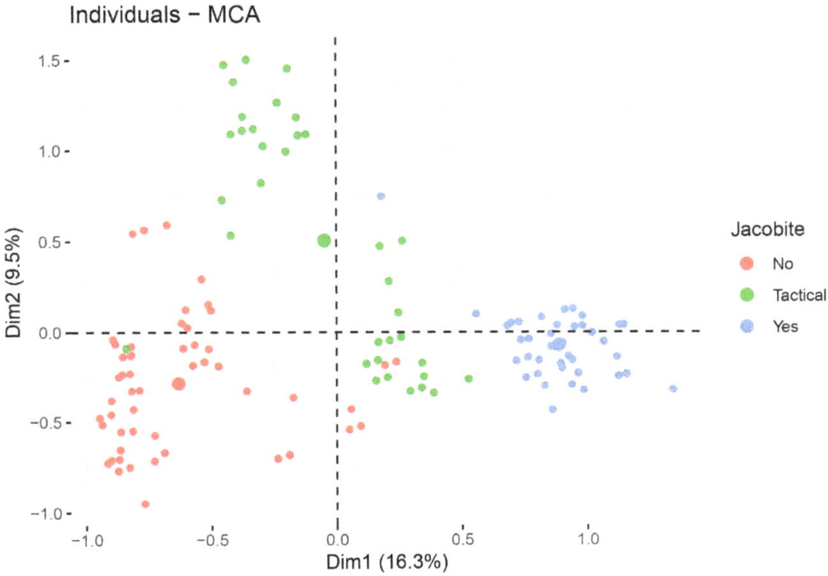

Figure 6.9: MCA individuals plot for predictor 'Jacobite'.

both Dimension 1 and 2, whilst 'Tactical' is spread across both axes and has a less clear relationship with either dimension. 'Yes' is situated to the right and has a strong positive relationship with Dimension 1, falling within the area of highest Scots probabilities. This indicates that the likelihood of using Scots increased among those who were Jacobites, as opposed to those who weren't or wavered in their loyalties. Given that the dimensional space occupied by 'Yes' is also linked to 'Anti-Union', 'Episcopalian' and 'Country' party, it goes without saying that this result is expected – these factors are all highly correlated. The analysis has already established that these categories favour Scots, and ergo, those who were Jacobite demonstrate a greater Scots preference.

This does however suggest the coherent nature of the group in terms of linguistic behaviour, which in many ways mirrors the tightly clustered nature of the Squadrone Volante seen earlier, in Figure 6.7. Perhaps they too formed a cohesive Community of Practice (CofP) bound by their religious and ideological principles that united them not only in the parliamentary scene, but even spurred a number of Jacobites to risk their lives in armed uprisings and rebellions. Their common cause, with its overt links to an ancient, unbroken Scottish heritage, derived from a divinely sanctioned dynastic legitimacy that professed strong, nationalistic overtones, has a clear and salient connection to Scottish interests, and local identity. Such themes could naturally have aligned with use of 'Scottish' variants, and perhaps this relatively close-knit group utilised such forms within their shared linguistic practice, to reinforce their collective aim.

The plot also gives insight into the behaviour of the 'Tactical' group, which forms two relatively distinct clusters: one located in the top-left quadrant, and the other closer to the origin of the two axes. The first cluster corresponds with the weaker concentration of Scots probabilities identified in Figure 6.5. This suggests that the Pro-Union, Court Party Episcopalians identified earlier were also tactical Jacobites. This group is most likely composed of Court politicians who had underlying Jacobite sympathies, but felt these had to be suppressed in order to advance their political careers, such as the Earl of Mar (Ehrenstein, 2015). They may have similarly kept their Episcopalian beliefs quiet to avoid scrutiny. The combination of these features again seems to have created a unique sub-group within the corpus, whose linguistic behaviour differed slightly from other members of the multiple groups they were part of. This group is predicted to choose Scots variants more frequently than their Court and Pro-Union contemporaries, but less frequently than their fellow Episcopalians and Jacobites, perhaps mirroring their compound political identity, and the conflicting local and national demands they faced. The motives of the political Jacobites were paradoxical after all; while they vested moral authority in their 'good old cause' and clearly disagreed on the constitutional fundamentals of Kirk and State, they were also involved in the running of central and local government which was debating exactly these fundamentals (Macinnes, 2007: 246).

The second cluster of tactical Jacobites are clustered on the right side of Dimension 1 but are based relatively close to the axes origin. Yet, while they are behaving differently from the 'No' group to the left, they are also not integrated with the 'Yes' group further along to the right. Examining the previous plots, this subgroup largely corresponds to a small collection of Presbyterians who were also Anti-Union and Country party members.

These writers thus represent the Presbyterian, (non Squadrone) wing of the Country party. While they shared the Anti-Unionist sentiments of their Jacobite party members, their cooperation was uneasy at best. Issues around Scottish nationhood may have driven them to temporarily embrace Jacobitism in a bid to prevent incorporation, but they were never devoted to the cause. Their positioning in the plot might reflect this dichotomy of interests. They are associated with decreasing probabilities of Scots in relation to their Jacobite, Episcopalian counterparts, but demonstrate slightly higher probabilities of Scots than the Court and Squadrone Presbyterians. Again, perhaps this reflects the conflicting influences shaping written Scots use, in which party identity, political or Jacobite ideology and ecclesiastical loyalties all simultaneously played a role. The conglomerate nature of identities and ambitions within the Scottish parliament infiltrated the written sphere, influencing the linguistic behaviour of these men.

So far, the first four factors have all been highly correlated with one another, and have enabled the analysis to gradually build up a picture of political and ideological layers influencing probabilities of language choice, through specific group memberships. The dataset however also included a number of factors not immediately linked to the political machinations of the Scottish parliament and its members. These include the geographical factors *Address, Location* and *Birthplace*. Yet the factor map in Figure 6.2 indicated that *Location* and *Address* were not captured adequately by the first two dimensions, possibly because these were captured by other dimensions as previously discussed. *Birthplace* however did show a strong relationship with both Dimensions 1 and 2, and its relationship is shown in Figure 6.10 following.

Examining the plot, the patterning is somewhat less distinct than the previous plots analysed, though certain trends are still observable. A certain clustering of birthplaces within the political groups is observable, suggesting the role of familial and kinship ties in forming the parties within the Scottish parliament. Social connections stemming from marriage and lineage, as well as landowning interests across similar geographical areas, could accordingly create regional areas of shared political interest that manifested in geopolitical alliances within the parliamentary scene. This might highlight their locally rooted kinship connections – writers who

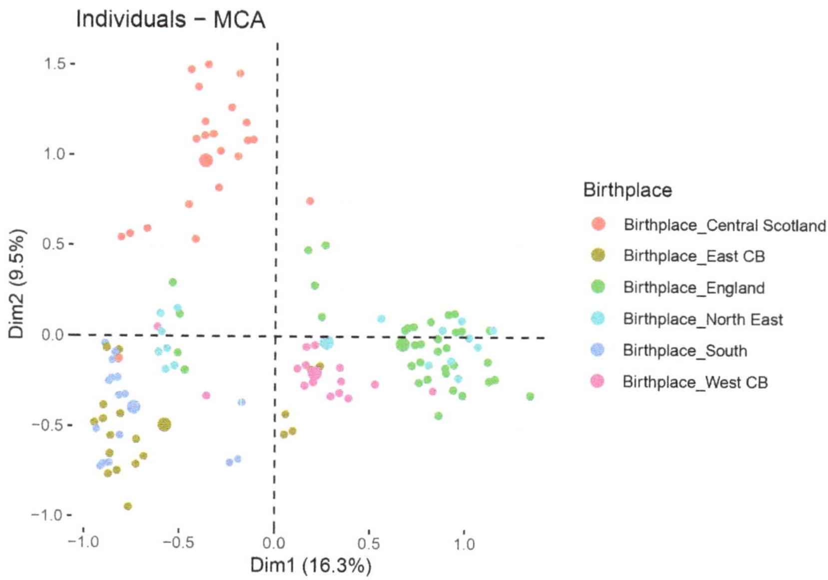

Figure 6.10: MCA individuals plot for predictor 'Birthplace'.

demonstrate a similar portfolio of characteristics and political motivations were also connected at a deeper level by their family associations. While tensions could easily break out between neighbouring estates or contended claims to land, it was desirable to maintain a level of congeniality between associated families and properties. Such factors may have led them to form a social and political unit of their own that differentiated them from the larger groups of which they held membership.

However, rather unexpectedly, 'England' is clustered on the far right of Dimension 1, closest to the space of highest Scots probabilities. Yet we would naturally predict that authors born in England[8] would not have acquired written Scots variants in their repertoire to the same degree as their Scottish counterparts. This would seem to contradict earlier findings, such as Aitken's (1997) analysis of writing produced in the Older

8 The few authors included who were born in England were from ruling Scottish families and, moreover, moved back to Scotland at a young age.

Scots period, which found the most heavily anglicised documents almost always originated from Scots based in England, even when writing to fellow Scots. Cruickshank's (2012) analysis of Lord Fife similarly indicated heightened anglicisation when he was based in London, though neither analysis considered birthplace itself.

However, as the previous four biplots have already made clear, this patterning might only be part of a story involving other factors. Each of these can contribute complementary or additional influences. Furthermore, fully interpreting the strength of this predictor requires detailed knowledge of the social and educational background of the authors, something that is not always accessible even when analysing the high-ranking noblemen of Scottish society. During the eighteenth century many leading families employed a private tutor to oversee their children's education rather than sending them to a local grammar school (A. Auer, 2015: 136), which may have introduced vernacular variants in their writing style. Moreover, family estates could be relatively self-contained and enclosed from the surrounding area, potentially minimising direct contact with local speech. Finally, the few authors in the corpus who were born in England all moved to Scotland early on. The Duke of Atholl for instance was born in Lancashire to a Scottish family, but moved to Scotland at a young age, and was actively involved in military and anti-Covenanting activities within Scotland by the time he was eighteen (Young, 2004b).

Examining Figure 6.10 further, it appears the 'North East' is also generally associated with a higher probability of Scots use. This follows along more expected lines – previous historical analyses have found peripheral areas such as the north of Scotland to show slower propensity for change toward the incoming standard (Meurman-Solin, 1993), and even today, the North East continues to constitute a recognisable dialect area in which varieties of 'Doric' are still regularly spoken (J. Smith, 2001, 2002; Millar, 2007; Leslie, 2020, 2021). The location's increased distance from the administrative capital of Edinburgh may have enabled local forms and features to persist for longer, compared to those based near urban concentrations along the Central Belt. Authors born in these areas could thus have had less exposure to incoming anglicised variants, as well as greater familiarity with local, vernacular variants through their correspondence with fellow land-owners.

The plot appears to reflect this generalisation, given 'South' and 'East CB (Central Belt)' cluster in the bottom left quadrant – the area of associated with the lowest probabilities of Scots use. For authors born in these locations, the anglicising influence of print and administration, and interaction with Scottish Standard English which was emerging in Edinburgh (Jones, 1997a; Dossena, 2005: 14–19), may have encouraged greater adoption of anglicised variants. This cluster also comprises almost entirely of the Squadrone members, who exercised considerable influence in East Lothian and the Border shires (Macinnes, 2007: 296, 264). Their place of birth may have gone some way to forging links with neighbouring landed families, forming social connections that flowed through to their correspondence, and possibly even to their written practices.

Birthplace therefore adds an extra layer of nuance to the picture, highlighting possible geographic locations in Scotland (or indeed outwith the country) that resisted the anglicisation trend for longer, while suggesting the interconnected nature of the political groupings within the Scottish parliament. *Birthplace* is clearly tied up within the larger political groupings of the parliament, but also determined their constellation to a considerable extent in the first place, and Scots use has related though not parallel interactions with both factors in consequence. A particular advantage to utilising the bidimensional space is that we can acquire this layered and interlinked picture of the data, slowly accumulating associations whereby the intricate nature of the historical time period, and the actors operating within it, are gradually brought to light.

So far, every factor analysed has demonstrated a clear clustering across the dimensional space, and these map in interesting and insightful ways onto the predicted probabilities of Scots. Recall however that not all predictors demonstrated a strong relationship with Dimension 1 or Dimension 2, as shown in the correlations plot (Figure 6.2). *Address* and *Location* were spaced in the middle of biplot, suggesting a weak relationship to either dimension, and *Relationship* was located by the origin, suggesting it is relatively unimportant to the interpretation of the data (Kassambara, 2017). To demonstrate how this appears within the dimensional space, the patterning for *Address* and *Relationship* are shown in Figures 6.11 and 6.12 below.

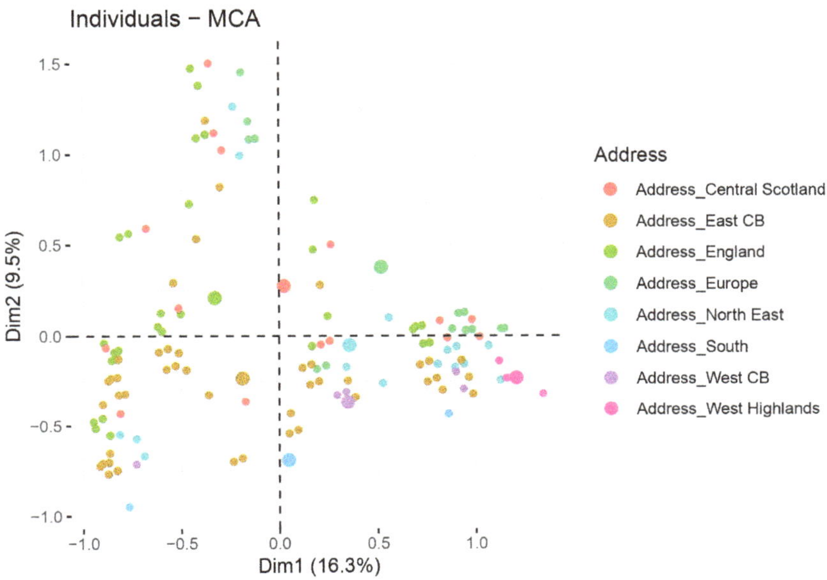

Figure 6.11: MCA individuals plot for predictor 'Address'.

In both cases the different predictor values are scattered quite evenly around the bi-dimensional space, and the clear clusters observed in the earlier graphs are not present. Their wide dispersal suggests these levels are well mixed into the data, which we might expect. The same writer in the corpus could be represented by multiple values within *Address* or *Relationship* – especially if their social network comprised of several correspondents located at various addresses, who represented different relationships. As the writers are clustered according to political factors, *Address* and *Relationship* will be distributed randomly across them, rather than localising to neat, well-defined locations in the variation space. This does not mean these factors might not explain some of the variation in the data, indeed they merit ongoing exploration, to determine whether they pattern along similar lines to previous analyses (c.f. Meurman-Solin, 1993, 2000), or perhaps indicate new geographical patterns that were emerging.

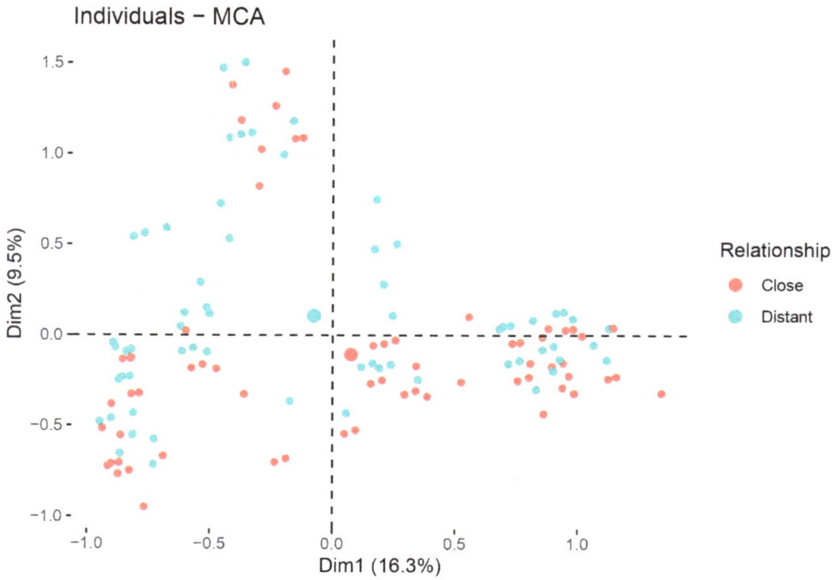

Figure 6.12: MCA individuals plot for predictor 'Relationship'.

Summary

This chapter has sought to take a First Wave, macrosocial and exploratory approach to identifying the factors influencing Scots use within the corpus, comparing writers in aggregate through pre-defined sociolinguistic categories to determine their effect on variation observed. By applying an exploratory and multi-model approach, different trends within the data have been highlighted as a result, identifying a range of values interweaving with linguistic choices in this corpus, rather than seeking a single predictor to explain what encouraged Scots usage. This seems appropriate and historically intuitive, given the complexities of this historical time period previously highlighted, and the transitional nature of written Scots by 1700. The combined MCA and brms model have highlighted the mosaic composition of historical identity in early eighteenth-century

Scotland, within which political factors including party, religious affiliation and Jacobite ambitions *do* seem to have influenced language choice. There were of course numerous pressures operating on this group of historical actors, both in their role as politicians and as Scotland's aspiring elite, and the picture we have been able to gradually construct reflects that process. The diverse and dynamic nature of these results suggests a complex combination of identities and goals could have played the ultimate role in guiding linguistic choices.

Of course, quantitative statistical methods naturally provide broad oversights across a population at large, rather than nuanced insights into individuals, thus these patterns might not hold for every writer in the corpus. This by no means discredits the findings, rather, it offers a comprehensive understanding of the conditioning factors operating on a community of writers and their choice to use Scots or anglicised variants in general. The next chapters complement this analysis, exploring these patterns in a more fine-grained manner across four individuals and their written behaviour, utilising Second and Third Wave perspectives into audience-focused and stylistic motivations to consider how they might influence Scots use. This chapter has paved the way for such an analysis, providing way markers for plausible conditioning effects, and an overview of the unique, complicated and intricate nature of written Scots in the early eighteenth century.

CHAPTER 7

'I think I have quite wearied you and almost myself too by soe long a scroll': A micro-analysis into intra-writer variation and the role of political and stylistic goals in written Scots use

The previous two chapters painted a picture of written Scots use across time and socio-political groups within the corpus. They have each elucidated interesting patterns, providing a window into the uniqueness of the time period and these political actors when exploring written Scots in eighteenth-century correspondence. To complement these findings, we now turn to a micro-analysis exploring individual differences in linguistic behaviour. This seeks to provide a bottom-up, 'worms-eye' (Elspaß, 2007: 4) perspective into the stylistic, indexical and contextual uses of variation. Applying the socially marked and stylistic approach current in Third Wave analyses (Purnell et al., 2009) can encompass the complexity and finesse with which writers might utilise the field of variation available to them, whilst locating statistical trends within the social practices and identities of language users.

This final analytical chapter therefore focuses on four individuals and their intra-writer variation. Specifically, this will examine when, where and how their written Scots patterns across their different recipients, and whether we can observe the same multi-layered, in-group identity being formed within their social network as that identified in Chapter 6. This can allow us to observe whether the potential association of Scots with particular constellations of politically and religiously linked figures was realised or recognised by these writers, as representatives and participants of these sub-groups within parliament. The exchange of news by personal letters often served to strengthen friendships and to affirm relationships of patronage (Raffe, 2022), and sensitivity to group language norms might assist in constructing such convivial networks. Yet writers may also have sought to project a particular persona that did not necessarily align with their recipients, dependent on their socio-political ambitions. Both internal and external perspectives are thus important – audience, accommodative desires, identity-marking and stylistic moves all have potential to condition variation in this setting.

Accordingly, a Country, Court and Squadrone commissioner and a clergyman were selected from the corpus. They are, respectively, George Lockhart of Carnwath, John Erskine the Earl of Mar, John Hay the Marquess of Tweeddale and Robert Wodrow. Each produced a sizeable volume of correspondence to a considerable network of recipients and were central members of their respective parties or groups: Tweeddale was the leader of the Squadrone Volante, Wodrow was one of the most outspoken clerical figures against the Union, Lockhart very much embodied the Episcopalian, Jacobite wing of the Country party and Mar was a 'court politician proper' (Ehrenstein, 2015), successfully establishing himself as a major power in Scottish politics during his time in parliament. Interests are balanced in terms of religious affiliation; Lockhart and Mar were Episcopalian, Tweeddale and Wodrow were Presbyterian, and they represent a range of locations within the Central Belt; Tweeddale was based in the east, in Haddington, Wodrow in the west, near Glasgow, Mar in centre, at Alloa and Lockhart to the south, in Lanark. Lockhart and Wodrow's correspondence came primarily from the Scottish History Society publications, while Tweeddale and Mar's correspondence was collected as manuscript material. A summary of their correspondence and word counts is given below (Table 7.1).

Table 7.1: Letter, word and variable counts for Lockhart, Mar, Tweeddale and Wodrow.

Author	Count of letters	Word Count	Variable count
George Lockhart	250	56,529	12,844
Earl of Mar	34	20,752	1,965
Marquess of Tweeddale	87	43,170	3,905
Robert Wodrow	137	85,984	7,553

Firstly, we can observe the overall proportions of Scots and anglicised variants within each writer, in Figure 7.1, giving an overview of their *general* behaviour, plotted using **ggplot2** (Wickham, 2016).

Examining Figure 7.1, it is clear the three politicians are highly anglicised: all demonstrate less than 10 per cent variable Scots features within their correspondence. Wodrow is a glaring exception to this trend, with almost 40 per cent of all variable written features realised as Scots, which might suggest the distinctive nature of the politicians in the corpus. Out of the three politicians, Tweeddale surprisingly shows the highest proportion of Scots features. Recall that the Squadrone's probability of Scots usage was predicted to be lowest within the corpus overall, but this is not apparent here. Lockhart and Mar demonstrate very similar proportions of Scots (with 5.1 per cent and 4.4 per cent, respectively), although considering Lockhart was an Episcopalian-Jacobite member of the Country party, we might expect a greater difference between him and Court politician Mar. While Mar was an Episcopalian member of the Court party, which was

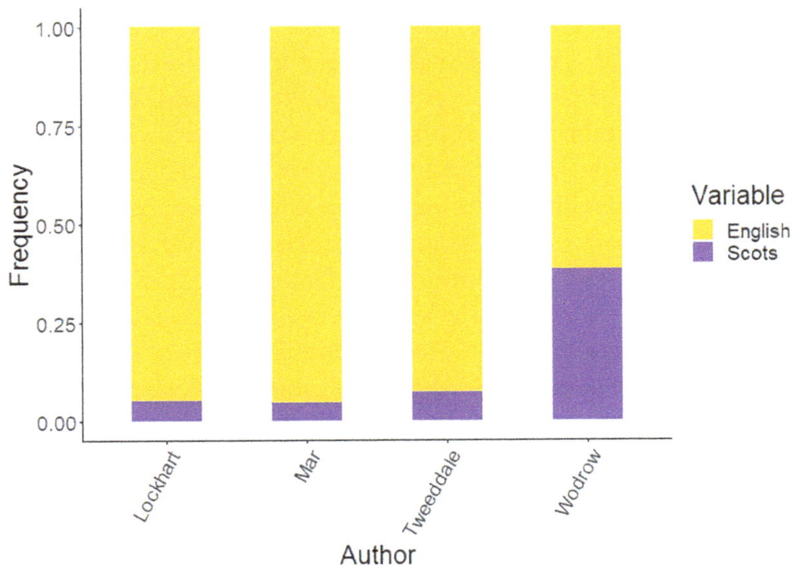

Figure 7.1: Proportions of Scots and anglicised variants across selected writers.

associated with slightly elevated probability levels, the model would still predict Lockhart's Scots use to be higher.

This highlights the difficulties in interpreting descriptive frequencies alone, given the very narrow perspective they provide into an individual's linguistic profile. Lockhart was clearly capable of anglicising his writing when required, but *how* he might use more or less Scots to different recipients remains inaccessible. Equally, it is not clear for instance whether a particular recipient or a categorical preference for certain Scots spellings encouraged Wodrow's heightened Scots levels. To come closer to understanding their behaviour, a detailed, close-up analysis of these writers and their letters is needed, and accordingly, each will now be individually analysed in turn, starting with George Lockhart of Carnwath.

George Lockhart of Carnwath

George Lockhart of Carnwath (1681–1731) was a Country politician who wrote to a large social network that stemmed from all levels of the social elite, including Catholics, Episcopalians and Presbyterians, Whigs, Tories and Jacobites (Szechi, 2002: 26). Lockhart was inevitably living during a time period in which traditional social structures and alignments were rapidly changing and restructuring, and he could not necessarily afford the outright alienation of opposing elite contacts. Indeed, he was fondly connected with the most powerful Whig families of post-Revolutionary Britain (Szechi, 1989: xiii), and he became a wealthy and economically successful estate manager, interested in agricultural and social advancement. His unique social, political and ideological ambitions probably stemmed from the network he created and maintained throughout his life.

However, his upbringing almost certainly played a role in his aspirations as well. Lockhart experienced tragedy early on when his father, a successful lawyer from a well-established legal dynasty, was murdered. As a result, the eight-year-old heir inherited a very rich estate, but was simultaneously pitched into the volatile political situation of 1689. This may have had quite a decisive role in moulding him, both in terms of his adherence to the Episcopalian faith, as well as his strong sense of family ties and filial obligations (Szechi, 2002: 16, 25). His uncle and new guardian, Sir John Lockhart of Castlehill, was a firm supporter of the Revolution, and he ensured Lockhart and his siblings were exposed to a thorough grounding in the Presbyterian and Revolution interest. Lockhart's Episcopalian tutor John Gillane was removed, and Lockhart was sent to live with the Presbyterian ducal family of Argyll. Contrary to the intended outcome, Lockhart developed a deep aversion to Presbyterianism and the first Duke of Argyll, although he formed lifelong friendships with his playmates John and Archibald Campbell. Upon the death of his uncle, he personally secured the Episcopalian Sir James Scougall as his tutor, and made Gillane his chaplain, suggesting a consistent devotion and allegiance to the church and its members, but also a growing estrangement from the mainstream political (Presbyterian) alignment (Szechi, 1989: xvii; 2002: 17).

Lockhart's ideology was informed by his dedication to the parallel causes of a Jacobite restoration of the deposed Stuart line, and (from 1707) the attainment of an independent Scotland (Szechi, 2011). His political career took off after he was nominated as a Commissioner to negotiate the terms of the Union. Initially reluctant, he was persuaded to accept the role by Andrew Fletcher and the Duke of Hamilton, who suggested he could act as a spy for the opposition, and he did so with enthusiasm and dedication (Szechi, 1989: xviii). Lockhart became an ardent opponent of the Union and Hanoverian Succession, developing an unequivocally hostile stance toward the agreement. His firm Episcopalian and Jacobite adherence naturally led to his alignment with the Cavalier[1] wing of the Country party, though he became personally attached to the party's Presbyterian leader, the fourth Duke of Hamilton. These twin alliances did not always form an easy coalition, and Lockhart seems to have had occasional misgivings about Hamilton's commitment to the Jacobite cause (Szechi, 1989: xviii). Nonetheless, he remained devoted to Hamilton until his death. Following the passing of the Union, Lockhart joined the British parliament where he continued to lobby for Scottish interests, but after the discovery of his

1 Recall that this refers to the Jacobite (and naturally, Episcopalian) clustering of commissioners within the Country party.

Memoirs, which painted a number of his political contemporaries in an unflattering light, he fell out of favour with Scottish noblemen across the political spectrum. Thereafter he dedicated himself to Jacobite plotting, remaining a committed Jacobite until at least 1728.

It seems likely that, had he toed the line and adhered to the Court party platform, Lockhart would have been rewarded politically as well as socially. However, whilst recognising the personal gain at stake, Lockhart remained committed to his ideological principles despite the costs they incurred (Szechi, 2002: 40). He was certainly not lacking in social ambition; his efforts had placed the family in the top echelon of Scotland's landed elite in terms of wealth by the 1720s (Szechi, 2011). These factors might partially explain his highly anglicised correspondence: social climbers often demonstrate a greater sensitivity to prestige forms than noble-born authors (Conde-Silvestre and Hernández-Campoy, 2004: 145), while association with social superiors could also have encouraged Lockhart to adopt the emerging, pan-national variety appropriate for civic discourse between intellectuals as a mark of respect. Lockhart's dedication to the Jacobite cause did not blindside him to contemporaries of a different ilk, nor did it destroy his very strong and cordial bonds with members of the Whig elite, especially the Duke of Argyll and Earl of Ilay. It was thanks to their intervention that Lockhart was frequently saved from arrest, imprisonment, and interrogation as a result of his Jacobite dealings (Szechi, 2002: 42). Despite this, Lockhart remained committed to the quasi-national philosophy and dynastically conceived Scottish nationhood of his fellow Jacobites.

Lockhart played multiple roles simultaneously, much like most historical actors involved in the top levels of Scottish society at this time (Szechi, 2002: 7), being informed by both staunch Scottish patriotism and heightened social ambition. Historical identities and ideologies are multilayered constructs, encompassing seemingly contradictory stances into unique subcultures within the broader, political playing field, and in many senses, Lockhart is a microcosm of the complex layering of identities and influences already glimpsed at in the quantitative exploration in Chapter 6. To peel back the layers of detail, however, Lockhart's behaviour across recipients and within letters needs to be examined individually.

Proportions and letters

Firstly, Lockhart's proportions of Scots and anglicised variants across his network of correspondents were collated and plotted using a mosaic plot, from the **ggplot2** package in R. A mosaic plot indicates the proportions of different variants in relation to total volume or quantity – in this case, the proportion of Scots or English across the total volume of writing in which they occur. The length of the bar indicates proportions of the different variants – Scots is represented by the blue, and the anglicised variants ('English' for short) by the red section of the bar. The width of the bar represents the volume of material; the wider the bar, the higher the wordcount. This puts the proportions into perspective, giving an idea of relative proportions. Figure 7.2 indicates Lockhart's variable Scots use in a mosaic plot accordingly.

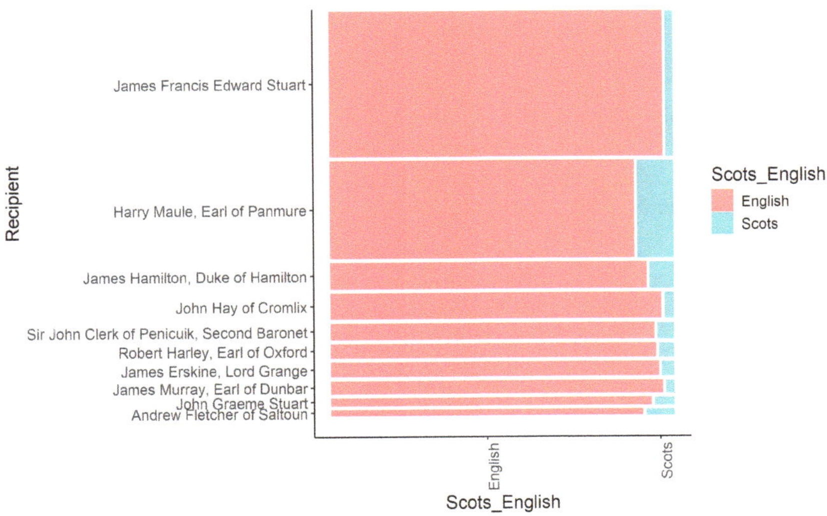

Figure 7.2: Mosaic plot of Lockhart's Scots and English frequencies by recipient.

Examining the mosaic plot, the recipient who sees the largest volume of material is at the top of the graph. This is written to James Francis

Edward Stuart, the son of the exiled King James VII and II, who died in 1701. Lockhart's use of Scots in these letters is very minor, given the small proportion that is shaded blue, despite the large volume of correspondence. This may suggest the deference he demonstrates to a member of the exiled royal family. If Lockhart associated the emergent English standard with prestige, it would not be incongruous to employ such variants in higher frequencies when corresponding with a high status recipient, who naturally commanded respect and obeisance when being addressed. Yet many of the letters exchanged between Lockhart and James were not necessarily of the highly decorous and formulaic nature that royal correspondence often reflects. Lockhart frequently wrote to James using a cipher or code names, following the infiltration and discovery of previous Jacobite lines by Court spies, and such letters are noteworthy for their more informal style. An example extract, from a letter dating 23 April 1722 is shown below. The code-names are translated in square brackets.

> I told him that I knew Turner liked him much better than the Sheep [Squadrone], and he knew that against these he woud willingly have joined with him [...] I had often told him he woud never be trusted by Warts's [the English Whigs'] ministry unless he sold his estate with Swift [Scotland] and gave up his interest with Scrimger [Scotsmen] [...] so soon as Warrington [Walpole] got the better of Stonehouse [the Earl of Sunderland], he'd retain Skelton [Montrose], well knowing he woud serve and trukle under him or the devil himself for wages.

The extract is peppered with code-names, some which seem to have been rather artfully chosen – the Squadrone are referred to as 'sheep', possibly in reference to their political movements in the new British parliament post-Union, while the English Whigs are referred to as 'Warts'. There are also personal anecdotes, such as the reference to the Duke of Montrose and his countenance, and the content is conversational in nature. The combination of these features suggests the confidential nature of their correspondence. Despite this however, there are no instances of Scots features in this extract, even though the use of less formulaic language choices including vernacular variants, as a means to demonstrate authenticity, reliability and psychological proximity, has been identified in previous Scots research (Dossena, 2019). However, James VIII was born in

England and grew up on the continent, having left for France with his exiled father as an infant. Concurrently, he may not have encountered Scots written features, nor would it necessarily have been part of the written medium he acquired. Scots features were unlikely to have much currency with James as a consequence, and perhaps the status and language of the exiled king himself stymied any tendency to use Scots on Lockhart's behalf.

Moreover, Lockhart held an unfavourable opinion of James as a result of his political mismanagement and inability (Szechi, 1989: xxxvi). The exiled court also gave less weight to Scottish agents under James VIII and III, compared to English and Irish personalities, which became a festering grievance among the Scottish Jacobites, including Lockhart (Macinnes, 2007: 244). Alongside status differences this may have increased the social distance between them, resulting in the use of formal linguistic behaviour that manifested as the avoidance of variants associated with conviviality and commonality. While Lockhart has a highly anglicised register overall, it seems he shifted even further along the continuum when addressing James, regardless of the contents of their letters.

By comparison, Lockhart's next most frequent correspondent, Harry Maule of Panmure, sees a much higher proportion of Scots, presenting clear evidence of style-shifting. Lockhart, it seems, was able to vary among his correspondents despite his overall anglicised style, and Harry Maule in particular encouraged use of written Scots features. The brothers James and Harry Maule of Panmure were Episcopalians and Jacobite sympathisers who refused to recognise the authority of William and Mary in 1689. They walked out of parliament in protest and neither of them ever sat in parliament again. Both however continued to be involved from the sidelines as open opponents to the Union and maintained a steady stream of correspondence with fellow Jacobites such as Lockhart (Handley, 2006). The heightened levels of Scots between Lockhart and Harry Maule might stem from their staunch commitment to the Jacobite cause, and dedication to the Episcopalian church, leading them to become prominent advocates for toleration (Blair-Imrie, 2011). They developed a close working relationship as leaders of the Lowland Jacobites, and shared a joint interest in early Scottish history, particularly its religious and political developments

(Szechi, 2002: 106). Their alignment along ideological and personal fronts may have encouraged Lockhart to accommodate towards a close friend and fellow Scot, as well as build a positive and authentic social identity (c.f. Johnstone, 2000; Moore and Podesva, 2009) by using Scots features to subtly index a shared Scottish identity founded upon Episcopalian and Jacobite lines.

While Lockhart, James Stuart and Harry Maule were part of the same Jacobite community, Lockhart's linguistic behaviour does not parallel across these two recipients, and it seems likely that different social and stylistic desires were important contributing factors.

To explore this further, an extract of a letter to Harry Maule, written during the last session of the Scottish parliament on the 4th of June, 1706 is presented below. All Scots features are italicised (my emphasis).

> I told you before yt trade & lawe were allmost over, wee'r now proceeding to setle *qt* the equivalent will amount to, *qch* wee are to demand in res-pect of ye proportion of ye debts of Engld which will be payd by Scotlds entring into *ane* equality of ye taxes in Engld & appropriated for paying of debts [...] This Callcull is made by ye proportion *qch* ye Engl: customs, & excise at prest bear to ye Scots as theyr att present *farmed* [...] now this I take to be *doun* right buying & selling [...] as farr as concerns themselves & as far as ther *pouer* goes ther obsequious.

There are a number of different Scots features present in the text, including the use of <quh> in abbreviated form as *qt* and *qch*, 'wt [what]' and 'wch [which]', <u> spellings in the MOUTH set such as *doun*, 'down' and *pouer*, 'power', and other features such as *farmed*, 'formed'. Lockhart's Scots is not limited to a single feature, and includes salient variants such as <quh>. However, this only ever occurs in abbreviated form in this tract, suggesting its presence might be due to conventionalised scribal practices integrated within the stylistic norms of everyday correspondence (see van Eyndhoven, 2024 for further discussion). Although at first glance Lockhart's Scots seems relatively limited, such observations need to be put in perspective. Lockhart is highly anglicised overall, thus such quantities and occurrences may reflect a considerable shift towards greater vernacularity for him, particularly when we compare it to the earlier tract written to James Stuart which saw no instance of Scots features.

Here, Lockhart is discussing the *Equivalent* – the compensation to be paid to Scotland in return for accepting the future burden of English debt. Lockhart outright rejected the Equivalent and his opinion of commissioners in its favour comes through clearly – he labels them 'obsiquious' and suggests that the whole proposal is '*doun* right buying & selling' This may have encouraged Lockhart to distance himself from the Court and Squadrone members accepting the Equivalent. Recall from Chapter 6 that their predicted Scots use was lower than the Country party members, particularly the Episcopalian-Jacobite wing of the party, of which Lockhart was part. In light of this, Lockhart might be subconsciously laying claim to an in-group identity rooted in dynastic and ecclesiastical legitimacy, by shifting away from the stylistic patterns of the Court. Given that speakers can utilise linguistic features in ideological and indexical moves to invoke ways of belonging to certain groups (Kiesling, 2001; Podesva, 2011; Eckert, 2012: 94), Lockhart's Scots variants may delineate this in-group association, to which Maule belonged through his Jacobite and theological devotions. An increase in Scots thus marks their affiliation and collective opposition to the Court, who are distanced and disgraced in Lockhart's letter.

A similar pattern emerges in two other letters to Maule, written several years apart, extracts of which are shown below. Scots features are again emphasised.

> The Scots Commissioners omitted to give any answer to the equality of all excises, without wch there coud not be *ane* intire Union, of *qch* they were so desirious that they'd give *ane* equivalent for *qt* the Scots shoud be burdned by the English debts [...]. It woud have been too bare-faced to have acquieced att once to all, and therfore they drew up *ane* answer to be presented on Monday in these terms; [...] they proposd that they shoud be exempted from all other taxes *qtsoever* for such a period of time as shoud hereafter be *condeshended* on. This is the substance when they explain the equivalent, which I hear's a good summ of mony (alies bribe).
>
> 4 April 1706.

> The Chancelr having this day reported this answr to ye house my Ld wharton sd he was sorry to see such *ane* answer from ye throne to ye H: of Peers, *qch* was fitter to be given to a litle *bussie* medling fellow or a news monger [...]. I was told this day by one has heard D of Argyle yesterday say yt ere 2 months went about this ministry woud *bepish* ymselves if they knew what was in a litle time coming on ym.
>
> 13 April, 1714

In the first extract, Lockhart's negative portrayal of the Scottish commissioners is again clearly observable. They are portrayed as self-serving individuals, desperate to ensure the Union takes place, to the point where they would be willing to burden the nation with English debts by agreeing to the Equivalent. He suggests the payment is an 'alies bribe'[2] and sarcastically notes it would have been 'too bare-faced to have acquieced att once to all' for the commissioners involved. Alongside Lockhart's regular use of abbreviated <quh> and *ane,* he also demonstrates use of the sibilant interchange, in *condeshended*, 'condescended', with the sense of 'to agree on, or upon, something' (DSL, 2022), a sense which is mostly Scottish or northern (OED, 2022). This use of a distinctive feature that represents 'Scottishness' on not just orthographic, but also phonological and semantic levels, would arguably have increased its salience within the context of the letter. Moreover, the sibilant interchange – a Scottish shibboleth – was no longer frequent in elite correspondence, indeed it had almost disappeared from such writing (van Eyndhoven, 2023a). Its use here might accordingly suggest that stylistic or identity-marking goals were once again influencing the occurrence of Scots.

As before, Lockhart seems to position himself outside the Scottish parliament and the commissioners debating the terms of the treaty, despite the fact that he was a commissioner himself, a position that was likely conflicting and at odds with his Jacobite ideology. It seems almost ironic that Lockhart has used a Scots spelling for an item denoting 'to agree on something' when it was well-known he did not agree at all with the Equivalent or its terms. By utilising a feature both Lockhart and Maule would likely have recognised, given its distinctive nature, Lockhart might thus position himself in opposition to these commissioners.

A similar effect appears to be at work in the second extract, written several years after the Union had taken place, in which Lockhart again

2 Although originally sourced from the SHS publications, having had the opportunity at a later date to check the manuscript from which this letter is taken, my reading of these words differs from Szechi (1989), who has 'a clear bribe'. I have opted to keep my interpretation but note that either option may be possible.

reflects use of <sh>, rather unflatteringly, in the word *bepish,* 'bepiss' – to wet oneself. In this context, the word is referring to the British ministry, which, like the Scottish commissioners, Lockhart was also part of. Likewise, he might seek to distance himself from them, using salient Scots features to emphasise the odious terms with which he describes his opponents to Maule. Scots could thus be used to denigrate the figures being described, painting the ministry in a sordid, distasteful light, whilst implying Lockhart's divergence from the English and incorporationist figures making up the majority of the British parliament. By using selective, locally rooted features, Lockhart could tap into the linguistic norms of the Episcopalian-Jacobite collective of which he and Maule were both part, underscoring their collective, Anti-Unionist identity or group membership.

Lockhart's increased levels of Scots in letters to Maule, especially within these contexts, might, at a broader level, index their concordant aims to restore the exiled Stuart dynasty and maintain Scotland's independence – the very topics being debated by these commissioners. His language use in the second extract, furthermore, suggests a high level of conviviality and confidentiality between them, perhaps enabling the selective use of such salient and colloquial features. By seeking to foreground their friendship, and the Jacobite ideology they shared, with all its nationalist associations, Lockhart's variable usage lays claim to the in-group identity he shares with a fellow Jacobite like Maule. The desire to assert group membership could be achieved through use of variants linked to the wider political platform that incorporated Maule and Lockhart's ideological commitments, and excluded the politicians who did not share these ideals. Rather, Lockhart's selective use of salient Scots features appears to be deliberately moving away from the written norms of these out-group members.

To identify whether Lockhart's Scots was being encouraged by association with a narrow Episcopalian-cum-Jacobite identity or broader, party-wide association, letters to the Duke of Hamilton, leader of the Country party, need to be examined. Lockhart's Scots use to Maule already suggested the possible construction of a shared repertoire to highlight their membership and their mutual engagement in shared practices, indicating patterns resembling a Community of Practice (CofP) (Eckert and McConnell-Ginet, 1992: 464; Meyerhoff, 2002; Kopaczyk and Jucker, 2013: 6). It is plausible that this community stretched beyond close-knit Jacobite links to the Country party at large, particularly once they became more cohesive following the break-away of the Squadrone. In addition, Lockhart was attached to Hamilton despite his wavering commitments (Szechi, 1989: xvii, Szechi, 2011), which could plausibly encourage the utilisation of shared linguistic resources specific to the affiliation or group-membership they might index.

Examining the mosaic plot, Hamilton clearly sees a lower proportion of Scots than Maule, but he receives a higher proportion of Scots than most other recipients, adding tentative support to the above possibility. Again, however, exploring some of the letters themselves can provide a window into Lockhart's linguistic choices. In the following letter, Lockhart writes to Hamilton on the 14th of December, 1704 about proceedings in the parliament.

> The report of our having a new Parliament is revived again and much more possitively asserted since our statesmen came *doun*, than before [...] This is all I know that the land of cakes *affoords* att present worth your Grace's knowledge [...] the Abby Close is as *throng* just now with brokn *lairds* and tradesmen.

There is use of the lexical item *throng* – a feature that was present in Middle English but became chiefly Scottish and northern English in later use (OED, 2022) – to suggest the crowded and miserable state of affairs in the Scottish capital. This is accompanied by *lairds*, 'lords', originally indicating Scots variation in the MORE subset, though in later usage *laird* became lexicalised as a Scottish title, rather than a descriptive item in its own right (DSL, 2022). Lockhart might be tying the issues created by the parliamentary processes to a specifically Scottish context, through use of these lexical items. Both their semantic meaning – particularly the use of *throng* with its negative connotations in this tract – and nature as lexical items would likely have increased their salience in this instance, perhaps positioning Lockhart in a firmly opposition stance and aligning with Hamilton in the process. Given their shared party platform, the use of Scots lexical variants in particular when discussing the adversity brought upon by the proposed Union might thus seek to underline Lockhart and Hamilton's shared defence of Scottish interests.

However, in general Lockhart's proportion of Scots features in correspondence to Hamilton is more limited than to Maule. Lockhart might be sensitive to Hamilton's Presbyterian background, considering the quantitative results suggested that Presbyterian, non-Jacobite members of the Country party were less likely to use Scots than their Cavalier contemporaries. Furthermore, they shared an asymmetrical social relationship, as Hamilton was a duke from one of the leading Scottish families, while Lockhart was a member of the minor gentry. Lockhart thus had to balance stylistic and social desires to construct common ground with the need to recognise the status and ideological standing of his recipient. His Scots may thus have been chosen selectively for deliberate effect, which can be seen for example in a further letter to Hamilton, written on the 20th of January, 1706.

> But, by what I coud pick up in England, as I look upon the fare pretences the English make of doing us right, to be only a *plaisture* to skinn over the wound which the approaching division is likely to make.

The use of *plaisture*, 'plaster'[3] seems to reflect a caustic interpretation of English intentions, especially as it is the only Scots item within the page of text. It underscores Lockhart's disdain for the English parliament and their weak promises, whilst possibly indexing the 'national' position claimed by the Country party that Hamilton and Lockhart both belonged to.

Of Lockhart's remaining recipients, the other Country party member who sees a considerable proportion of Scots is Andrew Fletcher of Saltoun, though within a much smaller volume of correspondence. Lockhart developed a frank admiration of Fletcher, whom he later characterised as the ideal Scottish patriot and whose ideas profoundly influenced him (Szechi, 2002: 56). Yet despite being labelled as a 'Scottish patriot' within his own lifetime, it is estimated Fletcher spent thirty five years (he lived for forty eight) out of Scotland, enjoying the civil life, culture and metropolitan

3 This feature was classified as 'Other' due to its complicated phonological history and the fact that it was the only example of its kind. 'Master' and 'plaster' originally had Middle English/Older Scots /ai/, giving Modern Scots /e/, but in English this became /a:/ (for uncertain reasons).

environments of various European capitals and London much more than his home country (Robertson, 1997). Lockhart, on the other hand, did not embark upon a 'Grand Tour' of Europe, and in general never went willingly further afield than England. As a result, he was well-read and intellectually astute, but with perhaps a somewhat narrow mind-set in comparison (Szechi, 2002: 19). Fletcher and Lockhart also differed in terms of ideological and religious convictions – Fletcher was not a Jacobite or Episcopalian, but rather a firm Erastian with a largely latitudinarian outlook, though one that tended towards Presbyterianism (Robertson, 2008). Yet they shared a common commitment to protecting certain Scottish liberties, and increasingly sought each other's company in the aftermath of the Union. This may have induced Lockhart to adopt a more convivial writing style, in which Scots features would not appear incongruous. Lockhart's bid to construct a shared in-group membership is particularly salient in the extract below, written on the 25th of December, 1711.

> But give me leave to say, that I hope both I & all my bretheren in ye Commission, are above being led by malice [...] agst you or any other whatsoever wee have each of us our particular Eni-mys as *weel* as you've yrs [...]. The rules & orders of ye house are you know very misterious; especially to us Scotsmen, Ld I dont know by *qt* rule they make up ye votes. The kind assurances of yr *freindship*, I take as a very great honour, & shoud be more vain therof [...]. I wish you a *mirry* Christmas.

In this extract Lockhart constructs a discourse that overtly includes Fletcher as part of a conceived 'in-group' of Scottish representatives (presumably Scottish Tories) within the British parliament, claiming 'wee have each of us our particular Enimys as *weel* as you've yours' and referring to themselves as 'us Scotsmen' when disparaging the workings of the parliamentary system. Lockhart posits himself at the centre of this in-group, appearing to speak on their behalf when he suggests that 'I hope both I & all my bretheren in ye Commission, are above being led by malice', and his polite and cordial overtures to Fletcher suggest he conceives of a common alignment between Fletcher and this group. Lockhart's style is overall more formal, but several Scots features occur, including not just <quh> but also <i> for <e> in *mirry*, and the Scots words *weel* and *freindship*. These might serve to index their shared Scottish patriotism, and position as 'outsiders' within the British parliament, given both their Scottish and Tory background.

The content overall suggests Lockhart felt great respect for Fletcher, and Scots variants might serve to emphasise the commonality and convergence he overtly refers to throughout the text. Perhaps Lockhart is seeking to construct and maintain a positive self-evaluation of their in-group membership (Turner and Brown, 1978; Ting-Toomey, 1999: 40), which includes himself, his Scottish Tory associates, and Fletcher, as part of a larger, 'outsider' identity of which their Scottish background forms the common ground. Convergence is thus signalled both on a group level as Scotsmen, and on an individual level between Lockhart and Fletcher as fellow patriots, along a complex interindividual-intergroup continuum (Tajfel and Turner, 1979) that encompasses both large-scale and local identities (Bucholtz and Hall, 2005: 22).

This possibility becomes more tangible if we consider Lockhart's correspondence with opposition members. Lockhart was well connected to such figures, often serving as a communication link between Court and Country interests (Szechi, 2002: 56). Yet his proportion and range of Scots is noticeably reduced when writing to them. For instance, Baron John Clerk, Second Baronet (upon 1722 following his father's death) was a Court politician but also Lockhart's neighbour, and they had an uneasy relationship, frequently arguing over matters relating to land boundaries and access. Matters were not improved by Lockhart's tendency to poach coal miners from Clerk's pits to work in his own (Szechi, 2002: 25, 33). Scots features in correspondence directed to the baron are comprised almost entirely of lexical items, as opposed to spelling features. Two extracts are shown below.

> seing you form so many objections against my working the coal on that part of the *brae* opposite to my Engine [...]. I can do more *convenientlie* if both sides of the *burn* were mine [...]. I shall apply to my Lord Polton and Mr Baird to see if they'l appoint some day next week for the *excambion*.
>
> 3 April, 1723.

> On this day sennight, I found 5 *nolt* belonging to John Hunter within my plated enclosures, which I seized [...]. *Nixt* day I returned 4 of them and keept the 5th [...] *earlie* this morning, a *slap* was taken down in the dike.
>
> 28 October, 1723.

In the first extract, Lockhart uses the terms *brae*, 'hillside', *burn*, 'stream/ river', and *excambion*, which stems from Scots law, and refers to exchange or barter, specifically of land (DSL, 2022). The second extract contains *nolt*, an individual bull or cow in Scots (OED, 2022), and *slap*, which refers to a 'gap' in a wall or dike, and stems from Older Scots, with origins in Dutch and Low German (OED, 2022). This use of agricultural or legal lexis is not unexpected given the context of the correspondence, and the fact that agricultural and legal spheres tended to retain Scots lexis (Aitken, 1971; Millar, 2003, 2004; Kopaczyk, 2013b). The other Scots features present are common features likely below the level of consciousness as a result of their indistinct nature, including <i> for <e> in *nixt*, 'next' and <ie> in *convenientlie* and *earlie*. Given their non-distinctive and widespread nature, these features were perhaps less likely to function as identity-marking tokens or reflect in-group accommodative behaviour.

Thus, recipients who did not share personal, ideological, religious or political links with Lockhart tended to reduce the frequency and scope of his written Scots. It seems Lockhart could and did shift his language use along a formality and politeness cline, but also along a vector of familiarity and identity, of which Scots features formed a part. In general, he reflects the macro-social patterning observed in Chapter 6; while alignment with fellow Country-party members was important, the biggest influence behind his choice to employ Scots features was his Jacobite-Episcopalian identity. Hence, we see the highest level and widest range of Scots features when he writes to Harry Maule, a fellow Jacobite and Episcopalian, slightly lower levels to Country party members Hamilton and Fletcher, and the lowest levels to James Stuart and Baron John Clerk, Second Baronet. Whether similar awareness is demonstrated by the other politicians requires further investigation, and accordingly the patterning of Scots features will now be examined in the correspondence of the Earl of Mar.

John Erskine, Earl of Mar

The Court politician John Erskine (bap. 1675, d. 1732), styled twenty-second or sixth earl of Mar (dependent on a disputed creation in 1565) was a major player in Scottish politics during and after the Union debates. Mar was a complex character whose wavering nature and unclear sympathies stemmed from a fundamental internal conflict, which on the one hand drove his ambition and desire for political, social and economic success, and on the other his sentimental association with Jacobitism and an undercurrent of Scottish patriotism. Born in Alloa, Clackmannanshire on his family estates, his early education has been described as somewhat 'eclectic' (Ehrenstein, 2015), and he does not seem to have completed a university education. He did not learn another language, bar some rudimentary French quite late in life, nor did he embark upon a 'Grand Tour' through Europe as many leading Scottish nobles did during this time. He was and remained a committed Episcopalian, something he kept largely quiet during his time in parliament, but which set him apart from most Court party contemporaries.

Mar's curtailed educational opportunities, however, did not dampen his high opinion of his aristocratic background. He took great pride in the ancient lineage of his family, whose status as hereditary keepers of Stirling Castle and guardians of the royal princes had granted them special ties to the royal Stuart dynasty (Gregg, 1982: 179; Ehrenstein, 2015). Yet this pride masked the acute financial difficulties Mar inherited, as a result of crushing debts accumulated during the civil war and further economic mismanagement. This made a Court position very appealing, given the financial security and boost to self-esteem it offered (Smout, 1963: 58), and Mar maintained adherence to the Court party throughout his nineteen years in parliament. He enjoyed being in the thick of political life, seeking to follow in the footsteps of his ancestors by acquiring leading political roles, and was astute in his political manoeuvring. Mar quickly worked his way into the Court's inner circle, though following the failed Queensberry plot he temporarily aligned himself with the Jacobite Tories, forging links with Hamilton and the Country party and switching so convincingly that many believed it to be genuine (Lockhart, 1995: 85). However, after the events of 1704 he swiftly integrated back into the Court party and became an active speaker for Union, demonstrating energy and zeal as an effective leader of the house (Ferguson, 1964: 108; Macinnes, 2007: 299). Though probably not applied during his lifetime, this kind of behaviour led to his nickname later on as 'Bobbing John'.

Mar's devotion to the cause of Union, and his cultivation of close contacts within English Tory circles secured his selection as one of sixteen representative Scottish peers in the newly formed British parliament. He became the leader of the Scottish Court party in 1710, but also patron to Scottish Jacobite MPs following the death of the Duke of Hamilton, partly as a result of his underlying Jacobite sentiments. In this latter role, Mar began to publicly voice concern about the supposed benefits of the Union, stating to his brother 'we had fine hopes ... and I think not without good reason, but these hopes have proved vain' (Mar to James Erskine, 1714, NL Scot., MS 5072, fol. 26). For while Mar only really engaged with Jacobitism following the death of Queen Anne in 1714, it seems likely he had always harboured underlying sympathies for the cause, but felt the need to keep these hidden in order to acquire profitable Court positions (Ehrenstein, 2015). When Mar fell from favour and was dismissed from the British parliament, he became involved in plotting the Jacobite rising of 1715, organising supplies and distributing propaganda. Unfortunately, as a military strategist he was less adept, and his decisions were 'marked with a disastrous combination of chronic indecision and strategic incompetence' (Macinnes, 1996: 200). Nonetheless, Mar was offered a role by James VIII as his advisor and secretary of state in the Jacobite court in Paris. Yet, always wavering between one position and the other, Mar acted as double agent for both the Stuart court and Westminster for several years, before his duplicity was eventually discovered.

It seems Mar's personal ambitions, pride and desire for status frequently overrode his ideological persuasions, which ultimately became one of his biggest weaknesses (Gregg, 1982: 179). Yet Mar's writings and architectural drawings do suggest a resolute Scottish patriotism was central to his beliefs, and Lockhart characterised him as 'a man of good sense but bad morals' (Lockhart, 1995: 85). His persistent homesickness for Scotland after his exile, moreover, implies a certain devotion to his country of birth, subtly present throughout his dealings and decisions. Thus, Mar epitomises the complex internal struggle facing Scottish politicians, in which their personal and economic motivations were counterbalanced by a desire to protect Scottish interests. Social ambition and Episcopalian-Jacobite sympathies dove-tailed Mar's movements and decisions, though whether these conflicting loyalties and ambitions might interact with his Scots usage to different recipients representing those interests, remains to be explored.

Proportions and letters

Accordingly, the proportions of Scots and anglicised variants in Mar's correspondence were extracted from POLITECS and plotted in a mosaic plot, depicted in Figure 7.3.

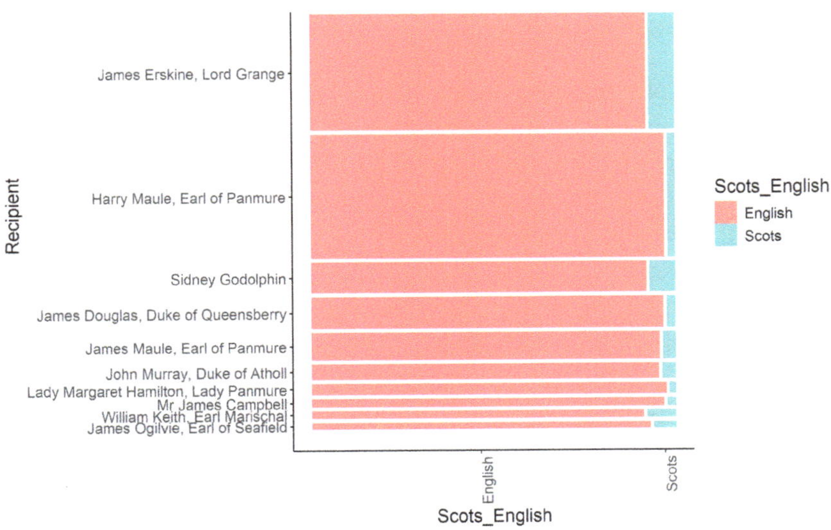

Figure 7.3: Mosaic plot of Mar's Scots and English frequencies by recipient.

The plot suggests that Mar writes by far the greatest amount of correspondence to the top two recipients: James Erskine (Lord Grange) and Harry Maule, Earl of Panmure. Lord Grange was Mar's younger brother, and they seem to have been personally close. His brother was similarly fluctuating and unclear in his political and religious sympathies (Scott, 2006), but given Mar's dedication to the family name, a high level of familiarity was likely. Indeed, Mar successfully campaigned for Grange to gain an influential legal office towards the end of 1706, and he was able to secure a number of positions for his relatives during his time in parliament and the Jacobite court (Ehrenstein, 2015). This familiarity might explain Mar's high proportion of Scots features to Grange, as he may have felt less need to shift towards an anglicised register when corresponding with family, and an extract from a letter written to Lord Grange on 12 March, 1709 demonstrates ample use of Scots features.

> I had a great *dale* to do & less time to *spair*, so pray be not surpriezed that I wryt not more frequently [...]. Wee hear a great *dale* of noice of the severitys to the Episcopale *clargie* in putt- putting them out [...]. I *nather* would nor cou'd protect him; since Glenkindie is to *cairie* it [...]. Thers nothing yet determined as to yt lord of Session, but will now *e'er* long I belive Lord Tillicull offers to *demitt* both his places in favours of Dougall wch is likly to do [...]. I shall *mind* the gift of Escheat now since I've got to get it post as soone I can.

Scots features are scattered liberally throughout the letter, including the <ai> spelling for MATE in *spair*, 'spare', <ie> in *cairie,* 'carry', <ar> in *clargie*, 'clergy', the Front Vowel Merger in *nather*, 'neither' and *dale*, 'deal', a deleted consonant in *e'er*, 'ever' and use of lexical items such as the legal term *demitt*, 'to let go, send away or dismiss, chiefly used by Scottish writers' (OED, 2022), and *mind*, 'remember'. Unlike Lockhart, Mar uses a much greater range of Scots features within his correspondence. This might indicate the different upbringing and schooling the two had – certainly Mar's education was far less extensive than Lockhart's. It might also point to the nature of their recipients. Grange was a highly familiar correspondent which may have enabled greater freedom of expression and a reduced monitoring of language use, in which a wider range of Scots features in higher proportions could occur. This suggests relatively equal family connections encouraged increased vernacularity and ergo, written Scots features.

To consider this further, another extract written to Grange on 13 January, 1709 is shown below.

> I send you incloased a Paper wch will direct you [...] they say the submission expirse soon, so pray *mind* it. I had a letter last post from my Lord Bowhill, & he sayes he *had spoke* to you. Give him my service & tel him that at this time to be sure the Queen will do nothing in re-lation to the Justiciary *nather* by *receaveing* demissions nor filling up any places tho they were vacant, but I should be *glade* if it were in my power to serve him.

This extract is composed of a series of demands: Mar orders his brother to *mind*, 'remember' the paper he is sending, and to give Lord Bowhill his service. There is less recognition of epistolary politeness conventions than might be expected among upper-class writers, particularly when a request is involved (see, among others Elsweiler, 2023), presumably because Mar did not feel the need to use them with his own brother. Alongside this, a range of Scots features are observed within the letter, including both orthographic variants such as *nather*, 'neither', *receaving*, 'receiving' and *glade*, 'glad', as well as the lexical item *mind*, and the past tense form *had spoke*, a Scots and northern morphosyntactic feature.[4] This provides additional evidence that the influence of a familiar recipient could perhaps enable the increased presence of Scots features in Mar's correspondence, which might also be responsible for the reduction in epistolary norms observed here.

However, this does not mean they were entirely negligible, and in this instance, Scots features could provide an additional function of softening the request being made. Rather than having to include formulaic politeness models, the use of features associated with a 'domestic' or vernacular register might assist in reducing the impact of the request by establishing common ground. Indeed, such patterns were identified in Cruickshank's (2011, 2012) analyses of Lord Fife's letters to his estate factor, in which Scots

4 Although morphosyntactic features were not included in the categories identified during the methodological process, nor in the quantitative analyses of Chapters 5 or 6, some of these features came to light during the micro-analysis. To ignore these features would be to ignore the linguistic behaviour characterising these individuals, thus they are pointed out in these extracts as they occur.

features accompanied instances of scolding or demands. This served to reduce the face-threatening act being performed, despite the considerable difference in status and power between the correspondents (Cruickshank, 2012: 116–117). Similarly, though Mar had no pressing need to defer to his brother, maintaining cordial relations was essential all the same, and Scots forms might invoke increased amicability between them by drawing on resources from a common plane of written variation. Mar might for instance seek to foreground his close relationship with his brother through variants linked to a locally rooted identity and upbringing, pertinent interests to him considering his pride in their ancient family lineage within Scotland. Language users are able to construct interactionally specific stances and participant roles within their discourse (Bucholtz and Hall, 2005: 592), and these stylistic moves can occur across multiple levels synergistically rather than independently of one another (Campbell-Kibler et al., 2006; Moore and Podesva, 2009: 448–449). Mar's use of Scots variants, which include not just orthographic but also lexical and morphosyntactic features, might accordingly aid in constructing an authoritative but nonetheless brotherly persona, enabling him to make a potentially face-threatening request.

In this vein, it is worth considering whether alongside the recipient, the topic of the letter may also have influenced Mar's use of Scots features. Intention or agency could equally underpin his variable usage, particularly in salient contexts that created a conflict between his multiple identities. To explore this possibility, an earlier extract from the same letter to Grange, written 13 January, 1709 is shown below. In this section, Mar is defending his actions in the British parliament following the aftermath of the failed Jacobite rising of 1708.

> Our being in the Queen's service made it impossible for us to show our haveing [deleted] no hand in this before now, but only saying as we did that it was not as it was given out, but now I hope all our countrymen will be convinced of it. I cou'd wish for my own *shair* that all my papers were printed, but of tho they be not, by being laid before the house they will be *pritty* publick [...] & my being against the bring-ing up the prissoners haveing past in Councill so will not appear so clearly by my own papers [...] all wch I hope will be known in Scotland since there was so much pains taken to asperss us wt the *contrarie*.

The letter again contains a range of Scots spellings, including <ai> in *shair*, 'share', <i> for <e> in *pritty*, and <ie> in *contrarie*. The nature of the extract might reflect not just audience influences, but also the indexing of Scottish identity conceived through a popular, Jacobite-inspired lens. Mar expresses the wish that his papers would be printed, to clear his name among his fellow 'countrymen' of any association with the imprisonment of the Jacobites. Despite his focus on personal advancement and political aggrandisement, Mar was clearly concerned with his image and reputation at home. His social ambitions did not entail an indiscriminate embrace of Court politics, and it is trivial to assume an individual's ideological stance is unitary and lacking in contradiction (Millar, 2020: 103). There were diverse pressures acting on Scottish politicians during this time, and the sentiments Mar professes in this letter are indicative of the conflicting influences operating on his multilayered identity. His use of features associated (whether consciously or subconsciously) with his homeland might thus seek to index and reinforce the undercurrent of patriotism in Mar's ideological make-up.

By comparison, Harry Maule of Panmure, as the next most common recipient, sees much less Scots despite sharing family and political connections with Mar. Harry Maule was Mar's uncle, and although he gave up his parliamentary career in 1689, at the time of the Union debates Maule was allied personally and politically with Mar (Blair-Imrie, 2011). Considering Mar's behaviour to his brother, it seems unusual that their family connection would suppress the prevalence of Scots. Yet, unlike Lockhart, who used the highest levels of Scots with Maule, Mar seems to distinctly disfavour using Scots when corresponding with his uncle. Perhaps Mar acknowledged the age and status difference between himself and Maule, given their familial connection was nonetheless hierarchical. Maule may have represented a senior and authoritative figure to Mar, whereas Lockhart and Maule shared perhaps a more symmetrical relationship, based around analogous political ideals and academic pursuits. Maule was an exceptional scholar whose political and intellectual abilities came to be widely recognised by the Scottish elite across the political spectrum (Blair-Imrie, 2011), while Mar was meanwhile aware of his own limited schooling, of which he remarked to his son 'you have been more luckie in your education than I was' (Erskine, 1896: 178). In addition, Maule was outwardly Jacobite and Episcopalian, whereas Mar kept such sympathies hidden at least until 1714. These factors may have induced a shift towards variants considered 'polite', given the increased association of Scots with traditional and informal usage by this time. Mar's accommodation patterns may not have necessarily operated along a simple vector of kinship relations, but could well have been tied up in complex social and political identities.

To turn now to some of Mar's correspondence to Maule, the first extract, taken from a letter written 26 May, 1717, shows a noticeable reduction in both Scots and non-standard features in general, compared to the previous extracts written to Grange.

> My Dear Hary. It was a very great pleasur to me to hear by Sr Hugh that *you was* well & I came here in expectation of meeting a near friend wch hap-ned accordingly some time ago & to be in the way in case a certain thing had gone on, wch for a twelve month before had *cast* us a good *dale* of pains to bring to that pass the dissapointment in that was no great surprize to me.

The letter is formal in tone, and there is a recognition of epistolary norms in Mar's reference to the correspondent's health. The spelling and word choices are also much closer to the incipient standard, and there are only a few Scots features present throughout. The features that are present in the text include *you was*, a morphosyntactic feature present in Scots but also many non-standard English dialects, as well as *dale*, 'deal' (Front Vowel Merger), which seems to be largely invariable for Mar. The consistent nature of these features might indicate Mar's lack of awareness of their Scots origins, though it is less clear whether his use of *cast*, 'cost' (<a> – <o>) falls into this category, given this feature was disappearing from correspondence by this time (van Eyndhoven, 2023a), which might suggest its salience as a Scots feature. Nonetheless, taken together, these characteristics are suggestive of a shift towards politeness, perhaps because of the learned character and social standing of Mar's recipient. This implies Mar associated Scots with an informal or less-polite register, which is supported by his behaviour to his brother.

Despite Mar's reduction in written Scots features when conversing with Maule, Scots could be employed for effect, plausibly to reduce the impact of a difficult or potentially face-threatening communicative act, just as we saw earlier with Grange. We can observe this in a letter to Maule, dated 9 March, 1706. The subject matter is delicate – Mar is discussing the Union debates, and is suggesting that incorporation is inevitable, perhaps justifying his stance. Mar spoke out in favour of Union agreement, but this ran counter to Maule's Jacobite principles, and Mar was likely all too aware that Maule would disagree with his news.

> The Affair of the *Treatie* will now be the great sub-ject of discourse. The English nation *were* never in so good a disposition towards Scotland as at this time, but I'm affraid they will be unwilling to treat of anything but an *Intear* Union. A federall union they think a jest & I *realie* belive they will give us no terms (*simplie*) of any *valow* for going into their succession [...]. You certainly have heard Annandale's *storie* so I will not *fash* you with it.

There appears to be an almost deliberate choice of the lexical item *fash*, 'to afflict, annoy, trouble, vex, bother or weary' (OED, 2022). The utilisation of a local feature might reduce the impact of the message and emphasise their shared Scottish heritage, within a context that highlighted the clear breach in their political ideologies. Mitigation strategies are apparent within the letter – Mar suggests there is a certain inevitability to incorporation, but takes an opportunistic view, stressing the need for Scottish politicians to capitalise on the favourable political climate. Yet he recognises the irritation his news might cause Maule and his use of *fash* might seek to repair the common ground between them. The use of Scots to minimise the difficult subject matter has been identified in other studies (c.f. Dossena, 2002; Cruickshank, 2012) and in a similar vein, Mar may be using a Scots lexical item to signal linguistic and cultural solidarity. Utilising features that index a shared linguistic code between two Scotsmen when discussing matters relating to the heart of Scottish politics thus enables him to shape an alternative social identity, one that is acceptable to Maule.

Interestingly, the exact opposite appears to happen in one of Mar's letters to Sidney Godolphin, the English High Treasurer and a recipient who interestingly sees higher proportions of Scots. Written on the 26th of October 1706, the letter concerns negative Scottish reactions towards the proposed Union treaty, and the tone differs considerably from the letter written to Maule. Here, Mar takes a pro-Union viewpoint, in line with the stance of his recipient.

> Tho we have still as good hopes as ever of succeeding in Parliament, yet I must *acquent* your Lordship that the humour in the country against the *treatie* of union is much increst as late [...] and the opposeing *pairties* misrepresenting every article of the *treatie* makes the comonality believ that they will be opprest with taxes [...]. Yet the union will certainly do in the Parliament.

The letter makes excuses for parliamentary delay, whilst overall attempting to take a reassuring tone, perhaps because Mar felt the Scottish parliamentary process reflected on the competence of the Court party in securing the agreement. Mar wanted to establish connections with Godolphin to ensure political success post-Union, thus impressing him and portraying an image of capability was an important consideration. Yet while Mar would clearly have sought his receiver's social approval, he is not doing so by accommodating toward Godolphin's register as would be expected (c.f. Labov, 1990), considering the range of Scots features identified here. Rather, as we saw earlier with Lockhart, Mar may similarly be distancing himself from an identified out-group within the Scottish parliament, seeking to align with Godolphin instead. In this case the out-group is the Country party members who are causing problems in parliament, and Mar uses the PART variable in *pairties* to describe them. In utilising a Scots variable when discussing the opposition, Mar might seek to remove himself from association with these figures and their actions, especially given that he is writing to a politically important Englishman who could potentially secure his political future.

To do so, Mar might be drawing on the 'rustic', even 'backwards' status that Scots had been slowly acquiring over the past century, as the result of a prestige-shift in the linguistic landscape of Scotland. The PART variable was a distinctly northern phenomenon and as a result, Godolphin may have recognised this as a Scots, or at least non-standard, feature. Accordingly, Mar might be correlating the increasingly negative associations of Scots features with the Country party. Interactional positions can accumulate ideological assumptions that come to be associated with both large-scale and local categories of identity and social categories, which in turn feed back into language choices (Bucholtz and Hall, 2005: 22), and Mar may similarly be tapping into local identity politics and relating these to broader macro-social associations around Scots and its users, forging links between the Country party and the undertones that regional varieties, especially Scots, were acquiring by this time.

Thus, while both Lockhart and Mar use Scots features to paint their adversaries in a bad light, Lockhart's usage foregrounds a shared, local, in-group identity with his fellow Country or Cavalier recipients in opposition to the Court, whereas Mar's use rather draws upon the broader, supra-regional connotations Scots was acquiring as a 'domestic' variety to characterise the opposition. Moreover, the fact that it is the word *pairties* itself which attracts this variable, is indicative of a deliberate move on the part of Mar. Politically charged language can reflect and promote political cohesion (Hall-Lew et al., 2012: 61), and such behaviour could plausibly span political parties and national borders in eighteenth-century Scotland. Rather than referring to a shared Scottish background, Mar instead creates an alternative alignment along political lines, one that incorporates Godolphin by delineating their 'in-group' from the opposition party through his disparaging language use.

In another letter to Godolphin, written 22 September, 1706, Mar's use of Scots features similarly seems to portray the Anti-Union stance in an unfavourable light.

> The Queen's Advocat did not like it, and he *continows* of his own oppinion, and *argowd* against it to us all together [...]. His main arguments against it are the loosing of our *soverainity* and that a toleration will ruin the *Presbitrie* [...] acting the *pairt* he does most be with a designe, for a man of his sence cou'd never be convinced with those *waik* reasons and arguments he makes use of.

In this instance, Mar is discussing the Lord Advocate's negative opinion of the Union articles, which he rejected. Rather than being described as a genuine political or ideological stance, the Advocat is instead playing a *pairt*, his whole opposition platform is based on *waik* reasons, with a focus on constructs deemed unimportant by Mar or Godolphin, such as Scottish *soverainity* and the *Presbitrie* (as Mar was Episcopalian). As with his previous letter, Mar's use of particular Scots spellings may seek to discredit the opposition through use of vernacular language features and their associated connotations, particularly when writing to an English recipient based firmly at the source of the emerging English standard.

While's Mar's behaviour between Maule and Godolphin seems almost polar opposite, in many senses his relationship with them also spanned the two poles of the political spectrum. Mar was both a Court politician motivated by personal ambition, and a tactical Jacobite with hidden sympathies and a strong loyalty to family. Consequently, Mar's use of Scots to his Jacobite uncle and to his English political patron could be employed for quite radically different effects, though ultimately in both cases he seeks to close the gap between them through careful positioning and alignment. This does not necessarily form a contradiction in stance therefore, given Mar's twin loyalties to family and fortune. The social relationships Mar sought to build through his letters was an important influence in his choice of spelling and lexical features, in which Scots could act as a mitigation strategy, or as an alignment device with his recipients, positioning Mar within their political remit.

How Lockhart and Mar compare to Tweeddale, however, as a Squadrone member with complex bilateral relations across the political spectrum, will now be explored, to ascertain whether these patterns hold in this instance also.

John Hay, Second Marquess of Tweeddale

John Hay, second Marquess of Tweeddale (1645–1713) was the leader of the Squadrone Volante in the Scottish parliament. Born into a distinguished family, Tweeddale became firmly associated with the Williamite regime after the Revolution, despite being seen as 'sadly out of his depth at court and, for that matter, in most other places' (Riley, 1979: 49). It seems that Tweeddale lacked interpersonal skills which hindered his political advancement, despite his prominence in the Scottish and first British parliament. While he eventually became an active proponent for incorporation, in the opening years of the eighteenth century Tweeddale was a spokesman for the Country party, and his early political activity can be seen as a firm defence of Scotland's independent institutions and enterprises, naturally aligning him with many Country party members. His political platform was based around safeguarding the Kirk and freedom of trade, with a heavy focus on Scottish ecclesiastical liberties and securities (Russell, 1995: 237).

When Tweeddale was approached by the Crown in 1704 to form a new administration, he broke with the Country party and instead came to support the Court, but this shift was occasioned by a fundamental mismatch between his religious and political ideals and those of the opposition, rather than pure political expediency. This led to the formation of the Squadrone, as previously discussed in Chapter 1, who became crucial in securing the Union treaty as it passed through the final session of the Scottish parliament between 1706 and 1707 (Young, 2004a). They were linked by a relatively cohesive set of political and ecclesiastical goals, as well as close-knit social connections through their kinship ties, and they maintained a presence for several years in the ensuing British parliaments post-Union (Simpson, 1970; Scott, 1981). Tweeddale played a leading role in its formation, with some contemporaries even labelling them 'Tweeddale's party' (Ferguson, 1964: 98; Macinnes, 2007: 261–262), but despite his active political involvement, both contemporary and later historical accounts have suggested Tweeddale was of a rather simple nature, well-meaning and modest, but not particularly driven by political success (Macky, 1733: 186; Riley, 1979: 50; Lockhart, 1995: 66). Tweeddale it seems, was not driven by socio-political ambition as Lockhart and Mar were, nor was he strongly oriented toward personal aggrandisement. Perhaps as a result, Tweeddale felt less need to shift his variable usage along the 'politeness' cline toward a more anglicised register, explaining why his Scots proportions are slightly elevated. To gain more perspective on his language use, however, Tweeddale's behaviour across individuals must now be examined.

Proportions and letters

Accordingly, Tweeddale's Scots and anglicised variants were extracted from POLITECS, compiled, and plotted in the mosaic plot shown in Figure 7.4.

Figure 7.4 suggests that overall, Tweeddale barely differentiated between his recipients, which might indeed point to his lack of interpersonal skills within parliament. Tweeddale writes to a mix of Squadrone, Court and Country party members, and yet, unlike Lockhart and Mar, there is no single recipient who is clearly favoured or disfavoured when it comes to Scots usage. This is not the result of minute levels of Scots, indeed Figure 7.1 suggested that Tweeddale was the most Scotticised out of the politicians. Instead, he might not have been sensitive to the same audience pressures or stylistic concerns as Mar and Lockhart, while his changing allegiances may have hindered his ability to construct a coherent political persona through discourse.

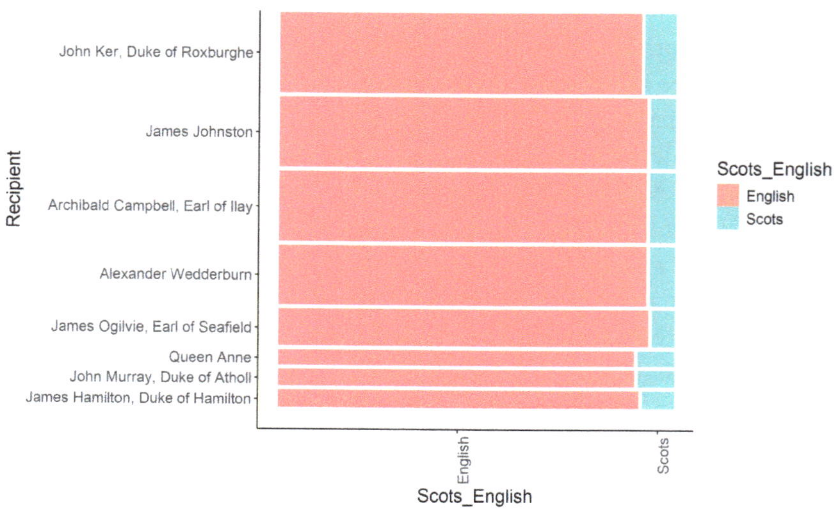

Figure 7.4: Mosaic plot of Tweeddale's Scots and English frequencies by recipient.

Honing in on micro-level differences however, there is a very small split within Tweeddale's recipients. He uses very similar proportions of Scots to Roxburghe, Johnston and Wedderburn – all Squadrone members – as well as the Court politicians Ilay and Seafield. The remaining recipients see slightly higher proportions of Scots. These include Queen Anne, the Dukes of Atholl, Hamilton and Marlborough, and the Earl of Cromartie – a somewhat eclectic mix of royalty, Country party members and English commissioners. It is not immediately clear what might motivate this patterning across these two groups of recipients. The Queen, for instance, seems unlikely to have encouraged use of Scots features given her status and English upbringing, while the close-knit nature of the Squadrone would, if anything, be predicted to encourage vernacular language use, especially considering the family ties between them. The minimal differences between recipients might reflect Tweeddale's personal inability to cultivate political connections; he seems to have been rather stiff, withdrawn and introverted when it came to personal relations, failing to network effectively with the right patrons and associates, and gaining a reputation for being inflexible and staid in his communications (Riley, 1979: 50).

Nonetheless, Tweeddale's behaviour to his Squadrone recipients in particular is notable for its consistency. John Ker of Roxburghe is Tweeddale's most frequent correspondent and like Tweeddale, he was a central member of the Squadrone Volante, serving as its secretary from October 1704 to May 1705. Roxburghe played a particularly prominent role in the party – it was through his intervention that Queensberry was sacked and the 'New Party' emerged under Tweeddale, and he has been credited for the Squadrone's alignment with the Court position regarding Union (Simpson, 2005; Macinnes, 2007: 264). Tweeddale and Roxburghe were furthermore connected by kinship connections, as Roxburghe was Tweeddale's nephew. James Johnston, meanwhile, was a key member of the Squadrone; he pushed for the adoption of the 1641 constitutional settlement together with Tweeddale. Johnston had also previously worked with Tweeddale's father in parliament (Young, 2008), and was concerned to cultivate Tweeddale himself (Riley, 1979: 50, 83). They shared a firm adherence and loyalty to Presbyterianism and their political careers continued post-Union in the British parliament, suggesting a similar political agenda bound by theological concerns.

Tweeddale uses fairly uniform levels of Scots across these Squadrone addressees in Figure 7.4, which might reflect the homogeneous composition of the party. Their congruity in terms of political goals, Presbyterian orthodoxy, geographical proximity and marriage ties has been noted in previous historical scholarship (Simpson, 1970; Fergusson, 1977: 216-218; Riley, 1978: 115–118; Scott, 1981; Macinnes, 2007: 246), and was identified in the statistical analysis, which found Squadrone commissioners to be particularly tightly clustered within the bi-dimensional space. Such factors have also been found to determine the strength of a social network (Fitzmaurice, 2007); when mutual relationships within a network affect more than one sphere, such as profession, family and friends, individuals are under greater pressure to maintain the circumscribed linguistic variety (Conde-Silvestre, 2012: 333). This tight-knit nature might have encouraged less variability in internal correspondence, perhaps constructing a CofP that drew from and contributed to this shared linguistic repertoire (Wenger, 1998: 72–85; Tieken-Boon van Ostade, 2000), especially as dispositions (whether linguistic or otherwise) are learned interactively through participation in practices most typical for members of a particular group or class (Bourdieu, 1977).

Thus, Tweeddale's patterns of Scots use observable here might reflect a linguistic similitude between the Squadrone, derived from his frequent correspondence with his fellow party members. Micro-patterns of variation can accumulate into larger macro-social categories, continually informing and being reinforced by stylistic practice and group membership desires, and Tweeddale's behaviour plausibly demonstrates this interaction between different sociolinguistic frames of reference. This in turn reinforces the pattern we have already seen in the quantitative analysis – unlike the more nebulous composition of the Court and Country parties, Squadrone members reflect a relatively uniform identity.

Figure 6.5 of Chapter 6 also suggested the Squadrone figures were particularly anglicised, in fact, their probability of using Scots was among the lowest within the corpus. This might indicate that Scots features were not a resource they utilised to index relations with fellow members, rather their party membership may have instead encouraged the adoption of a highly anglicised register among them, which Tweeddale was sensitive to despite his clear ability to use Scots features. However, some extracts need to be analysed to provide more clarity on his behaviour. Following are several extracts from a letter written to Roxburghe, dated 11 December 1704. They demonstrate a preponderance of lexical items, particularly those that relate to Scots law and legal terminology.

> 'Treasury had resolv'd upon for *rouping* of ye Customes wherof a copy was sent yow *togither* with yt of their letter, to Her Majesty *theranent*.'
>
> 'I have showen ye Treasurer *deput* what yow write as to your meeting with yt person.'
>
> 'Might occasion a jealousy that it was not to be a free *Roup*, but that we were to pitch upon those we lik'd best which might hinder people to *engadge* to bid for it.'

The legal lexical items include *rouping*, 'to put up for public auction', *theranent*, 'concerning', *roup*, 'public auction', and *deput*, 'deputy' (OED, 2022), and their presence is not surprising given the natural link between politics and law. There is little evidence of other Scots features throughout the letter, apart from occasional occurrences of <i> – <e> in *togither* and dg~g in *engadge*. Similarly, when writing to the Squadrone members Wedderburn and Johnston, most of Tweeddale's usage is largely lexical, as demonstrated in the following extracts.

> 'It is true that I found it convenient immediatly after ye address *anent* ye plott was voted to make a short speech and in ye conclusion of it to adjourn'.
>
> Tweeddale to Wedderburn, 28 August 1704.
>
> I made a short speech thinking to divert the motion and to make ym fall again upon ye acts of Security and for ye *cesse*, but it would not do till I was forc'd to consent to go to ye nomination ye first *sederunt* next week.
>
> Tweeddale to Wedderburn, 6 August, 1704.
>
> The publick instructiouns seem *likewayes*[5] defective and therfor severall things desired to be added which it is supposed will not be stuck at particularly a clause to ye 4th article *anent* ye succession.
>
> Tweeddale to Johnston, 9 June, 1704.

5 Scots 'way' is pronounced 'wye', leading writers to misinterpret '-ways' as '-wise' or spell it phonologically. However, this confusion sometimes led to the reverse phenomenon, in which '-wise' becomes '-ways', as in this case.

In these letters Tweeddale uses lexical items such as *cesse* – the land tax in Scotland, though this is also still the official term in Ireland (OED, 2022), *sederunt*, 'A sitting of a deliberative or judicial body' (OED, 2022), and *anent*, 'concerning, about or in view of, frequently used in legal and quasi-legal phraseology' (DSL, 2022). Again they are linked to political and legal proceedings, or are associated with such discourse. Given a sufficient or appropriate English alternative did not always exist, their continuation is perhaps to be expected, especially within political discourse, private or otherwise. This does suggest however that when Tweeddale wrote to his Squadrone recipients, his use of Scots features was largely dictated by the need for precise legal or political terms, for which an anglicised alternative might not have been immediately accessible to him.

Tweeddale did also occasionally use instances of Scots spellings in his letters to these recipients, and such behaviour to his party associates is not unexpected, given that Tweeddale appears to be more conservative[6] in general in his linguistic behaviour. He was clearly unable to remove all instances of Scots from his correspondence, even those that may have attracted more attention. This does not necessarily negate the possibility that Tweeddale is subtly shifting into a more-anglicised register, however, and it is erroneous to assume that style or code-switching must necessarily involve a complete transition. What represents a 'shift' for Tweeddale is relative to his baseline behaviour and ability to do so, which may have been more limited than Lockhart's capabilities, for instance. Tweeddale does appear to be sensitive to the anglicised nature of his Squadrone recipients, reducing the range of Scots features largely to those that were required by the discourse. As a result, by seeking to avoid features that had less currency among the Squadrone, Tweeddale may have been tapping into a common alignment within the newly formed party, one that flowed along both political and linguistic lines, to ensure their continued homogeneity.

Alongside these Squadrone members, there are two recipients from the Court party with whom Tweeddale uses almost identical proportions of Scots. They are Archibald Campbell, Earl of Ilay, and James Ogilvie, Earl

6 By 'conservative', this refers to retaining multiple Scots features, rather than anglicising them.

of Seafield. Initially, Tweeddale's adherence to the Country party would likely have distanced him from such figures, but he shared their dedication to Presbyterian church government and the Hanoverian succession and came to vote with the Court after 1704. Tweeddale's correspondence to both recipients is dated between 1704 and 1705 – the exact time when the Squadrone were forming and shifting in their political adherence. This may have led Tweeddale to accommodate toward the linguistic behaviour of his Court recipients, as he did with his own Squadrone members, marking this transition. Indeed, in correspondence directed to Ilay and Seafield Tweeddale similarly uses mostly lexical items, as is demonstrated in the extracts below.

> all ye D. of Queensberries friends, and particular *dependers* went in to a man, and all those Her Majesty hath honoured with new Titles, except ye E. of Hoptoun, and on ye other hand none of D. Hamiltons ffriends, or any one of His family except my Ld Bargeny, both his brothers having quitt him particularly my Ld Selkirk who hath behav'd with a wonderfull firmness [...] circumstances with yow have had a *contrair* effect with us.
>
> Tweeddale to Ilay, 18 July 1704.

> 'According to ye articles of ye *Roup* which had been read to ym at ye Barre and wherof I here send your LoPP a copy'.
>
> Tweeddale to Seafield, 11 January, 1705.

Tweeddale uses the terms *roup*, 'public auction', *dependers*, 'dependants' and *contrair*, 'contrary'. The latter two variants are graphically similar to their anglicised equivalent, but both are chiefly Scottish (DSL, 2022; OED, 2022). The similar nature of the cognates may have meant Tweeddale was less likely to recognise their Scots status, given that speakers are considered to be more aware of variants that are radically different, or which are involved in the maintenance of contrast (Trudgill, 1986: 11). Salient features tend to be accommodated to in contact situations, with adjustments made to linguistic forms that are high in the speaker's consciousness (Trudgill, 1986: 16), thus the fact that Tweeddale does not adapt his spelling of these forms, despite writing to a Court politician, indicates they may have been below the level of consciousness for him. This would enable such non-distinct lexical items to persist. Moreover,

Ilay was born in England and his family estates were based in the Western highlands, where the common language spoken was Gaelic rather than Scots. Consequently, Tweeddale's use of Scots in correspondence directed to Ilay was unlikely to have promoted an increased socio-political association between them. On the other hand, Ilay was likely familiar with legal lexical items through his active role in parliament, sanctioning their use in Tweeddale's correspondence.

Tweeddale's behaviour might also suggest an alignment with the Court, in which he similarly recognised the more anglicised nature of their register. As we observed earlier in Chapter 6, Court party members, particularly those who were Presbyterian and non-Jacobites (like Ilay and Seafield), were associated with lower probabilities of Scots. Tweeddale may have sought to accommodate toward this, perhaps laying claim to a shared unionist identity, thereby garnering Court support and bolstering his position in the new parliament. Positioning is frequently linked to a desire to assert group membership (Bucholtz and Hall, 2005: 18), and we have already seen how Lockhart and Mar positioned themselves relative to the 'other' in a bid to affirm their membership of a particular group or identity. The extract to Ilay above hints at a similar motive for Tweeddale. Written in the aftermath of the failed Queensberry plot, it captures his gradual adherence to the Court political line and correspondingly, he appears to distance himself from the Country party that he had been part of. Tweeddale writes that the Queen had not honoured any of Hamilton's friends (all of whom were members of the Country party), and that even his family members had 'quitt' (left) Hamilton's party, his brother Lord Selkirk having done so with 'wonderful firmness',[7] suggesting his approval of the affair. Tweeddale had been condemned as a turncoat by his old Country associates, who refused to support his new parliament and its main objective of securing the Hanoverian Succession (Ferguson, 1964: 99–100). Such strained relations may have added to his desire to shift away from their usage patterns. Thus, Tweeddale was perhaps in the process

7 At the time when this letter was written, the reforged alliance between the Country party and its Cavalier wing disgruntled Presbyterians within the party, leading Hamilton's brother Charles, Earl of Selkirk and his kinsman, John, Lord Belhaven, to join Tweeddale's party instead (Macinnes, 2007: 264).

of changing his group membership to one that encompassed the Court political platform, a process that might be indicated both by his tone and the anglicised nature of these extracts.

Further evidence of his transition towards supporting the Court is suggested in another letter, written 30 May 1704.

> The honour I had of your LoPP letter gave me great satisfaction, and ye assurance I had by it of your concurrence for obtaining what may be thought fitt or *necessar* to promote her Majestys service and interest here which If I had not hoped for I should never had ventured to undertake ye trust she has been pleas'd to putt upon me. My Ld in ye memoriall sent, there was all consideration had to ye measures laid *doun* and circumstances there so farre as we thought our *oun* would admitt of.

Tweeddale notes the 'trust she [the Queen] has been pleas'd to putt upon me', suggesting his alignment with the Crown, and remarks upon Ilay's concurrence with Tweeddale's intentions, indicating shared political goals. Alongside this, the tone is polite and respectful, which may have favoured an increase in features associated with the incoming 'polite' standard from the South. The level of politeness demonstrated by writers is often moderated by the relative power and social distance between correspondents (Raumolin-Brunberg, 1996a: 14; Dossena, 2019: 71), and recipients of higher rank would likely induce greater politeness and formality than letters between family members, especially when asking a favour or making a request (Fitzmaurice, 2006; Palander-Collin et al., 2009: 12; Hernández-Campoy and Conde-Silvestre, 2015). As Ilay came from one of the largest aristocratic interests in Scotland (Murdoch, 2006), Tweeddale could not have failed to be aware of this, encouraging his adoption of politeness conventions.

Indeed, the only Scots features are the use of <u> in *doun* and *oun*, and *necessar*, 'necessary'. The considerable discrepancy in social status, and the extensive political power Ilay wielded in parliament may thus be responsible for Tweeddale's greater use of anglicised features, but this does not suggest such variation was bound by a simple shift along the cline of formality or attention to speech. Rather, Tweeddale might seek to demonstrate the respect required by his recipient, *in order to* achieve membership of the group or interest that Ilay represented. The content of the letter, its anglicised nature, semantic and pragmatic devices, and the politeness conventions used, all lend weight to this possibility.

In general, Tweeddale's letters to Ilay establish a prevailing sense of analogous motives, initiatives and goals. This might go some way to explaining why his letters to Court politicians pattern so similarly to the Squadrone figures, in which Tweeddale integrates himself into a new position within the pre-existing social structure by aligning himself on a linguistic front with their practices. This was not just a passive reaction to their influence and status, however, as his letters clearly suggest he actively sought to portray himself as a trustworthy, esteemed and valuable member of parliament. In his new role as high commissioner of the Scottish parliament, Tweeddale would have been keen to demonstrate his competency and ability to manage such a role of high standing, and did so using variants that were both associated with higher prestige, and had greater currency with his recipients. The Court party and Squadrone did harbour an active alliance during the final sessions of the Scottish parliament, evident in the Court's moves to recognise the Squadrone's reservoir of support by selectively distributing rewards promised after the ratification of the treaty (Macinnes, 2007: 304), and Tweeddale, as leader of the Squadrone, was well aware of this. Despite his difficulties in cultivating political connections (Riley, 1979: 50), Tweeddale does appear to have been sensitive to the linguistic and stylistic norms of his Court party associates, and subtly moves towards these.

In comparison, Tweeddale's correspondence to the Duke of Hamilton and Duke of Atholl, both Country party members, sees a small uptick in proportions of Scots. Perhaps, as with his Squadrone and Court correspondents, Tweeddale sought to index his affiliation with their political group, particularly if these letters were written prior to 1704. Considering the Country party was associated with higher probabilities of Scots, Tweeddale may likewise have increased his use as an initial member of their faction. Doing so could underline a common opposition identity and membership, encouraged perhaps by Tweeddale's own political insecurity and poor networking skills, which demanded greater effort on his part to align with his political patrons in parliament. Dossena's (2019) analysis of nineteenth-century Scottish correspondence found that writers frequently sought to express authenticity, reliability and psychological proximity through means of less formulaic choices such as vernacular usage, as well as utilising the vernacular for positive and negative politeness moves, reinforcing mutual bonds (Dossena, 2019: 70).

Similarly, Tweeddale's use of Scots could have reinforced his value to the leaders of the Country coalition, particularly as neither Hamilton nor Atholl were part of the Cavalier wing of the Country party, thus they concurred with Tweeddale on ecclesiastical and dynastic issues. This relationship changed after 1704, and we have already seen the comments Tweeddale made about Hamilton to Ilay in the earlier extract, which suggested a political distancing took place. Initially however, the Tweeddale and Hamilton families were 'allies in resentment and ambition' (Riley, 1979: 133) following the aftermath of the Darien failure. Both had invested in the Company of Scotland, and the two of them exploited popular anger in Edinburgh in a bid to put pressure on the English Court (Riley, 1979: 137). All of Tweeddale's letters to Hamilton were written between 1700 and 1702, a time when they were arguably most closely aligned, while letters to Atholl are dated mostly around 1703, prior to Tweeddale's shift away from the Country party. To explore this in further detail, an extract from a letter written to Hamilton on 12 January, 1702, is shown below.

> God *hes blist* you with a sone of *lait* which the news was *receav'd* with the greatest satisfactione of all such [...]. I did not againe meett with the D. of Arg: [...] however I think the loss was not great for either the advances he made *was* with the designe you *writt* or he would never have *engadg* furder for the publick then he found would be usfull for his owne private interest for that *hes* been *alwise* the maxime that familye *hes* gone upon.

Tweeddale's style in this letter is less formal than that observed in letters to his Squadrone and Court party recipients - the tone of the letter is almost tale-telling in nature, and Tweeddale's close working relationship with Hamilton is evident from the extract, in which he congratulates him warmly on the birth of his son. He also paints Argyll - the leader of the Court party - in a rather negative light, suggesting Argyll is motivated primarily by private interest rather than the good of the public which '*hes* been *alwise* the maxime that familye *hes* gone upon'. Yet just two and a half years later Tweeddale writes to Argyll's brother Ilay about Hamilton, whom he casts off. Tweeddale's changing political allegiances might subsequently be matched by a slight change in linguistic behaviour, suggesting a sensitivity to the usage patterns of whichever group he was seeking to integrate into.

Alongside this, he demonstrates a range of Scots features, including <i> – <e> in *blist*, 'blessed', <dg> in engadg, 'engage', the non-standard past tense form *was* and 'Other' features including *writt*, 'wrote', *hes*, 'has' and *alwise*, 'always'. The prevalence and type of Scots features are increased, especially in comparison to the Court recipients examined earlier. They might serve as a mark of familiarity, indexing Hamilton and Tweeddale's shared Scottish background and perhaps their joint opposition to the leader of the Court (Argyll), consequently enabling Tweeddale to make such observations by referencing this common ground and closing the socio-political distance between them. As with his Court recipients, Tweeddale appeals to a mutual understanding with his correspondent, this time based around othering the Court rather than opposition members, and such moves are accompanied by various instances of Scots, rather than increased levels of anglicisation.

In a letter to Atholl, dated 2 November 1703, we can similarly observe Tweeddale referring to their common understanding – in this case their suspicions regarding certain members who recently joined the Court party – and a subsequent scattering of Scots features are present throughout.

> As to my *oun* particular your Grace hath all alongst *knoun* so much of my mind in those matters having been as plain with yow as with any [...] if yow believe me sincere in what I professe as I hope yow do, and I am persuaded may ye same of all our other friends. I am *sorie* such pitifall tricks, and under hand insinuations should bear such weight after they have been so often *catched* in ym as to support a *partie* who have no other thing to recommend them and litle or no interest of their *oun* to do it but what favour they have gained at Court by indirect means gives them.

Tweeddale's letter underlines their similar interpretation of events, inferring a mutual distrust that reinforces their alliance within the Country party. This enables Tweeddale to be 'as plain with yow [Atholl] as with any', and he refers to 'all our other friends', alluding to a common network of political figures between them within the loose amalgamation of interests in the Country party. He also seeks to negatively portray the Court party, who 'have no other thing to recommend them' and 'little or no interest of their *oun*', given their primary motivation is the favour they have gained at (the English) Court. As with Hamilton, a distinction between the Court and Country interests is being foregrounded, and there are several Scots features present, including the use of <ie> in *sorie* and *partie*, the past tense form in *catched*, and the use of <u> in *oun*, 'own' and *knoun*, 'known'. While it seems Tweeddale did not distinguish his *range* of Scots features in writing to Atholl, he does slightly alter his *proportion* to incorporate more Scots features, which may have signalled increased authenticity and reliability to Country party members.

In many ways, Tweeddale's stylistic behaviour towards Hamilton and Atholl mimics his demeanour towards the Court politicians he would write to just two years later. The use of the vernacular has frequently been found to correspond with in-group convergence or out-group divergence (Llamas et al., 2009: 385–386), and Tweeddale seems to subconsciously recognise the more anglicised registers of his Squadrone and Court contemporaries, and the increased vernacularity of his Country associates with their slightly higher Scots probabilities. Moreover, while at first glance Tweeddale's behaviour might seem inconsistent, identities emerge only in relation to other identities, making them naturally dynamic, fractured, and discontinuous, and different roles will be projected in different circumstances (Bucholtz and Hall, 2005: 25; Hernández-Campoy and Conde-Silvestre, 2015: 15). In this case, the transformative events around 1704 led Tweeddale to change his group membership, and the combination of content, tone and written features suggest Tweeddale's attempts at alignment or integration with either party and political platform as the situation demanded. Groups and individuals in multi-lingual settings have the ability to negotiate identity in response to ideologies demanding conformity and uniformity (Blackledge and Pavlenko, 2001: 248) and similarly Tweeddale seems to be negotiating his own stance through slight changes in his stylistic behaviour, depending on the political climate he was operating in. Perhaps he was a more nuanced and politically astute narrator than previous scholarship has given him credit for, and this in turn points to the value of a micro-analysis in which these faint patterns can be illuminated.

To determine the extent to which the stylistic use of Scots for positioning and in-group/out-group membership claims was unique to these politicians or occurred more generally in educated, eighteenth-century Scottish society, the corpus must be explored from one final, non-parliamentary perspective. Accordingly, the proportions and range of Scots demonstrated by the Presbyterian clergyman Robert Wodrow are explored in the following section.

Robert Wodrow

Robert Wodrow was a Presbyterian minister based in the parish of Eastwood, near Glasgow, and was by far the least anglicised writer of the four analysed here. He was the second son of James Wodrow (1637–1707), a professor of divinity in the University of Glasgow and a devout Presbyterian. Wodrow similarly acquired an unwavering commitment to the Presbyterian cause, especially after experiencing the tumultuous events of pre-Revolution Scotland as a young child. He completed his divinity studies at the University of Glasgow and was ordained a minister at the parish of Eastwood on the 28th of October, 1703. A keen scholar with a range of intellectual interests, Wodrow was an astute ecclesiastical historian well-versed in literary pursuits, thus while he did not come from an elite or noble background, his education was certainly not wanting. His Scots use might instead be driven by the consistent retention of certain features connected to his clerical duties within the Presbyterian Kirk, given the tendency for Scots lexis and set phrases to continue in ecclesiastical fields.

During his years at Eastwood he also became an avid collector of manuscripts, pamphlets, and natural history specimens, corresponding frequently with his associates about their discoveries. A popular and active parish minister, Wodrow devoted much of his spare time to his scholarly interests, and resisted all attempts at moving him to higher-profile charges such as Stirling or Glasgow (Yeoman, 2004), or to make him chair of divinity at Glasgow University when it became vacant. While Wodrow's brother and many of his colleagues studied abroad in the Netherlands,

Wodrow himself never travelled much further than Edinburgh, instead establishing a network of couriers and correspondents across the British Isles and the continent to overcome his isolation (Sharp, 1937: xxix). His largely immobile and rooted nature within the surrounds of his local parish may have encouraged the maintenance of certain Scots features, given the lack of direct contact with southern English speakers.

Of course, Wodrow's correspondence provided avenues through which his written language use could be influenced, but such contact would have been less pervasive and less intense than spending long periods of time in the metropolitan capital, or even associating with contemporaries in Edinburgh, where Scottish Standard English was slowly emerging. This might add a layer of explanation for Wodrow's higher proportion of Scots in his writing, given the relatively quiet and localised life he led. In addition, his historical pursuits may have led him to work with older manuscripts that were more conservative and traditional in their nature, and his collector's interests would increase the chances of specific flora and fauna being discussed – both fields in which Scots lexis is historically retained.

Despite this preference for the quiet country life, Wodrow played an active role in the discussion around the Union, as a vocal and expressive opponent to the proposed agreement. He articulated an ardent and passionate defence of Scotland's religious and civil liberties and independence (Sharp, 1937: xxviii), and wrote both publicly and privately about his concerns for the security of the Presbyterian Kirk, which he believed the Union did not adequately accommodate for (Yeoman, 2004; Raffe, 2012a). Despite this involvement, Wodrow was not caught up in complex party politics that integrated ideological commitments, denominational differences, kinship ties and personal ambitions within their complicated socio-political composition. He did not seek to further himself in terms of economic and social enhancement, nor to secure a place post-Union in the new political order. He therefore had no interest in ingratiating himself with the right patrons in parliament, thus his correspondence was not predicated upon political networking and advancement. Rather, Wodrow was in many ways the very opposite. As a result, any sociolinguistic influences on his Scots are likely to be calibrated along quite different lines. Of particular interest is thus how

Wodrow compares to the politicians. This can illuminate whether the linguistic behaviour observed in the previous three writers was potentially reflective of Scottish society more broadly, or tightly localised to their specific community of practice(s).

Proportions and letters

Wodrow's Scots and anglicised features were accordingly extracted from POLITECS and plotted in a mosaic plot, shown by Figure 7.5.

Examining Wodrow's proportions across his different correspondents, the first observation is how strikingly consistent he is. Regardless of the volume of correspondence he sends his recipients, almost all see very similar proportions of Scots. This proportion falls around 30–40 per cent of the variable tokens within the letters, though some recipients, such as Patrick Smith and John McLean, see 50 per cent or more. The second thing

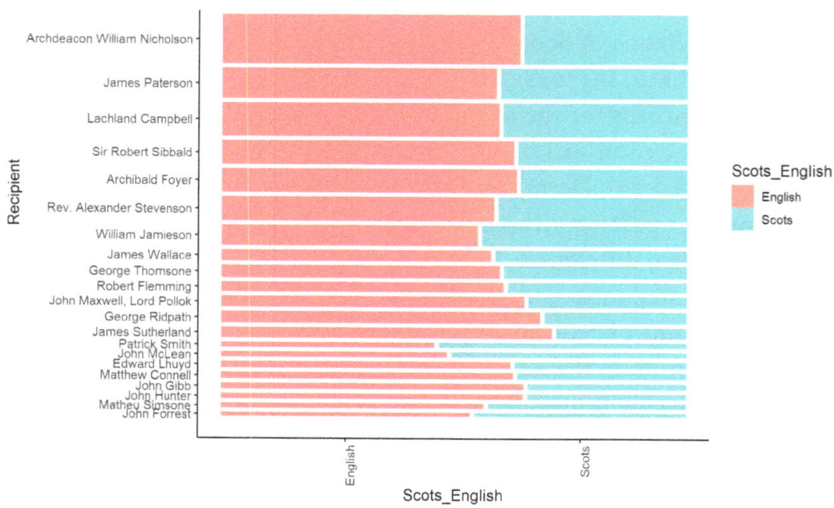

Figure 7.5: Mosaic plot of Wodrow's Scots and English frequencies by recipient.

to observe is just how Scotticised Wodrow is – unlike the previous three figures examined, Wodrow clearly uses much higher proportions of Scots features. This was already evident in Figure 7.1 and observing the patterns here, it is clear this higher Scots usage is applied across the board, rather than being driven by a handful of recipients.

Wodrow's Scots is not influenced by his audience in any obvious way, nor is there evidence of more subtle patterns like we saw with Tweeddale – Wodrow's usage barely fluctuates between letters written to established or esteemed literary figures such as the Archdeacon Nicolson, Edward Lhuyd and Sir Robert Sibbald, and his Glasgow colleagues from his divinity days, including George Thomson, the Simson brothers and Alexander Stevenson. This might suggest Wodrow's role in society did not place the same demands on his writing style as the socially mobile politicians seeking advancement and prestige. After all, Wodrow did not aspire to further his clerical ambitions, and was nowhere near as mobile as figures such as Lockhart or Mar, nor did he share their network of influential acquaintances in the English parliament. There are no letters to promising benefactors and regardless, Wodrow's main desire was to remain in his parish rather than seek promotion through the clerical system. This suggests that Scots features had not become available as a stylistic resource for him, but neither were they particular targets for anglicisation. Such patterning lends support to the idea that the Scottish politicians formed their own CofP in which their participation in the Union debates created a common objective that was enacted and reinforced through the shared activities and routines they participated in on a regular basis. While there was divergence, derived from their adherence to different ideological commitments underpinning the political agenda of the parliamentary groups, these historical actors were bound by mutual engagement and shared practices, and this seems to have stretched to their specific language use.

Moving on and examining Wodrow's letters individually might indicate how an eighteenth-century individual from a non-elite background was using written Scots. In Wodrow's single letter to Patrick Smith, written 5 August, 1699, it quickly becomes clear that the high proportion of Scots to this recipient is being driven almost entirely by his consistent use of <quh> in interrogative and relative clause markers. The only other instances of Scots features are <u> in *hou*, 'how' (MOUTH), *Neu*, 'New' and *knouledge*, 'knowledge'.

> 1. *Quhat* longitude & latitude *Neu* Edinburgh lyes in; *quhat* distance from Panama, Porto Bello, Cartagena, Jamaica and other adjacent places of note. 2. *Quhat* time of the year the raines in Caledonia begin; *hou* long they last; *quhat* are the ordinary antecedents of ther coming. 3. *Quhat* is the nature of the country, if mountanouse; if ther be good hopes of mettales in the hills and of *quhat* kind; *quhether* the ground be barren *quher* the mines are; As to the natives: *quhat* is ther disposition and genius, if sagaciouse or dull; if they have any *knouledge* of one God *quhom* they look upon as superiour to the rest.

This letter is a series of queries sent to his recipient, who was bound for 'Caledonia Nova' – the Scottish colony of Darien, established on the Isthmus of Panama.[8] As a result of these requests, Wodrow uses much more interrogative clause markers than would otherwise be expected in a regular letter, and he is highly consistent in using <quh> for these. Many of Wodrow's letters involve appeals to his recipients for information or news, drawing on their own scholarly or botanical knowledge or enquiring into their collections or findings, which is likely why his proportion of <quh> is exceptionally high. At first glance, it also appears that, unlike Lockhart, Wodrow consistently writes out the markers in full. However, examining the Scottish History Society transcription notes accompanying Wodrow's collection of letters, the editor L.W. Sharp notes that Wodrow regularly uses the contracted forms *qh, qt, qn* and *qr* for *quhich, quhat, quhen* and *quhere*, 'which', 'what', 'when' and 'where'. Sharp decided to expand these abbreviations into the Older Scots form 'in view of the archaic quality of much of Wodrow's vocabulary' (Sharp, 1937: li). In some of his later letters, however, Wodrow does write out these words in full, and always in the anglicised form, which indicates that his use of the Older Scots feature survives mainly in the contraction. Pietsch (2015) and Elspaß (2012a) have suggested that evidence of archaic grammatical

8 Confusingly, the same name was given to the Melanesian archipelago 'New Caledonia', which was only sighted by Captain James Cook in 1774.

structures in emigrant letters were likely remnants of 'standard' formulae that had been acquired in letter writing practice and similarly, the incorporation of abbreviated <quh> into standard writing practice might result in this near-categorical preference shown by Wodrow.

This would match the same pattern we have seen in Lockhart, suggesting that <quh> was no longer in everyday use as a full written form, being perhaps salient enough that authors were aware of its Scots nature and sought to anglicise this. This salience has been highlighted by previous research into <quh> in the Older and Middle Scots period, which has consistently found a rather abrupt change from <quh> to <wh> around the beginning of the seventeenth century, suggesting authors were aware of its status as a Scots marker (MacQueen, 1957; Devitt, 1989; Meurman-Solin, 1997; van Eyndhoven and Clark, 2019). In light of this, the continuation of <quh> into the eighteenth century is plausibly conditioned by its presence in abbreviated forms. Abbreviations and contractions, particularly of high frequency function words, were common in correspondence at this time (Markus, 2006: 125–126), given their time-saving nature and the utilitarian status of correspondence, along with its copious production and quick turnaround relative to other types of printed work (Kopaczyk, 2011: 95). Recent work on <quh> has indeed highlighted the near-categorical preference for its abbreviated forms in eighteenth-century Scottish correspondence, enabling it to persist in personal writings despite its disappearance from most printed and written genres by this point (see van Eyndhoven, 2024 for further discussion).

Nonetheless, given the variant had been disappearing from most text types since 1600, the retention of this feature and its highly consistent use does suggest a slightly more traditional or conservative linguistic behaviour. This might support the possibility that the relatively isolated and immobile lifestyle that Wodrow led, combined with the archaic language of the Kirk, influenced his own orthographic choices. The development of profession-specific standards including the preservation of precise forms has been identified for example in the use of Chancery standard among legal clerks in London (Fisher, 1977: 893–894; Richardson, 1980: 743–744; Conde-Silvestre and Hernández-Campoy, 2004), as well as in Scots law, in which specific lexical bundles required to validate legal documents were sites where Scots was preserved (Kopaczyk, 2013a, 2013b). This could lead to the preservation of <quh> forms, which were often present in legal and ecclesiastical texts, and which Wodrow may have concurrently had greater contact with through his scholarly pursuits and profession more generally.

Moving on to another tract, the consistent use of <quh> remains, but other features are also observable in Wodrow's letter written to John McLean, 13 April 1701.

> 4ly. *Ane* account of the fashions and customes that are peculiar to the Highlanders would be very acceptable; of their ancient bards, their peculiar games, the customes and *frites* [...] I hear there was *ane* accompt of all *thir write* by some body or other.

Alongside <quh>, *ane* and the lexical items *thir*,[9] 'these' and *frites*, 'a superstition, a superstitious belief, observance or act' (DSL, 2022) are all observed, as well as the use of *write* as a past participle – a feature that had been fading out of use in English throughout the 1600s, but carried on into the eighteenth century for Scottish writers (OED, 2022). Regarding this last example, Wodrow's use of a feature that was slowly becoming obsolete again seems to reflect his reduced levels of anglicisation, as well as perhaps the more archaic style of writing that Sharp (1937) referred to. The use of *frites* on the other hand was not a disappearing feature, having entered Scots from around 1420 onward and continuing throughout the nineteenth and twentieth centuries. It stems from the Older Scots word *frete* meaning 'superstition', and the nature of the lexical item itself might have encouraged its usage. Referring to a concept bound within cultural practice, it represents in many ways the traditional, everyday associations that Scots was increasingly acquiring by this time. It also reflects the nature of Wodrow's correspondence – both as a figure rooted in his local, rural and Scottish community, and as a correspondent who frequently wrote about topics connected to the land, folk and traditions that comprised his surroundings.

Indeed, the contents of Wodrow's letters provide another major reason for his heightened Scots use. He frequently discussed matters linked to agriculture, flora and fauna, as well as folklore and culturally specific rituals,

9 A Scots pronoun form, see Aitken (1971: 179).

alongside legal and ecclesiastical lexis relating to the Union debates. These fields encouraged use of Scots lexis, given the lack of appropriate, viable alternatives (Millar, 2003, 2004; Kopaczyk, 2013a, 2013b). In addition, the Scots lexical item may simply have been more accessible to the linguistically conservative Wodrow, mirroring his localised identity and traditional vocation, which was strongly grounded in local custom and national heritage.

Yet we do not see, as with Mar for example, a scattering of non-standard or even quasi-phonological spellings throughout Wodrow's letters – he uses certain Scots variants consistently, but the remainder of his letters are very standardised, perhaps reflecting his high level of education and well-read nature. Wodrow appears largely invariable, both in his Scots and his anglicised spelling features, adopting one or the other almost categorically. Occasionally he reflects plausible generational changes, as in the case of his adoption of <wh> toward the end of his life, but in general, he seems less aware of his Scots usage, making it unavailable as a target for anglicisation. This is supported by the passage below, written to John Forrest, on 28 May, 1702. Forrest was co-editor with John Gullon of the *Sedulius*, which was published at Edinburgh in 1701, and which forms the topic of the letter. Wodrow specifically discusses language, particularly the value of learning the classical languages, yet, his own written language does not overtly move towards the incipient English standard, despite its status being recognised in elite and educated circles within Scotland for quite some time.

> He is very *weel* satisfyed with the designe of a vocabulary for the use of the youth, I *knou* nothing more usefull for schools then a *weel* digested vocabulary ; at least I found nothing soe usefull to my self in *atteaning* and *reteaning* the small pittance of Latine, Greek and *Hebreu* as this kind of help I composed for my *oun* use in all the languages. I expect to wait on you *nixt* week at Edinburgh *quher* Mr Skirvine likwise *desings* to be, and then we shall discourse at more *lenth* on all these heads. Till then and ever belive me to be, Sir, your *oblidged* humble servant, R. Wodrow.

Wodrow does show variation in the use of <ng> in the word 'design' which sees both *designe* and *desings*, 'designs', but most features are consistently Scots, and Wodrow's diverse range of features in the text suggests he is not particularly altering or monitoring his language use when discussing this topic, despite the heightened focus on language it portrays.

Even as he reflects on his own language abilities Scots features emerge, when he discusses '*atteaning* and *reteaning* the small pittance of Latine, Greek and *Hebreu*'.

Overall, Wodrow's use of Scots might reflect the contents of his letters, as well as the retention of written practices acquired through his intellectual undertakings, and the traditional Scottish institution that he was part of. Wodrow's more conservative linguistic style might be at least partially driven by his belonging to a particular sub-culture within Scottish society, through which he accumulated aspects of his written repertoire. In that sense, Scots might still index his belonging to a particular group, though it was not an identity Wodrow consciously or subconsciously manipulated, foregrounded or suppressed to achieve particular socio-pragmatic goals. In this sense, he perhaps belonged to the ecclesiastical or Presbyterian discourse community operating in Scotland, especially considering that such members may not be conscious of sharing discourse practices, whereas members of communities of practice often are (Watts, 1999: 43). Comparing this behaviour with the likes of Tweeddale, for instance, the politicians thus seem to be operating within a Community of Practice much more obviously than Wodrow.

Concluding thoughts

The quantitative analyses in Chapters 5 and 6 were able to indicate how Scots patterned across time and across the writers of the corpus, including those analysed here, suggesting that the complex and interwoven identity politics characterising the Union debates played a role in shaping Scots usage. This micro-analysis was able to examine these tendencies up close within four selected authors, cautiously suggesting the extent to which they reflect the wider structural trends identified in the macro-social analysis, and the intricate role that relationships with their recipients alongside personal goals may have played in shaping their writing choices. While Lockhart, Mar and Tweeddale show sensitivity to the general conglomeration of political, religious and ideological interests encouraging greater levels of Scots or anglicisation, they do not necessarily embody these personae themselves. Their baseline levels of Scots, as indicated by their proportions in Figure 7.1, are not mere replicas of the general patterns identified in Chapter 6 – Tweeddale for instance is least anglicised out of the three of them, despite being a Squadrone figure. However, by exploring their individual relationships to different recipients, not only is there evidence that *audience design* influenced their linguistic behaviour – in line with the general patterns identified in the statistical chapter – but also highly specific *social* and *stylistic* goals. Scots features seem to have been available as a linguistic resource, enabling these writers to position themselves relative to their recipient or a collective 'other', or to reduce impositions or face-threatening requests by increasing amicability through use of shared, vernacular features.

Wodrow reflected a strikingly different patterning with a much higher proportion of Scots, albeit one that was being driven largely by his consistent use of certain features, such as <quh>. Nonetheless, his behaviour indicates that certain individuals remained much more Scots in their writing than others during the eighteenth century, particularly when they were localised, largely immobile individuals operating within traditional institutions such as the Kirk. Scots use, in some shape or form, does appear to reflect these writers' position within the larger, macro-social structure. Scots accordingly may have been developing into a resource to index the values particularly important to each individual analysed, whether they were necessarily aware of it or not.

CHAPTER 8

Eighteenth-century written Scots through macro and micro perspectives

There is no doubt that the turning of the eighteenth century, and the tumultuous time period around the parliamentary debates, was unique, unprecedented and complex in its scope and influence across large swathes of Scottish society. Not only the Union of the Parliaments itself, but also the increasingly tense lead-up to the debates, and the subsequent revolts, rebellions and popular uprisings in the aftermath, speak to the sentimental, emotionally charged and often quite personal relationship many in Scotland had with this moment in history. For the signing of the treaty was by no means a mere legal formality, solidifying tendencies that had been in motion for decades or even centuries prior. Equally, it would be unfair to suggest that incorporation materialised out of thin air, forced upon the negotiating table by the English during a moment of Scottish economic and political weakness. Rather, it captures an intricate web of interrelated and intertwined interests that combined, intersected and undermined each other throughout the progression of the debates, from the first serious discussions through to the treaty's final form and ratification. Political, religious, economic, local and national concerns, not to mention vested personal interests, all played a role in shaping perception and stance towards incorporation, and these factors have come back throughout this narrative again and again on a linguistic front as well.

Historical and contemporary accounts of the Union have already indicated the complexity of the situation and how these intervening factors influenced alliances and voting behaviour within the Scottish parliament. What has been less clear until now is whether they could also have influenced language use, particularly in terms of written Scots usage. This specific time period is promising to explore from a sociolinguistic perspective, particularly considering the links between language and the political sphere identified in contemporary variationist research. The thesis this book is based on sought to address this current gap, compiling a purpose-built corpus containing selected writings from relevant political individuals, incorporating a broad range of phonological-orthographic Scots features in the search criteria, and drawing upon the three waves of sociolinguistic investigation to interpret and analyse the patterning found. Given the convoluted, byzantine set of influences upon commissioners operating within the Scottish parliament, who had to navigate an increasingly complex cultural dualism, changes to form should be considered in the context of the dynamic interaction between extra and intra-linguistic processes and pressures (J. J. Smith, 1996b: 78). A thorough linguistic investigation of this historical event similarly needs to be polymorphic in its approach.

The combined insights of the macro and micro analyses provides a scope that is at once both broad and narrow, creating a more holistic view of eighteenth-century written Scots, whilst indicating the continual feedback loop between general and specific patterns of variation. As a result, this investigation has been able to explore this critical moment with greater depth, breadth and nuance than has previously been possible, across the temporal, social and linguistic landscape. This speaks more generally to the twin benefits of using data-driven, objective statistical models alongside careful, human insight in exploring collective and singular instances of variation. Consequently. we acquire a greater understanding of what was taking place at large within a language community, whilst never losing sight of what was happening on the ground. Historical sociolinguistic research is thus not only feasible through this approach, but also enhanced by it, and future studies examining diachronic variation might similarly benefit from applying the multiple lenses of the different frameworks to their data, in aggregate and across individuals.

Reflecting on the key findings, the temporal investigation indicated that this time period and the political scene *did* in fact have an impact on written Scots usage. Plotting the frequencies of Scots features over the time-period captured in the corpus, utilising Variability-based Neighbour Clustering (VNC), circumvented the potential shortfalls of partitioning data into arbitrary time chunks, and this was validated by the findings. The time period 1699–1704 – key years in the Union debates – was found to reflect a marked increase in the frequencies of Scots. Moreover, this increase took place at precisely the time of maximum political tension between Scotland and England. This provided the first plausible evidence that, alongside socio-political changes taking place at the time, the language use of Scottish politicians also changed during the Union debates, especially given the same body of writers produced the correspondence either side of this window. A traditional partitioning of the data would likely have split the timeline of the corpus at 1700, dividing the data of these crucial years in two and reducing their salience. Yet these five years in particular – only a very small window in the grand scheme of Scottish history – *were* able to indicate that the period around the Union debates saw heightened Scots use, precisely because the VNC analysis enabled them too. Future analyses wishing to explore subtle changes in variability within small corpora might thus benefit from utilising similar methodologies, rather than traditional partitioning.

This rise in Scots, and its subsequent tailing off just at the point where the Squadrone consolidated into a separate political body, might mirror the fluid and dynamic environment in which the Union debates took place. While some authors were committed to their position throughout the process, for others it encompassed a constantly shifting quicksand of emotional hostility, pragmatic concession, political acumen and social ambition, and the Squadrone can be considered to belong to the latter. The Squadrone may have been in the process of changing their group membership to one that encompassed the Court and ruling class – rather than their traditional domain within the Scottish gentry. In doing so, greater use of an anglicised writing style, which, as the following quantitative analysis made clear, was associated with a Presbyterian Court position, may have indexed this shift. They accordingly reflected their shift within the political spectrum not just by votes, but also through language. Conjectures aside, it is clear that something unique and distinct was going on specifically during these years, supporting the possibility that this time period was exceptional from a linguistic point of view. The complex series of events and the discourse constructed around the debates do appear to have influenced the language use of those most involved with them.

Given these findings, the potential factors interacting with these patterns were then examined through a quantitative exploration of the data in the following chapter. Utilising two statistical methodologies – MCA and Bayesian regression analysis – in tandem to explore the linguistic landscape provided a vantage point that proved highly beneficial to uncovering the multilayered nature of influencing factors and their patterning across groups of individuals. Different effects, including political and religious affiliations, party associations, Jacobite leanings, birthplace and family or landed connections all came to light. Rather than one factor trumping all others in terms of significance and predictive power, it seems multiple influences were operating at any one time, and it was their combination that could encourage or repress the use of Scots features, exercising complimentary or push-pull effects on different groups. Considering the diametric forces at work in 1700, perhaps it isn't surprising that influencing factors cannot be reduced to a single variable operating in isolation. The role of these interwoven identities was able to be suitably explored by combining the strengths of MCA and Bayesian regression modelling, offering a perspective of the data that is more sensitive and attuned to its historical reality. As a consequence, not only has early eighteenth-century Scots been explored for the first time using a comprehensive quantitative approach, but with the added insight from multiple modelling techniques to assist in illuminating trends taking place. Within the identified interests, it was the Country party writers who were Episcopalian and Jacobite (and it goes without saying Anti-Unionist) who were most likely to use written Scots features. Whilst recognising the multiplicity of the context, political identity *did* play a role in Scots use overall, and writers may have indexed their membership to particular platforms through subconscious changes in language use. This is in keeping with many of the contemporary analyses observing variation in modern-day political situations, in which politicians have been found to utilise lexical and phonological features to index their leadership or membership of particular political parties (e.g. Fairclough, 1989, 2000; Hall-Lew et al., 2010, 2012, 2017). Yet this was by no means a given in 1707, considering the fluid nature of the emergent Scottish political parties and the potential strength of other factors overriding stylistic moves to claim in-group membership. It is thus all the more interesting that such a link has been identified, albeit one tempered by other contributing factors.

Indeed, the likelihood of using Scots cannot be reduced to simple alignment along the apparent dichotomy between supporters and opponents of the Union, which, as mentioned throughout, was much more opaque and nontransparent than a binary set of choices. This aligns with what Chapter 1 highlighted about this time period already – the amorphous nature of the political parties (with perhaps the exception of the Squadrone), suggests their political identity was fluid and bound by deeper ties and commitments that went beyond mere party policy (Ferguson, 1964: 94). While this accumulates into a large-scale distinction between Pro and Anti-Union stances, the statistical analysis was able to uncover subtleties within the linguistic data, suggesting the landscape was more heterogeneous than might first appear. This was indicated in particular by the Cavalier wing of the Country party, who shared Episcopalian and Jacobite goals but also the highest probabilities of Scots. Similarly, the linguistic behaviour of the Squadrone Volante was strikingly uniform, and this came through again in the micro-analysis in Chapter 7. Just as speakers have been shown to utilise features in ideological and indexical moves that characterise certain groups, to invoke ways of belonging to that population (Kiesling, 2001; Podesva, 2011; Eckert, 2012: 94), so too these writers might be invoking their membership of these specific collections of interest within the Scottish parliament. These identities became increasingly salient around the events of 1704–1705, perhaps encouraging their use of specific features to index community ties, but also establish their collective entity in the process, creating a linguistic distinction between two groups who had previously been part of the same political unit. In many ways each respective group reflects the characteristics of a Community of Practice (CofP), bound by common goals, mutual practices, and a shared repertoire of resources (Wenger, 1998: 72–85), in which their variable language use both belonged to and constructed their socio-political identity. This manifested with a degree of consistency high enough to be identified within the statistical analysis, while the micro-analysis demonstrated this recognition on a more subtle layer.

The final analytical chapter unpicked this usage on an individual level, comprising of a micro-analysis into the language use of Country, Court and

Squadrone Volante politicians and a Presbyterian minister, to determine whether the macro-social patterns identified in Chapter 6 were reflected in their linguistic behaviour. This also gave an idea of what written Scots looked like in the letters themselves, and the extracts examined highlighted the individualised nature of Scots use by this time. Yet, while it may have diminished in frequency, it certainly hadn't diminished in complexity and the range of functions it could perform. The three political figures all suggested sensitivity to the overarching patterns found within the quantitative results – their proportions of Scots to recipients within their own political grouping tended to match the general baseline for that collection of writers. Hence we saw that the Country party politician Lockhart tended to use more Scots to other Country party members, and in particular to recipients who were Jacobite and Episcopalian.

Conversely, Tweeddale's behaviour towards his Court, Squadrone and Country party recipients suggests he was somewhat of a political chameleon, subtly emulating their writing style and aligning himself with whichever party he was cooperating with at that point in time. His overarching motives are not particularly surprising – this would have been the course of action for various parliamentary members who professed their own social and political agenda, and this was especially the case for the Squadrone who sought to act as political brokers. Unlike some of the more established members of the Court or Country parties, the changing loyalties of the Squadrone members meant that their alliances shifted over time, despite a common adherence to the Protestant succession and the security of the Presbyterian Kirk. Thus, it is all the more relevant that Tweeddale's greater Scots use occurs both to his Country recipients, and before 1705 – the point at which the Squadrone had consolidated into a separate interest, and the year the temporal analysis identified as the turning point in Scots frequencies, which began to decline following their sudden rise. From this point onward, Tweeddale writes only to Court and Squadrone recipients in the corpus, and his levels of anglicisation subtly increase. Such patterns do not suggest that Tweeddale was unaware of available Scots options, indeed his correspondence to Country party recipients, and the range of features he possessed overall, suggested that he could and did use a range of Scots variants within his correspondence. However, room for variability depends on the specific situation and relations between the groups or individuals in question (Blackledge and Pavlenko, 2001: 250), and in the case of Tweeddale, his language choices may have been curtailed by a need to ensure status and influence in the new political order. In doing so, his behaviour echoes the large-scale temporal trends identified in Chapter 5, and this micro-analysis was able to provide potential insight into that change.

Although compelling, audience design or accommodative desires alone could not explain all the variable patterns among the authors – it was not simply the case that they used the highest proportion of Scots features with the recipients they were closest to politically and personally. This was evident both in Mar's behaviour, which demonstrated a considerable reduction of Scots features when corresponding with his uncle, Harry Maule of Panmure, and in Tweeddale's language use to his Squadrone Volante members. Although both writers knew the recipient(s) well and were closely affiliated with them, they did not increase their proportions of Scots variants in these letters, even though they were addressing fellow Scotsmen. Yet all three politicians were capable of shifting, and shifting wasn't unidirectional either, encompassing both increases and decreases in written Scots, as well as the use of specific features to index particular associations or meanings, or the adoption of registers reflecting increased politeness or familiarity with their recipient along anglicised or vernacular lines. In some senses, these patterns also mirror the situation Scots speakers face today, in which individuals can code switch or style drift across a range of registers incorporating more or less Scots features depending on the interlocutor, but also the social context and personal motivations (Stuart-Smith, 2004).

The range of stylistic behaviours these writers demonstrated suggested that written Scots could additionally be used for the claiming of in-group membership with others, in which Scots features could be utilised not only to index congruous identities, but also to paint opponents in an unflattering light. Moreover, we observed Scots use in politeness strategies – which manifested sometimes through increased or specific Scots use to establish common ground with the recipient, and other times through elevated levels of polite, anglicised forms to demonstrate respect. In particular, Scots was important for positioning – either in opposition to the people being discussed, or in accordance with the recipient by highlighting a shared identity. This might reflect what Bucholtz and Hall (2005: 24) label the *tactics of intersubjectivity* – the idea that constructing identity revolves around more than just the simple dichotomy of sameness and otherness, but instead builds upon several, often overlapping, complementary relations, such as *adequation* and *distinction*. Differences that would run counter to groups or individuals will be downplayed, while similarities become more salient to and supportive of the immediate identity being constructed, and as such will be foregrounded. Such behaviour was evident in Tweeddale's correspondence to Court and Country party associates, each of whom saw dismissive comments about their opponents, in a bid to foreground his affiliation with their particular platform. Concurrently his writing style also came to approximate his recipients more closely, enabling Tweeddale to highlight similarities with whichever political orbit he was operating in, while downplaying characteristics that would set him apart, within the bounds and constraints of a letter.

Mar also sought to highlight different elements of similarity and difference to his recipients, thus when corresponding with his brother, familial connections and shared upbringing were plausibly foregrounded by his use of Scots features, reducing the impact of potentially face-threatening requests. Similarly, Scots could be used to mend the potential breach threatened by the contents of his letters to Maule, alongside epistolary politeness conventions and carefully worded phrases. In both cases, Scots was used to position Mar on a similar, locally rooted plane of identity to his recipients, to achieve pragmatically related means. It seems Mar employed similar *strategies* when it came to using Scots with family members, drawing upon their mutual background to minimise any damage done by his correspondence, despite demonstrating different *frequencies* between his brother and uncle. Distinction could likewise be underlined through vernacular features. In conversing with Godolphin, for instance, Mar positioned himself in opposition to the Scotsmen he describes through use of disparaging terms and possibly, Scots features. While such behaviour may seem contradictory, in both cases a positioning is taking place, the only difference being who is aligned with, and who is 'othered'. Moreover, language users can be subject to multiple loyalties, despite overarching discourses and the collective negotiation of identity seeking to reinforce a larger, national belonging (Blackledge and Pavlenko, 2001: 253). Despite Mar's personal drive for success, which may have dictated adherence to the emerging English standard and the new political order that was being developed, he may still have felt loyalty to his country of birth and the old order, a mixed loyalty that might be emergent in his writing choices and positioning.

The politicians explored in the micro-analysis thus suggested a complex combination of influences and motivations encouraging or suppressing the use of Scots features, in which themes from the Second and Third Wave frameworks became relevant at different moments and in different examples. Audience, interindividual-intergroup identities and membership claims, positioning, political indexicality, accommodation and divergence (or *adequation* and *distinction*), all had some role to play in the intricate patterning of Scots features within correspondence being produced at this time. Wodrow behaved remarkably differently to these three writers, suggesting that the politicians formed a CofP of their own. Their frequencies of written Scots were significantly lower than Wodrow, although contrariwise they demonstrated a wider range of features and stylistic applications of Scots. Given Wodrow did not share the aspirations or social pressures of the three political writers, he may not have utilised Scots as a stylistic resource to the same degree. Instead, his high frequencies seem to stem from the content of his writings themselves, and his nature as a relatively invariable writer. Wodrow's linguistic style was perhaps most influenced by the traditional institution he was part of, as well as his relatively immobile lifestyle, and lack of desire for social success.

The examination of individual letters also suggested the individuality, agency and creative ability of the politicians in using Scots features for their own purposes and intentions. That such patterns are suggested by the data is not inherently inconceivable, given the rich interplay of stylistic factors identified in contemporary studies on spoken variation. These have suggested that the individuality, stance, performativity and agency of the speaker as they navigate communicative situations, whilst negotiating and maintaining their social identity and authenticity, is as much responsible for determining variation as external influences (Johnstone, 2000: 72–73; Moore and

Podesva, 2009; Eckert, 2012: 90; A. Auer, 2015: 134; Hernández-Campoy and Conde-Silvestre, 2015: 15). Moreover, various historical sociolinguistic studies examining correspondence data have similarly found letter writers able to express social and stylistic facets by varying their use of particular constructions, and this applies even to aristocratic authors characterised by their classical education and expected awareness of the English standard (i.e. Fitzmaurice, 2015). Similarly, these politicians did not passively adopt a consistently anglicised register when corresponding with their social network. Rather, they used Scots in varying degrees across their different recipients, and across both lexical and orthographic levels. In the process they may have been performing certain alignment or positioning moves, whilst also maintaining their complex interpersonal identities.

These stylistic intentions not only draw from, but also inform, the extralinguistic factors identified in Chapter 6, reflecting the common feedback loop between macro and micro instances of variation that continually constructs and reinforces these categories and influences (Schilling-Estes, 2002: 389; Eckert, 2012: 91, 2016: 68; Hernández-Campoy and Conde-Silvestre, 2015: 15). In this vein, eighteenth-century politicians may have become subconsciously aware of the associations between style and social identity as they developed, leading for instance to the variable behaviour of the Squadrone. Their highly anglicised style was plausibly derived both from their long-standing kinship connections and presumably frequent correspondence, which enabled the transmission of a shared written style, and their shifting identity within the Scottish parliament toward one that sought incorporation and post-Union opportunities, perhaps encouraging the embrace of the emergent English standard. Plausibly, as members increasingly adopted anglicised variants, this accumulated into a community style that could be identified by the statistical analysis. Even figures who did not necessarily adopt the anglicised register as their baseline, such as Tweeddale, could still recognise and show sensitivity to it when corresponding with other members of their party. *Practice*, the fundamental cornerstone of a CofP, is emergent and reproduces previous practice or transforms it (Watts, 2008: 51), and it seems that these writers reflected some conscious or subconscious awareness of their community practice, in terms of their frequencies and range of Scots.

Of course, the question inevitably remains whether it is truly possible to know if the failure to conform to the anglicised standard was an instance of deliberate stance-taking in the indexical field of Scottish identity or something else, such as incomplete mastery of the standard or reference to something other than national identity. This notion is within itself somewhat problematic, given the incoming English standard was still in a process of flux, and though much less variable than Scots, it continued to be disputed and adapted throughout the eighteenth century. As a result, it could not necessarily be 'mastered' as such, and rather than viewing anglicisation as the blanket adoption of a fixed variety, it is perhaps more illuminating to think of this as a gradual transition from written Scots options – which may be shared with northern dialect areas – to those that reflect southern English spelling patterns or word choices.

In addition, the findings presented here suggest that the use of Scots variants was part of a wider stylistic repertoire that reflected political identities and loyalties, rather than being merely the result of writers still adapting to the incoming Southern English standard. This is demonstrated by the clear and sudden rise in Scots identified during the critical Union years, one that was not matched by the later section of the time-period. Considering that the same body of writers produced the material across this timeline, this suggests a sudden change in behaviour rather than unexplained 'blip' in the anglicisation abilities of these politicians. Secondly, the statistical analysis found repeated and observable differences between the three political parties in relation to their probabilities of Scots usage that aligned with what we would expect. If these writers demonstrated incomplete mastery of the standard, we would expect this to be reflected across the political spectrum, regardless of the social and ideological position of the politicians.

Instead, the highest probabilities of Scots were found precisely among the group whose ideology was based around nationalist sentiments, patriotism, and a staunch defence of Scottish independence and sovereignty – the Episcopalian and Jacobite wing of the Anti-Union Country party. Conversely, those at the very opposite end of this spectrum – the firmly Presbyterian, pro-Union Squadrone Volante, were the most anglicised. They had the most to prove in terms of being seen as fit to sit in the post-Union British parliament, making their increased use of anglicised features all the more pertinent. In many ways, they resemble the aspiring middle-class identified in contemporary sociolinguistic analyses and dialectal variationist studies, in which hypercorrection and adoption of pan-regional or national standards frequently characterises these speakers (c.f. Labov, 1966a). Similarly, the Squadrone's adoption of the incoming standard might reflect a desire to be recognised as an acceptable addition to the English (soon-to-be-British) ruling class, which could indicate that Scots features were to some degree marked for them and associated with a local, Scottish identity. While Scots features may have indexed other characteristics to some degree (as part of the wider indexical field (c.f. Eckert, 2008)), they were not the principle factors driving Scots usage, at least for these writers.

Finally, there was clear evidence of style-shifting through Scots use between various recipients that aligned with the large-scale statistical patterns identified in the macro-analysis. This suggests the awareness and sensitivity of these writers to these influences, rejecting the idea that these politicians and clergyman had simply failed to fully convert to anglicised norms. If there was incomplete grasp of the anglicised standard, we would expect this to be mirrored across their social network. Moreover, even the most highly educated writers (such as Tweeddale and Wodrow) demonstrated a variety of Scots features in their correspondence, while Lockhart, as the most anglicised, still used salient written Scots features. Ultimately, we can never be completely sure whether Scots was indeed indexing national identity or some other factor(s) entirely, perhaps influences that were not included in the analysis at all. Nonetheless, the consistent behaviour among this group of writers points to the influence of their political identity and ideology on their language and the role of Scots in constructing this, a not altogether-surprising effect considering the central nature of politics within their daily lives during the Union debates period.

Through a combination of quantitative and qualitative exploration, we have obtained a bicameral perspective on written Scots usage, recognising both the larger social forces at work on this small but significant group of historical figures, but also the range of abilities – some unique and some shared – that these writers possessed in utilising Scots variants in correspondence. As a result, eighteenth-century written Scots appears to be more resilient than previous accounts have given it credit for (c.f.

Aitken, 1979, 1997), or than would be predicted from its historical trajectory. Yet language change or decline does not necessarily follow a teleological, unwavering course to a natural endpoint, nor does it suggest a wholehearted abandonment by all sectors of society is the only plausible outcome. Written Scots did not disappear, even if it was heavily reduced in frequency and range by 1700. Rather, individual features and variants persisted, or were incorporated into a wider linguistic repertoire that included both Scots and English options, in which Scots features could be utilised to signal various allegiances or standpoints.

This is particularly evident in the political CofP operating within the Scottish parliament. Scots continued to be used in correspondence, even within the top tier of Scottish society, and could play an important role in establishing their connections within this elite layer and beyond the border. Perhaps it can even be said to have found a new vitality, to some extent, through its reinterpretation as a resource used to reflect wider social and interactive goals, and to index the relationships and identities therein. This has interesting links to the *Vernacular Revival* that took off some decades later, in which Scots has similarly been argued to have undergone a revitalisation and reinterpretation that was strongly informed by political and nationalist sentiments, although within the realm of poetry rather than correspondence. Perhaps these results suggest a certain line of continuity between the two, bridging time and genre. Both Scots and correspondence, it appears, was not rigid but flexible within its social context.

The findings presented here have shed light on the significance of this time period in influencing the form, function and use of written Scots in correspondence during the early eighteenth century, but they also inform and affirm a broader understanding of socio-politically inspired variation and change. Sociolinguistic analyses have suggested the importance of national identity, political allegiances and constructed idealisms of the self and other in influencing language usage, largely from contemporary perspectives (Chambers, 1995; Fairclough, 2000; Joseph, 2006; Llamas, 2007; Llamas et al., 2009; Krivoruchko, 2008; Hay and Drager, 2010; Hall-Lew et al., 2010, 2012; Fetzer and Bull, 2012; Dominic Watt, 2014; D'Onofrio, 2015; Kirkham and Moore, 2016; Shoemark et al., 2017; Devlin, 2017; Blas Arroyo, 2019; Woschitz and Yağli, 2019). Some diachronic studies have also been undertaken, as in the case of Welsh (Phillips, 2012) or English aristocratic networks (Fitzmaurice, 2000, 2007, 2015). Such research has found language users able to appropriate variants and varieties to signal allegiance or belonging to the identity, associations, and collection of interests indexed by their usage. Oftentimes, this manifests as resistance to overarching narratives demanding conformity to the standard, through use of local or vernacular variants in contested linguistic settings, but this can also develop along more subtle lines of variation, in which social allegiance, rather than outright rejection, is indexed.

Either way, use of the vernacular frequently corresponds to in-group convergence or out-group divergence (Llamas et al., 2009: 385–386), and these results align with such findings, suggesting the universality of indexicality within and outwith political contexts, spanning time, space and even language medium. The identities constructed through variable Scots use were by no means straightforward, indeed they have been found to be multilayered and malleable, but the connection between written Scots and these associations are there, all the same.

Along with politically inspired variation, patterns of convergence and divergence to claim membership of shared, socially constructed identities, have been identified time and again in studies exploring accommodative behaviour in various scenarios, political or otherwise. This includes both diachronic instances (Jaffe et al., 2012; Vosters, 2013; Vosters and Rutten, 2015) and synchronic examples (Hay et al., 2006; Babel, 2010; Drager et al., 2010; Hay and Drager, 2010; Llamas, 2010; Watt et al., 2010; Jungbluth et al., 2015; Sanchez et al., 2015; Walker et al., 2018), and such patterns can occur consciously, but also below the level of awareness in speech or writing. Similarly, the role of accommodation in supporting claims to social or local identities, mediated by recipients posing as representatives of their respective political groups, came through saliently in the micro-analysis. The Scottish politicians did appear to reflect a subconscious awareness of the language norms and written repertoires of the various political interests and subgroups within the parliament, and adjusted their behaviour accordingly. Their stance was thus informed and mediated by a range of factors, but crucially, these were largely interrelated political factors, intimating the universal nature of variation in politically charged settings.

This suggests that the overarching concepts informing contemporary sociolinguistic research on identity and indexicality, can be equally applicable to a historical setting and scenario, even one as complex as the unification of Scotland and England. This is not a given, considering we are dealing with written as opposed to spoken data, produced by an elite, highly mobile and socially ambitious group of writers, during a time when the local language variety had become increasingly relegated to domestic and spoken usage. Appearance and demeanour, both outwardly and in their correspondence, was an important consideration for these political figures, reflecting their education, manners, refinement, relative status and power, and ergo befitting of their social role. As such, these factors would predict a preference for anglicised features or those adopted from the nascent standard in their correspondence, rather than features increasingly associated with a 'rustic' and 'homely' agenda. Furthermore, while the researcher can posit an intuitive link between language use and political allegiance, this will not necessarily follow suit on the ground. The fact that consistent, politically inspired patterns of variation have been observable, both across individuals and across the corpus in total, is thus all the more intriguing.

Consequently, this reflects the power of national and political interests on language variation, even when the variety in question is disfavoured (at least in writing), and no longer supported by the establishment and the prestigious institutions that may once have been its stronghold. The persistence of varieties in the face of a dominant standard, despite the potential inconveniences, difficulties or even dangers this may pose to its users, is nothing new (c.f. Joseph, 2016). Yet, while there is no doubt that spoken Scots continued during this time, evidenced in particular by the fact that it is still spoken today across many parts of Lowland Scotland and the North East, written Scots had suffered a severe decline in context-suitability and prestige across most written domains. Even its revitalisation later in the century during the *Vernacular Revival*, took place largely in the realm of popular literature and poetry, where its use was sanctioned by the elite, rather than in public or personal writing. In these latter domains Scots features were instead remarked upon by grammarians as remnants of a 'barbaric culture', and they frequently became specific targets for anglicisation. The landed elite of Scotland, whose goals were often driven by a vested interest in furthering their political dominance, are thus the least likely candidates to demonstrate continued use of written Scots. Yet the persistence of written Scots in their writings does not derive from the invariable nature of these features, from accidental slips of the pen, or manifest as the forgotten residue of a time long since passed. Rather, these findings highlight a degree of universality between the diachronic and synchronic, in which the power of language users to resist domineering narratives of incorporation, adaptation and amalgamation, is as salient in historical settings as it is today. Simply because our objects of study are long deceased and a product of their time should not deny them the agency to carve out their own relationships with variation and change—relationships that may defy both the global linguistic trends taking place, as well as our expectations of them. Historical language users were not passive individuals acquiescent to broad language developments happening around them, but rather were at the forefront of local and large-scale change, in which they were instrumental in shaping the linguistic landscape they operated in.

In line with this, rather than framing language change through a narrowly constructed narrative of 'decline' and 'disappearance', perhaps we need to consider that reinterpretation and redevelopment of a language variety is also a plausible outcome, particularly in instances where concerns around prestige or social mobility collide with heightened national awareness and political tension. In lieu of generating an ultimate winner, a redistribution of functions is a possible alternative, in which the prestige variety dominates the medium, but individual features from the minority can be employed in subtle ways as the situation and stylistic goals of the writer requires. The outcome is not a guaranteed zero-sum game, but a situation much more nuanced and subtle in its colouring, one that sees an increase in scope by encompassing a greater range of options. These enable a broad range of highly specific styles, spanning multiple spheres of interest. In many respects, this is similar to the linguistic situation we observe with modern day spoken Scots and its 'bi-polar continuum' (Stuart-Smith, 2004), as well as the use of written Scots features on public platforms such as Twitter (Shoemark et al., 2017; Shoemark, Kirby and Goldwater, 2017). This might speak to a degree of historic continuity from the eighteenth century until today, in which these factors had a powerful and lasting impact on the language, even with the odds stacked against it. Agency should thus be accorded not just to the historical actors involved, but also to the variants under investigation – a reduction in range does not necessarily mean a reduction in vitality. Written Scots features weren't the washed-up leftovers of a fading language, delivering their swansong, but rather new tools in constructing the changing social and political world of these writers, and their relationships within it.

CHAPTER 9

Swansong or key-change? Concluding thoughts on written Scots at the turn of the century

This book has provided a detailed perspective of early eighteenth-century Scots, through which we can obtain a window into the fluctuating and ephemeral political landscape of pre-Union Scotland at the turn of the century. It offers a linguistic understanding of the convoluted and interlinked interests scaffolding the identities and ideologies of the ruling families and their representatives in the Scottish parliament. This time period has been understudied within historical Scots scholarship, situated as it is right on the cusp of 'Older Scots' and 'Modern Scots', between the ongoing anglicisation of the previous century and a half, and the emerging *Vernacular Revival* and orthoepist movements that were to take off just half a century later. In addition, an analysis into a corpus of writers as opposed to an individual author, has not yet been undertaken, nor have quantitative analyses utilising statistical techniques been particularly forthcoming. Finally, most previous work has focused on individual orthographic or lexical features, or has used selected wordlists to explore Scots variation, rather than taking a more holistic approach to 'Scots'. The methodology and analyses presented here have been able to address a number of these gaps, elucidating the nature of written Scots with greater depth, exploring the linguistic behaviour of a community of practice, and successfully incorporating statistical techniques to measure the effect of multiple macro-social factors simultaneously on written Scots variation during this time period. The results have been able to suggest the salience of the political context in influencing variation among this community of historical actors, highlighting the existence and continuity of written Scots in their writings, despite previous claims to the contrary.

However, large-scale corpus analysis alone misses much of the complexity and finer detail characterising variation, especially when examining a variety that has been retreating from the written sphere and is no longer as prolific in frequency and scope as it may have been. Thus, along with top-down influences from broad political characterisations, the active role of the writers themselves in utilising variation to reflect salient, socio-political identities, or position themselves in alternative camps, was shown to be a palpable possibility in the micro-analysis. The intricate role of stylistic desires working symbiotically with large-scale, macro-social patterns was posited, highlighting the value of a combined approach to uncover diachronic variation. Additionally, the benefit of combining the three waves of sociolinguistic investigation has been demonstrated, as concepts from each 'wave' added a layer of definition and insight into what was a multi-layered and convoluted historical setting. This enabled the persistence of Scots features and their dynamic potential in personal communication to become apparent.

That written Scots did continue, in large enough quantities for it to pattern in interesting and predictable ways across the corpus, suggests that pressure to anglicise was not absolute, even among highly educated, mobile and socially ambitious elite writers. Instead, we may be observing a reinterpretation of Scots features as elements in themselves, utilised for particular social and pragmatic goals that were sensitive to in-group memberships and political ideologies, rather than appearing as unwanted remnants in writing, to be removed if enough attention was paid to language choices. Scots features may have been shifting from being part of their own system to being incorporated into a new register. While this was based upon the anglicised standard emanating from the south, it nonetheless employed select Scots features in ways both conscious and subconscious, for various purposes. The fact that several of the extracts examined in the micro-analysis seemed to suggest an almost-deliberate application of Scots features, given the meaning, context or word, speaks to this possibility.

Persistence, continuity and room for resistance in the face of pressure to conform to an imposed standard, brought about by an established or higher political order, is not a simple numbers game, in which the higher the frequency and wider the scope, the greater the strength of the variety in question. Indeed, while overall frequencies of written Scots had clearly diminished by this time period, and anglicised tokens vastly dominated the dataset, a considerable range of different variants were still in use. All writers, from the most powerful dukes through to clergymen in their country parishes, continued to use Scots in their writings, often in creative and stylistically advanced ways. Instead of viewing such cases of 'decline' as a unidirectional movement toward ever-increasing decay, variation instead can be thought of as multitudinous in its application, used as part of an extended repertoire to mark or delineate a range of identities and communicative goals. Nor does it seem that historical instances of language preservation necessarily require a climate convivial to continuation, much in the same way that contemporary studies have highlighted the resilience of features or varieties in reaction to environments encouraging their reduction or loss. The linguistic situation in eighteenth-century Scotland was almost entirely geared toward adoption of the incoming standard, at least from a written point of view. This was especially the case for the Scottish political elite seeking social advancement and political success. As the Union progressed, the pragmatic need to acquire status, patronage or respect among English elite circles must have become increasingly clear. By 1705 incorporation was more and more likely, and the consequence of its passing was almost certain to be a social amalgamation of sorts among the elite. Yet written Scots did not disappear in their writings, even if it reduced after this point.

Accordingly, these results have hinted at the power of politically inspired identities and political change in encouraging the continuation, or even increase, in variants from a minority variety, despite all pressures operating to the contrary. Such processes form a continual feedback loop, in which these events or loyalties influence the use of certain language variants, which in turn accumulate into indexical associations that mark or characterise related identities in measurable ways. Political and ideological concerns can facilitate the construction, negotiation and renegotiation of identities in a multilingual setting, based on practices of language use. These practices become a central plank of such identities, rather than the by-product of a complex socio-political situation. Looking forward to Scots as it is both spoken and written today, such relationships seem as salient as ever (c.f. Shoemark et al., 2017; Shoemark, Kirby and Goldwater, 2017), suggesting a fine-spun line of continuity, stretching from the eighteenth century and possibly earlier, through to the present day. The desire to claim membership and belonging is universal in its scope after all, and diachronic variation and its users are no less unique than their contemporary cousins in this respect. Perhaps it was not the end of an auld song after all, but simply the beginning of the next verse, sung to a *neu* tune.

Bibliography

Abdi, H., and Williams, L. J. (2010). 'Principal Component Analysis', *Wiley Interdisciplinary Reviews: Computational Statistics, 2* (4), 433–59.

Agha, A. (2003). 'The Social Life of Cultural Value', *Language and Communication, 23*, 231–73.

Agha, A. (2005). 'Voice, Footing, Enregisterment', *Journal of Linguistic Anthropology, 15* (1), 38–59.

Agutter, A. (1988). 'The Not-So-Scottish Vowel Length Rule'. In J. M. Anderson and N. Macleod (eds), *Edinburgh Studies in the English language,* pp. 120–32. Edinburgh: John Donald.

Aitken, A. J. (1971). 'Variation and Variety in Written Middle Scots'. In H. Pálsson, A. J. Aitken and A. McIntosh (eds), *Edinburgh Studies in English and Scots,* pp. 177–209. London: Longman.

Aitken, A. J. (1977). 'How to Pronounce Older Scots'. In A. J. Aitken, M. P. McDiarmid and D. S. Thomson (eds), *Bards and Makars. Scottish Language and Literature, Medieval and Renaissance,* pp. 1–21. Glasgow: University of Glasgow Press.

Aitken, A. J. (1979). 'Scottish Speech: A Historical View with Special Reference to the Standard English of Scotland'. In A. J. Aitken and T. McArthur (eds), *Languages of Scotland,* pp. 85–118, vol. 4. Edinburgh: W. & R. Chambers.

Aitken, A. J. (1984). 'Scottish Accents and Dialects'. In P. Trudgill (ed.), *Language in the British Isles,* pp. 94–118. Cambridge: Cambridge University Press.

Aitken, A. J. (1985). 'A History of Scots'. In M. Robinson (ed.), *The Concise Scots Dictionary,* pp. ix–xvi. Aberdeen: Aberdeen University Press.

Aitken, A. J. (1997). 'The Pioneers of Anglicised Speech in Scotland: A Second Look', *Scottish Language, 16*, 1–36.

Alcorn, R., Molineaux, B., Kopaczyk, J., Los, B., and Maguire, W. (2017). 'The Emergence of Scots: Clues from Germanic *a reflexes'. In J. Cruickshank and R.M. Millar (eds), *Before the Storm: Papers from the Forum for Research on the Languages of Scotland and Ulster triennial meeting, Ayr 2015*, pp. 1–32, vol. 5. Ulster: Publications of the Forum for Research on the Languages of Scotland and Ulster.

Allen, B. (2015). 'A Non-Standard Standard? Exploring the Evidence from Nineteenth-Century Vernacular Letters and Diaries'. In A. Auer, D. Schreier and R. J. Watts (eds), *Letter Writing and Language Change,* pp. 202–22. Cambridge: Cambridge University Press.

Anderson, J. M. (1987). 'System Geometry and Segment Structure: A Question of Scots Economy', *North East Linguistics Society, 18* (1), 22–37.

Auer, A. (2008). 'The Letter Which That I Wrote – Self-Corrections in LModE Letters'. In M. Dossena and I. Tieken-Boon van Ostade (eds), *Studies in Late Modern English Correspondence: Methodology and Data*, pp. 213–34. Bern: Peter Lang.

Auer, A. (2015). 'Stylistic Variation'. In A. Auer, D. Schreier and R. J. Watts (eds), *Letter Writing and Language Change,* pp. 133–55. Cambridge: Cambridge University Press.

Auer, A., Peersman, C., Pickl, S., Rutten, G., and Vosters, R. (2015). 'Historical Sociolinguistics: The Field and its Future', *Journal of Historical Sociolinguistics, 1* (1), 1–12.

Auer, A., Schreier, D., and Watts, R. J. (2015). 'Epilogue: Where Next?'. In A. Auer, D. Schreier and R. J. Watts (eds), *Letter Writing and Language Change,* pp. 277–87. Cambridge: Cambridge University Press.

Auer, P. (2007). *Style and Social Identities: Alternative Approaches to Linguistic Heterogeneity*. Berlin: Walter de Gruyter.

Auer, P., and Hinskens, F. (2005). 'The Role of Interpersonal Accommodation in a Theory of Language Change'. In P. Auer, F. Hinskens and P. Kerswill (eds), *Dialect Change: Convergence and Divergence in European Languages,* pp. 335–57. Cambridge: Cambridge University Press.

Baayen, R. H. (2008). *Analysing Linguistic Data: A Practical Introduction to Statistics Using R*. Cambridge: Cambridge University Press.

Baayen, R. H. (2010). 'A Real Experiment is a Factorial Experiment?', *The Mental Lexicon, 5* (1), 149–57.

Baayen, R. H., Davidson, D. J., and Bates, D. M. (2008). 'Mixed-effects Modelling with Crossed Random Effects for Subjects and Items', *Journal of Memory and Language, 59* (4), 390–412.

Babel, M. (2010). 'Dialect Divergence and Convergence in New Zealand English', *Language in Society, 39* (4), 437–56.

Bailey, G., and Tillery, J. (2004). 'Some Sources of Divergent Data in Sociolinguistics'. In C. Fought (ed.), *Sociolinguistic Variation: Critical Reflections,* pp. 11–30. Oxford: Oxford University Press.

Banerjee, S., Carlin, B. P., and Gelfand, A. E. (2015). *Hierarchical Modelling and Analysis for Spatial Data,* 2nd edn. Boca Raton, FL: CRC Press.

Bann, J., and Corbett, J. (2015). *Spelling Scots: The Orthography of Literary Scots, 1700–2000*. Edinburgh: Edinburgh University Press.

Bates, D. (2005). 'Fitting Linear Mixed Models in R: Using the lme4 Package', *R News, 5* (1), 27–30.

Bates, D., Maechler, M., Bolker, B., and Walker, S. (2014). *lme4: Linear Mixed-Effects Models Using Eigen and S4* (version 1.1-35.3) [R Package], <http://CRAN.R-project.org/package=lme4.182>.

Beal, J. C. (1997). 'Syntax and Morphology'. In C. Jones (ed.), *The Edinburgh History of the Scots Language,* pp. 335–77. Edinburgh: Edinburgh University Press.

Beal, J. C. (2004). 'Marks of Disgrace: Attitudes to Non-Standard Pronunciation in 18th Century English Pronouncing Dictionaries'. In M. Dossena and R. Lass (eds), *Methods and Data in English Historical Dialectology,* pp. 329–50. Bern: Peter Lang.

Beal, J. C., and Sturiale, M. (2012). 'Prescriptivism and Pronouncing Dictionaries: Past and Present', *Language & History*, *55* (1), 1–4.

Beaugrande, R de. (2006). 'Speech Versus Writing in the Discourse of Linguistics', *Miscelánea: A Journal of English and American Studies*, *33*, 31–45.

Beebe, L., and Giles, H. (1984). 'Speech-Accommodation Theories: A Discussion in Terms of Second-Language Acquisition', *International Journal of the Sociology of Language*, 46, 5–32.

Bell, A. (1984). 'Language Style as Audience Design', *Language in Society*, *13*, 145–204.

Bendixen, M. (2003). 'A Practical Guide to the Use of Correspondence Analysis in Marketing Research', *Marketing Bulletin*, *13* (2), 1–15.

Bergs, A. (2012). 'The Uniformitarian Principle and the Risk of Anachronisms in Language and Social History'. In J. M. Hernández-Campoy and J. C. Conde-Silvestre (eds), *The Handbook of Historical Sociolinguistics*, pp. 80–98. Chichester: John Wiley & Sons.

Biber, D. (1995). *Dimensions of Register Variation: A Cross-Linguistic Comparison*. Cambridge: Cambridge University Press.

Biber, D., and Finegan, E. (1989). 'Styles of Stance in English: Lexical and Grammatical Marking of Evidentiality and Affect', *Text*, *9*, 93–124.

Blackledge, A., and Pavlenko, A. (2001). 'Negotiation of identities in multilingual contexts', *The International Journal of Bilingualism*, *5* (3), 243–57.

Blair-Imrie, H. (2011). 'Maule, Harry, Styled Fifth Earl of Panmure (1659–1734), Jacobite Army Officer and Scholar', *Oxford Dictionary of National Biography*, <https://www.oxforddnb.com/view/10.1093/ref:odnb/9780198614128.001.0001/odnb-9780198614128-e-18366>, accessed 15 Nov. 2021.

Blas Arroyo, J. L. (2019). 'Español a la catalana: Variación vernácula e identidad en la Cataluña soberanista', *Oralia: Análisis del Discurso Oral*, *22* (1), 7–40.

Bourdieu, P. (1977). *Outline of a Theory of Practice.* Cambridge: Cambridge University Press.

Bowie, K. (2007). *Scottish Public Opinion and the Anglo-Scottish Union, 1699-1707*. Woodbridge: Boydell Press.

Bowie, K. (2008). 'Popular Resistance, Religion and the Union of 1707'. In T. M. Devine (ed.), *Scotland and the Union 1707–2007,* pp. 39–53. Edinburgh: Edinburgh University Press.

Bowie, K. (2015). 'A 1706 Manifesto for an Armed Rising Against Incorporating Union,' *The Scottish Historical Review*, *94* (2), 237–67.

Brown, S. J., and Whatley, C. A. (2008). 'Publicity, Parties and Patronage: Parliamentary Management and the Ratification of the Anglo-Scottish Union'. In S. J. Brown and C. Whatley (eds), *The Union of 1707: New Dimensions,* pp. 78–95. Edinburgh: Edinburgh University Press.

Brulard, I., and Carr, P. (2013). 'Variability, Unconscious Accent Adaptation and Sense of Identity: The Case of RP Influences on Speakers of Standard Scottish English,' *Language Sciences*, *39*, 151–55.

Bucholtz, M. (2010). *White Kids: Language, Race, and Styles of Youth Identity*. Cambridge: Cambridge University Press.

Bucholtz, M., and Hall, K. (2005). 'Identity and Interaction: A Sociocultural Linguistic Approach', *Discourse Studies*, *7* (4–5), 585–614.

Bugaj, J. (2004). 'Middle Scots as an Emerging Standard and Why It Did Not Make It', *Scottish Language*, *23*, 19–34.

Bukhari, S. S., Kadi, A., Jouneh, M. A., Mir, F. M., and Dengel, A. (2017). 'anyOCR: An Open-Source OCR System for Historical Archives', *14th IAPR International Conference on Document Analysis and Recognition (ICDAR)*, *1*, 305–10.

Bürkner, P. C. (2017). 'Brms: An R Package for Bayesian Multilevel Models Using Stan', *Journal of Statistical Software*, *80* (1), 1–28.

Campbell-Kibler, K., Eckert, P., Mendoza-Denton, N., and Moore, E. (2006). 'The Elements of Style', Poster presented at *New Ways of Analyzing Variation (NWAV), Columbus, Ohio.*

Carr, P., and Brulard, I. (2006). 'Anglo-English Influences on Scottish Standard English Speakers: Trap/Bath/Palm/Start and Lot/Cloth/Thought/North/Force', *Scottish Language*, *25*, 31–46.

Chambers, J. K. (1995). *Sociolinguistic Theory: Linguistic Variation and its Social Significance*. Oxford: Blackwell.

Conde-Silvestre, J. C. (2007). *Sociolingüística Histórica*. Madrid: Gredos.

Conde-Silvestre, J. C. (2012). The Role of Social Networks and Mobility in Diachronic Sociolinguistics. In J. M. Hernández-Campoy and J. C. Conde-Silvestre (eds), *The Handbook of Historical Sociolinguistics,* pp. 332–52. Chichester: John Wiley & Sons.

Conde-Silvestre, J. C. (2016). 'A 'Third-Wave' Historical Sociolinguistic Approach to Late Middle English Correspondence: Evidence from the Stonor Letters'. In C. Russi (ed.), *Current Trends in Historical Sociolinguistics,* pp. 46–66. Warsaw & Berlin: De Gruyter Open.

Conde-Silvestre, J. C., and Hernández-Campoy, J. M. (1998). *An Introduction to the History of English II: Middle and Early Modern English*. Murcia: ICE & Diego Marín.

Conde-Silvestre, J. C., and Hernández-Campoy, J. M. (2004). 'A Sociolinguistic Approach to the Diffusion of Chancery Written Practices in Late

Fifteenth-Century Private Correspondence', *Neuphilologische Mitteilungen, 105* (2), 133–52.

Conde-Silvestre, J. C., and Hernández-Campoy, J. M. (2013). 'Tracing the Generational Progress of Language Change in Fifteenth-Century English: The Digraph in the "Paston Letters"', *Neuphilologische Mitteilungen, 114* (3), 279–99.

Corbett, J. (2013). 'The Spelling Practices of Allan Ramsay and Robert Burns', *Scottish Cultural Review of Language and Literature, 19* (7), 65–90.

Corbett, J., McClure, J. D., and Stuart-Smith, J. (eds), (2003a). *The Edinburgh Companion to Scots.* Edinburgh: Edinburgh University Press.

Coretta, S. (2020). 'Vowel Duration and Consonant Voicing: A Production Study', PhD thesis, University of Manchester, Manchester.

Coretta, S., Casillas, J. V., and Roettger, T. (2021). 'Why Bayesian?', *learnb4ss blog* (2021), <https://learnb4ss.github.io/learnB4SS/articles/why-bayes.html>, accessed 7 March 2023.

Coupland, N. (2001). 'Language, Situation and the Relational Self: Theorizing Dialect-Style in Sociolinguistics'. In P. Eckert and J. R. Rickford (eds), *Stylistic Variation in Language,* pp. 185–210. Cambridge: Cambridge University Press.

Coupland, N. (2007). *Style: Language Variation and Identity.* Cambridge: Cambridge University Press.

Coupland, N., and Giles, H. (1988). 'Introduction: The Communicative Contexts of Accommodation', *Language & Communication, 8* (3–4), 175–82.

Craigie, J. (1940). 'Fowler's Language'. In H. W. Meikle, J. Craigie and J. Purves (eds), *The Works of William Fowler*, pp. li–lxxix, vol. 3. Edinburgh: Scottish Text Society.

Cruickshank, J. (2011). 'The Emergence of Scottish Standard English: The Evidence of the Correspondence of 2nd Earl Fife 1764–1789', PhD thesis, University of Aberdeen, Aberdeen.

Cruickshank, J. (2012). 'The Emergence of Scottish Standard English and the Role of the Second Earl of Fife' *Scottish Language, 31,* 111–27.

Cruickshank, J. (2013). 'The Role of Communities of Practice in the Emergence of Scottish Standard English'. In J. Kopaczyk and A. H. Jucker (eds), *Communities of Practice in the History of English* (pp. 19–45). Amsterdam & Philadelphia: John Benjamins.

Cruickshank, J. (2017). 'The Language of Lord Fife in Letters to George Grenville 1763 to 1769'. In J. Cruickshank and R.M. Millar (eds), *Before the Storm: Papers from the Forum for Research on the Languages of Scotland and Ulster Triennial Meeting, Ayr 2015*, vol. 5, pp. 212–31. Edinburgh: Forum for Research on the Languages of Scotland and Ulster.

Curtis, F. J. (1894). *An Investigation of the Rimes and Phonology of the Middle-Scotch*. Halle: Romance Clariodus.

De Cuypere, L. (2015). 'The Old English To-dative Construction', *English Language and Linguistics*, *19* (1), 1–26.

Dekker, R. (ed.) (2002). *Egodocuments and History: Autobiographical Writing in its Context Since the Middle Ages*. Hilversum: Verloren.

Devitt, A. J. (1989). *Standardizing Written English: Diffusion in the Case of Scotland, 1520–1659*. Cambridge: Cambridge University Press.

Devlin, A. M. (2017). 'Lard-eaters, Gay-ropeans, Sheeple and Prepositions: Lexical and Syntactic Devices Employed to Position the Other in Russian Online Political Forums', *Russian Journal of Communication*, *9* (1), 53–70.

Dittmar, N., Schlobinski, P., and Wachs, I. (1986). *Berlinisch. Studien zum Lexikon, zur Spracheinstellung und zum Stilrepertoire*. Berlin: Berlin Verlag.

Dobreva, S. (2023). 'Bayesian inference vs frequentist approach: Same data, opposite results', *365 Data Science* (2023), <https://365datascience.com/trending/bayesian-vs-frequentist-approach/>, accessed 8 Mar. 2023.

Dobson, E. J. (1968). *English Pronunciation, 1500–1700. Volume II, Phonology*. Oxford: Clarendon Press.

Donaldson, W. (1989). *The Language of the People: Scots Prose from the Victorian Revival*. Oxford: Pergamon Press.

D'Onofrio, A. (2015). 'Persona-based Information Shapes Linguistic Perception: Valley Girls and California Vowels', *Journal of Sociolinguistics*, *19* (2), 241–56.

Dossena, M. (1997). 'Attitudes to Scots in Burns's Correspondence', *Linguistica e Filologia*, *4*, 91–103.

Dossena, M. (2002). 'A Strong Scots Accent of the Mind: The Pragmatic Value of Code-Switching Between English and Scots in Private Correspondence: A Historical Overview', *Linguistica e Filologia*, *14*, 103–27.

Dossena, M. (2005). *Scotticisms in Grammar and Vocabulary: 'Like Runes upon a Standin' Stane'?* Edinburgh: John Donald.

Dossena, M. (2011). 'Scottishness and the Book Trade: Print and Scotticisms'. In S. W. Brown and W. McDougall (eds), *The Edinburgh History of the Book in Scotland. Volume 2, Enlightenment and Expansion 1707–1800*, pp. 545–50, vol. 2. Edinburgh: Edinburgh University Press.

Dossena, M. (2012a). 'A Highly Poetical Language? Scots, Burns, Patriotism and Evaluative Language in 19th-Century Literary Reviews and Articles'. In C. Percy and M. C. Davidson (eds), *The Languages of Nation: Attitudes and Norms*, pp. 99–119, vol. 148. Bristol: Multilingual Matters/Channel View Publications.

Dossena, M. (2012b). 'The Study of Correspondence: Theoretical and Methodological Issues'. In M. Dossena and G. Del Lungo Camiciotti (eds), *Letter Writing in Late Modern Europe*, pp. 13–30. Amsterdam & Philadelphia: John Benjamins.

Dossena, M. (2013). 'Mixing Genres and Reinforcing Community Ties in Nineteenth-Century Scottish Correspondence', *Communities of Practice in the History of English, 235*, 47–60.

Dossena, M. (2019). 'Singular, Plural, or Collective?: Grammatical Flexibility and the Definition of Identity in the Correspondence of Nineteenth-Century Scottish Emigrants'. In R. Hickey (ed.), *Keeping in Touch: Emigrant Letters Across the English-Speaking World*, pp. 67–84, vol. 10. Amsterdam & Philadelphia: John Benjamins.

Drager, K., Hay, J., and Walker, A. (2010). 'Pronounced Rivalries: Attitudes and Speech Production', *Te Reo, 53*, 27–53.

Dictionary of the Scots Language/Dictionar o the Scots Leid [DSL], <http://www.dsl.ac.uk/>, accessed 7 April 2020.

Du Bois, J. W. (2007). 'The Stance Triangle', *Stancetaking in Discourse: Subjectivity, Evaluation, Interaction, 164* (3), 139–82.

Eckert, P. (2000). *Linguistic Variation as Social Practice*. Oxford: Blackwell.

Eckert, P. (2008). 'Variation and the Indexical Field', *Journal of Sociolinguistics, 12* (4), 453–476.

Eckert, P. (2012). 'Three Waves of Variation Study: The Emergence of Meaning in the Study of Variation', *Annual Review of Anthropology, 41*, 87–100.

Eckert, P. (2016). 'Variation, Meaning and Social Change'. In N. Coupland (ed.), *Sociolinguistics: Theoretical Debates*, pp. 68–85. Cambridge: Cambridge University Press.

Eckert, P., and McConnell-Ginet, S. (1992). 'Think Practically and Look Locally: Language and Gender as Community-Based Practice', *Annual Review of Anthropology, 21*, 461–490.

Eckert, P., and Rickford, J. R. (eds) (2001). *Style and Sociolinguistic Variation*. Cambridge: Cambridge University Press.

Ehrenstein, C. V. (2015). 'Erskine, John, Styled Twenty-Second or Sixth Earl of Mar and Jacobite Duke of Mar (bap. 1675, d. 1732), Jacobite Army Officer, Politician, and Architect', *Oxford Dictionary of National Biography*, <https://www.oxforddnb.com/view/10.1093/ref:odnb/9780198614128.001.0001/odnb-9780198614128-e-8868>, accessed 15 Nov. 2021.

Elder, C. M. (2022). 'Anglicisation in the Letters of Marie Stewart, Countess of Mar and her Family: A Sociolinguistic Perspective', MPhil(R) thesis, University of Glasgow, Glasgow.

Elspaß, S. (2005). 'Language Norm and Language Reality. Effectiveness and Limits of Prescriptivism in New High German'. In N. Langer and W. Davies (eds), *Linguistic Purism in the Germanic Languages*, pp. 20–45. Berlin & New York: Walter de Gruyter.

Elspaß, S. (2007). 'A Twofold View 'From Below': New Perspectives on Language Histories and Language Historiographies'. In S. Elspaß, N. Langer, J. Scharloth, and W. Vandenbussche (eds), *Germanic Language Histories 'from Below' (1700–2000)*, pp. 3–10. Berlin & New York: De Gruyter.

Elspaß, S. (2012a). 'Between Linguistic Creativity and Formulaic Restriction. Cross-Linguistic Perspectives on Nineteenth-Century Lower Class Writers' Private Letters'. In M. Dossena and G. Del Lungo Camicioti (eds), *Letter Writing in Late Modern Europe*, pp. 45–64. Amsterdam & Philadelphia: John Benjamins.

Elspaß, S. (2012b). 'The Use of Private Letters and Diaries in Sociolinguistic Investigation'. In J. M. Hernández-Campoy and J. C. Conde-Silvestre (eds), *The Handbook of Historical Sociolinguistics*, pp. 156–69. Chichester: John Wiley & Sons.

Erskine, J. (1896). 'The Earl of Mar's Legacies to Scotland, and to his Son, Lord Erskine, 1722–1727'. In S. Erskine (ed.), *Wariston's Diary and Other Papers*, pp. 139–248, vol. 26. Edinburgh: T & A. Constable.

Etz, A., Gronau, Q. F., Dablander, F., Edelsbrunner, P. A., and Baribault, B. (2018). 'How to Become a Bayesian in Eight Easy Steps: An Annotated Reading List', *Psychonomic Bulletin & Review*, *25* (1), 219–34.

Eyndhoven, S. van. (2018). '"An Eye for an Aye?": Linguistic and Political Backlash and Conformity in Eighteenth-Century Scots', Masters thesis, University of Canterbury, Christchurch.

Eyndhoven, S. van. (2021). '"An Eye for an Aye?": Linguistic and Political Backlash and Conformity in Eighteenth-Century Scots', *Journal of Historical Sociolinguistics*, *7* (2), 243–82.

Eyndhoven, S. van. (2023a). '"Ane end of an auld song?" Macro and Micro Perspectives on Written Scots in Correspondence during the Union of Parliaments Debates', PhD thesis, University of Edinburgh, Edinburgh.

Eyndhoven, S. van. (2023b). 'Eighteenth Century Scots in Correspondence During the Union Debates: An Intra-Writer Perspective'. In M. Schiegg and J. Huber (eds), *Intra-Writer Variation in Historical Sociolinguistics*, pp. 271–94, vol. 5. Oxford & New York: Peter Lang.

Eyndhoven, S. van (2024). '"Quhen I am begun to write I really knou not what to say": Inter- and Intra-Writer Variation in the Use of <quh-> in Early Modern Scots'. In L. Caon, M. Gordon and T. Porck (eds), *Unlocking the History of English. Pragmatics, Prescriptivism and Text Types. Selected Papers From the 21st ICEHL*, pp. 225–49. Amsterdam: John Benjamins.

Eyndhoven, S. van, and Clark, L. (2019). 'The <quh-> – <wh-> switch: An Empirical Account of the Anglicisation of a Scots Variant in Scotland during the Sixteenth and Seventeenth Centuries', *English Language and Linguistics*, *24* (1), 211–36.

Eyndhoven, S. van, Gotthard, L. and Filgueira, R. (forthcoming) '"Scots for the masses"? Exploring the Use of Scots in Late Modern Print'. In M. Laitinen and P. Rautionaho (eds), *Data-intensive Investigations of English*. Cambridge: Cambridge University Press.

Fairclough, N. (1989). *Language and Power.* London & New York: Longman.

Fairclough, N. (2000). *New Labour, New Language?* London & New York: Routledge.

Fairman, T. (2008). 'Strike-throughs: What Textual Alterations Can Tell Us About Writers and their Scripts, 1795-1835'. In M. Dossena and I. Tieken-Boon van Ostade (eds), *Studies in Late Modern English Correspondence: Methodology and Data,* pp. 193–212. Bern & New York: Peter Lang.

Fairman, T. (2015). 'Language in Print and Handwriting'. In A. Auer, D. Schreier and R. J. Watts (eds), *Letter Writing and Language Change,* pp. 53–71. Cambridge: Cambridge University Press.

Ferguson, W. (1964). 'The Making of the Treaty of Union of 1707', *The Scottish Historical Review, 43* (136), 89–110.

Ferguson, W. (1977). *Scotland's Relations with England: A Survey to 1707.* Edinburgh: Saltire Society.

Fetzer, A., and Bull, P. (2012). 'Doing Leadership in Political Speech: Semantic Processes and Pragmatic Inferences,' *Discourse & Society, 23* (2), 127–144.

Finlay, R. J. (1999). 'Keeping the Covenant: Scottish National Identity'. In T. M. Devine and J. R. Young (eds), *Eighteenth Century Scotland: New Perspectives,* pp. 121–33. East Linton: Tuckwell Press.

Fisher, J. H. (1977). 'Chancery English and the Emergence of Standard Written English', *Speculum, 50*, 870–78.

Fitzmaurice, S. M. (1998). 'The Commerce of Language in the Pursuit of Politeness in Eighteenth-Century England', *English Studies, 79* (4), 309–28.

Fitzmaurice, S. M. (2000). 'The Spectator, the Politics of Social Networks, and Language Standardisation in Eighteenth-Century England'. In L. Wright (ed.), *The Development of Standard English, 1300–1800: Theories, Descriptions, Conflicts,* pp. 195–218. Cambridge: Cambridge University Press.

Fitzmaurice, S. M. (2002). *Familiar Letter in Early Modern English: A Pragmatic Approach.* Amsterdam & Philadelphia: John Benjamins.

Fitzmaurice, S. M. (2004). 'Orality, Standardization, and the Effects of Print Publication on the Look of Standard English in the 18th Century'. In M. Dossena and R. G. Lass (eds), *Methods and Data in English Historical Dialectology,* pp. 351–84. Bern: Peter Lang.

Fitzmaurice, S. M. (2006). 'Diplomatic Business: Information, Power, and Persuasion in Late Modern English Diplomatic Correspondence'. In M. Dossena and S. M. Fitzmaurice (eds), *Business and Official Correspondence: Historical Investigations,* pp. 77–106. Bern: Peter Lang.

Fitzmaurice, S. M. (2007). 'Questions of Standardization and Representativeness in the Development of Social Networks-Based Corpora: The Story of the

Network of Eighteenth-Century English Texts'. In J. C. Beal, K. P. Corrigan and H. L. Moisl (eds), *Creating and Digitizing Language Corpora: Diachronic Databases,* pp. 49–81, vol. 2. Basingstoke & New York: Palgrave Macmillan.

Fitzmaurice, S. M. (2015). 'English Aristocratic Letters' in A. Auer, D. Schreier and R. J. Watts (eds), *Letter Writing and Language Change,* pp. 156–84. Cambridge: Cambridge University Press.

Fonteyn, L., and van de Pol, N. (2016). 'Divide and Conquer: The Formation and Functional Dynamics of the Modern English ing-clause Network', *English Language and Linguistics, 20* (2), 185–219.

Fox, A. (2020). *The Press and the People: Cheap Print and Society in Scotland, 1500–1785*. Oxford: Oxford University Press.

Fromont, R., and Hay, J. (2008). LaBB-CAT (formerly ONZE Miner) [software], 2008, <https://labbcat.canterbury.ac.nz/system/>, accessed 8 April 2020.

Gal, S. (1979). 'Peasant Men Can't Get Wives: Language Change and Sex Roles in a Bilingual Community', *Language in Society, 7*, 1–17.

Giampapa, F. (2001). 'Hyphenated Identities: Italian-Canadian Youth and the Negotiation of Ethnic Identities in Toronto', *International Journal of Bilingualism, 5* (3), 279–315

Giles, H. (1973). 'Communicative Effectiveness as a Function of Accented Speech', *Speech Monographs, 40*, 330–31.

Giles, H. (1984). 'The Dynamics of Speech Accommodation', *International Journal of the Sociology of Language, 46*, 1–155.

Giles, H., Coupland, N., and Coupland, J. (1991). 'Accommodation Theory: Communication, Context, and Consequence'. In H. Giles, J. Coupland and N. Coupland (eds), *The Contexts of Accommodation: Developments in Applied Sociolinguistics,* pp. 1–68. Cambridge: Cambridge University Press.

Giles, H., Mulac, A., Bradac, J. J., and Johnston, P. (1987). 'Speech Accommodation Theory: The First Decade and Beyond', *Annals of the International Communication Association, 10*, 13–48.

Giles, H., and Powesland, P. (1975). *Speech Styles and Social Evaluation*. London: Academic Press.

Glassey, L. K. J. (1987). 'William II and the Settlement of Religion in Scotland, 1688–1690', *Records of the Scottish Church History Society, 23*, 317–29.

Glauser, B. (1974). *The Scottish-English Linguistic Border: Lexical Aspects*. Bern: Francke Verlag.

Görlach, M. (1996). 'And Is It English?', *English World-Wide, 17* (2), 153–74.

Görlach, M. (1999). *English in Nineteenth-Century England: An Introduction*. Cambridge: Cambridge University Press.

Görlach, M. (2001). *A Dictionary of European Anglicisms: A Usage Dictionary of Anglicisms in Sixteen Selected European Languages*. Oxford: Oxford University Press.

Graham, E. J. (2005). *Seawolves: Pirates & the Scots*. Edinburgh: Birlinn.

Grant, W. (1931). *The Scottish National Dictionary: Designed Partly on Regional lines and Partly on Historical Principles, and Containing all the Scottish Words Known to be in Use or to have been in Use Since c. 1700*. Edinburgh: The Scottish National Dictionary Association.

Greenblatt, S. (1980). *Renaissance Self-Fashioning from More to Shakespeare*. Chicago: Chicago University Press.

Gregg, E. (1982). 'The Jacobite Career of John, Earl of Mar'. In E. Cruickshanks (ed.), *Ideology and Conspiracy: Aspects of Jacobitism, 1689–1759*, pp. 179–200. Edinburgh: John Donald.

Gries, S. T., and Hilpert, M. (2008). 'The Identification of Stages in Diachronic Data: Variability-based Neighbor Clustering', *Corpora, 3* (1), 59–81.

Gries, S. T., and Hilpert, M. (2010). 'Modeling Diachronic Change in the Third Person Singular', *English Language and Linguistics, 14* (3), 293–320.

Gries, S. T., and Hilpert, M. (2012). 'Variability-Based Neighbor Clustering: A Bottom-Up Approach to Periodization in Historical Linguistics'. In T. Nevalainen and E. C. Traugott (eds), *The Oxford Handbook on the History of English*, pp. 134–44. Oxford: Oxford University Press.

Gumperz, J. J. (1982). *Discourse Strategies*. Cambridge: Cambridge University Press.

Hall-Lew, L., Coppock, E., and Starr, R. L. (2010). 'Indexing Political Persuasion: Variation in the Iraq Vowels', *American Speech, 85* (1), 91–102.

Hall-Lew, L., Friskney, R., and Scobbie, J. M. (2017). 'Accommodation or Political Identity: Scottish Members of the UK Parliament', *Language Variation and Change, 29* (3), 341–63.

Hall-Lew, L., Starr, R. L., and Coppock, E. (2012). 'Style-Shifting in the U.S. Congress: The Vowels of "Iraq(i)"'. In J. M. Hernández-Campoy and J. A. Cutillas-Espinosa (eds), *Style-Shifting in Public: New Perspectives on Stylistic Variation*, pp. 45–63. Amsterdam: John Benjamins.

Handley, S. (2006). 'Maule, James, Fourth Earl of Panmure (1658/9–1723), Jacobite Sympathizer', *Oxford Dictionary of National Biography*, <https://www.oxforddnb.com/display/10.1093/ref:odnb/9780198614128.001.0001/odnb-9780198614128-e-18367>, accessed 3 July 2022.

Hay, J., and Drager, K. (2010). 'Stuffed Toys and Speech Perception', *Linguistics, 48* (4), 865–92.

Hay, J., Nolan, A., and Drager, K. (2006). 'From Fush to Feesh: Exemplar Priming in Speech Perception', *The Linguistic Review, 23*, 351–79.

Heal, F., and Holmes, C. (1994). *The Gentry in England and Wales, 1500–1700*. Basingstoke: Palgrave Macmillan.

Hernández-Campoy, J.M. (2016). Authorship and Gender in English Historical Sociolinguistic Research: Samples from the Paston Letters. In C. Russi (ed.), *Current Trends in Historical Sociolinguistics*, pp. 108–42. De Gruyter Open.

Hernández-Campoy, J. M., and Conde-Silvestre, J. C. (1999). 'The Social Diffusion of Linguistic Innovations in Fifteenth Century England: Chancery Spellings in Private Correspondence', *Cuadernos de Filología Inglesa*, *8*, 251–74.

Hernández-Campoy, J. M., and Conde-Silvestre, J. C. (2005). 'Sociolinguistic and Geolinguistic Approaches to the Historical Diffusion of Linguistic Innovations: Incipient Standardisation in Late Middle English', *International Journal of English Studies*, *5* (1), 101–34.

Hernández-Campoy, J. M and Conde-Silvestre, J. C. (eds), (2012). *The Handbook of Historical Sociolinguistics*. Chichester: John Wiley & Sons.

Hernández-Campoy, J. M., and Conde-Silvestre, J. C. (2015). 'Assessing Variability and Change in Early English Letters'. In A. Auer and R. J. Watts (eds), *Letter Writing and Language Change*, pp. 14–34. Cambridge: Cambridge University Press.

Hernández-Campoy, J. M., and Cutillas-Espinosa, J. A. (eds), (2012). *Style-Shifting in Public: New Perspectives on Stylistic Variation*. Amsterdam & Philadelphia: John Benjamins.

Hernández-Campoy, J. M., and García-Vidal, T. (2018). 'Persona Management and Identity Projection in English Medieval Society: Evidence from John Paston II', *Journal of Historical Sociolinguistics*, *4* (1), 1–31.

Hernández-Campoy, J. M., and Schilling, N. (2012). 'The Application of the Quantitative Paradigm to Historical Sociolinguistics: Problems with the Generalizability Principle'. In J. M. Hernández-Campoy and J. C. Conde-Silvestre (eds), *The Handbook of Historical Sociolinguistics*, pp. 63–79. Chichester: John Wiley & Sons.

Heuser, W. (1897). Die Lautveränderung von ā, ē, ī im Mittelschottischen. *Anglia*, *19*, 405–8.

Hill, J. (1999). 'Styling Locally, Styling Globally: What Does It Mean?', *Journal of Sociolinguistics*, *3*, 542–56.

Hilpert, M. (2013). *Constructional Change in English: Developments in Allomorphy, Word Formation, and Syntax*. Cambridge: Cambridge University Press.

Jackson, C. (2008). 'Conceptions of Nationhood in the Anglo-Scottish Union Debates of 1707'. In S. J. Brown and C. A. Whatley (eds), *The Union of 1707*, pp. 61–77. Edinburgh: Edinburgh University Press.

Jackson, C. (2012). 'Union Historiographies'. In T. M. Devine and J. Wormald (eds), *The Oxford Handbook of Modern Scottish History*, pp. 339–54. Oxford: Oxford University Press.

Jaeger, T. F. (2008). 'Categorical Data Analysis: Away from ANOVAs (Transformation or Not) and Towards Logit Mixed Models', *Journal of Memory and Language*, *59* (4), 434–46.

Jaffe, A. (2000). 'Introduction: Non-Standard Orthography and Non-Standard Speech', *Journal of Sociolinguistics*, *4* (4), 497–513.
Jaffe, A., Androutsopoulos, J., Sebba, M., and Johnson, S. (2012). *Orthography as Social Action: Scripts, Spelling, Identity and Power*. Berlin: De Gruyter.
Johnson, D. E. (2009). 'Getting off the GoldVarb Standard: Introducing Rbrul for Mixed-Effects Variable Rule Analysis', *Language and Linguistics Compass*, *3* (1), 359–83.
Johnston, P. (1984). 'Variation in the Standard Scottish English of Morningside', *English World-Wide*, *4* (1), 133–85.
Johnston, P. (1997a). 'Older Scots Phonology and its Regional Variation'. In C. Jones (ed.), *The Edinburgh History of the Scots Language*, pp. 47–111. Edinburgh: Edinburgh University Press.
Johnston, P. (1997b). 'Regional Variation'. In C. Jones (ed.), *The Edinburgh History of the Scots Language*, pp. 433–513. Edinburgh: Edinburgh University Press.
Johnston, P. (2007). 'Scottish English and Scots'. In D. Britain (ed.), *Language in the British Isles*, pp. 75–104. Cambridge: Cambridge University Press.
Johnstone, B. (1996). *The Linguistic Individual: Self-expression in Language and Linguistics*. Oxford: Oxford University Press.
Johnstone, B. (2000). *Qualitative Methods in Sociolinguistics*, vol. 50. Oxford: Oxford University Press.
Johnstone, B. (2010). 'Locating Language in Identity'. In C. Llamas and D. Watt (eds), *Language and Identities*, pp. 29–36, vol. 31. Edinburgh: Edinburgh University Press.
Jolliffe, I. T. (2002). *Principal Component Analysis*. New York: Springer-Verlag.
Jones, C. (1995). *A Language Suppressed: The Pronunciation of the Scots Language in the 18th Century*. Edinburgh: John Donald.
Jones, C. (1997a) (ed.), *The Edinburgh History of the Scots Language*. Edinburgh: Edinburgh University Press.
Jones, C. (1997b). 'Phonology'. In C. Jones (ed.), *The Edinburgh History of the Scots Language*, pp. 267–334. Edinburgh: Edinburgh University Press.
Jones, C. (2010). 'Nationality and Standardisation in Eighteenth-Century Scotland'. In R. Hickey (ed.), *Eighteenth-Century English: Ideology and Change*, pp. 221–34. Cambridge: Cambridge University Press.
Joseph, J. E. (2006). *Language and Politics*. Edinburgh: Edinburgh University Press.
Joseph, J. E. (2016). 'Historical Perspectives on Language and Identity'. In S. Preece (ed.), *Routledge Handbook of Language and Identity*, pp. 19–33. London & New York: Routledge.
Jucker, A. H., and Kopaczyk, J. (2013). 'Communities of Practice as a Locus of Language Change'. In J. Kopaczyk and A. H. Jucker (eds), *Communities of*

Practice in the History of English, pp. 1–16. Amsterdam & Philadelphia: John Benjamins.

Jungbluth, K., Zinkhahn Rhobodes, D., and Rosenberg, P. (2015). *Linguistic Construction of Ethnic Borders*. Bern: Peter Lang.

Kahle, P., Colutto, S., Hackl, G., and Mühlberger, G. (2017). 'Transkribus – A Service Platform for Transcription, Recognition and Retrieval of Historical Documents', *14th IAPR International Conference on Document Analysis and Recognition (ICDAR), 4*, 19–24.

Kassambara, A. (2017). *Practical Guide to Principal Component Methods in R*, (vol. 2). United States: Sthda.

Kassambara, A., and Mundt, F. (2020). Factoextra: Extract and Visualize the Results of Multivariate Data Analyses. [R Package Version 1.0.7]. <https://CRAN.R-project.org/package=factoextra>, downloaded 8 Aug. 2021.

Kay, B. (1986). *Scots: The Mither Tongue*. Edinburgh: Mainstream Publishing.

Kidd, C. (1999). *British Identities Before Nationalism: Ethnicity and Nationhood in the Atlantic World, 1600–1800*. Cambridge: Cambridge University Press.

Kidd, C. (2008). *Union and Unionisms: Political Thought in Scotland, 1500–2000*. Cambridge: Cambridge University Press.

Kiely, R., McCrone, D., Bechhofer, F., and Stewart, R. (2000). 'Debatable Land: National and Local Identity in a Border Town', *Sociological Research Online, 5* (2), 66–79.

Kiesling, S. (2001). 'Stances of Whiteness and Hegemony in Fraternity Men's Discourse', *Journal of Linguistic Anthropology, 11* (1), 101–15.

Kirby, J., and Sonderegger, M. (2018). 'Mixed Effects Design Analysis for Experimental Phonetics', *Journal of Phonetics, 70*, 70–85.

Kirk, J. M. (2001). 'Scots Language and the Song Tradition'. In J. M. Kirk and D. P. Ó Baoill (eds), *Language Links: The Languages of Scotland and Ireland,* pp. 233–36. Belfast: Cló Ollscoil na Banríona.

Kirkham, S., and Moore, E. (2016). 'Constructing Social Meaning in Political Discourse: Phonetic Variation and Verb Processes in Ed Miliband's Speeches', *Language in Society, 45* (1), 87–111.

Kniezsa, V. (1997). 'The Origins of Scots Orthography'. In C. Jones (ed.), *The Edinburgh History of Scots,* pp. 24–46. Edinburgh: Edinburgh University Press.

Kopaczyk, J. (2011). 'A V or not a V? Transcribing Abbreviations in Seventeen MSS of the "Man of Law's Tale"'. In J. Thaisen and H. Rutkowska (eds), *Scribes, Printers, and the Accidentals of their Texts,* pp. 91–106, vol. 33. Frankfurt: Peter Lang.

Kopaczyk, J. (2012). 'Communication Gaps in Seventeenth-Century Britain: Explaining Legal Scots to English Practitioners'. In B. Kryk-Kastovsky (ed.), *Intercultural Miscommunication Past and Present*, pp. 217–43. New York: Peter Lang.

Kopaczyk, J. (2013a). 'How a Community of Practice Creates a Text Community: Middle Scots Legal and Administrative Discourse'. In J. Kopaczyk and A. H. Jucker (eds), *Communities of Practice in the History of English,* pp. 225–47. Amsterdam & Philadelphia John Benjamins.

Kopaczyk, J. (2013b). *The Legal Language of Scottish Burghs: Standardization and Lexical Bundles (1380–1560)*. Oxford: Oxford University Press.

Kopaczyk, J. (2013c). 'Rethinking the Traditional Periodisation of the Scots Language'. In R. M. Millar and J. Cruickshank (eds), *Selected Papers from the Forum for Research on the Languages of Scotland and Ulster*, pp. 233–60. Aberdeen: Aberdeen University Press.

Kopaczyk, J., and Jucker, A. H. (eds), (2013). *Communities of Practice in the History of English*. Amsterdam & Philadelphia: John Benjamins.

Krivoruchko, J. G. (2008). 'Prepositional Wars: When Ideology Defines Preposition'. In D. Kurzon and S. Adler (eds), *Adpositions: Pragmatic, Semantic and Syntactic Perspectives,* pp. 191–208. Amsterdam & Philadelphia: John Benjamins.

Kruschke, J. (2015). *Doing Bayesian Data Analysis: A Tutorial with R, JAGS, and Stan* (2nd edn). Amsterdam: Academic Press.

Labov, W. (1962). 'The Social History of a Sound Change on the Island of Martha's Vineyard', Masters thesis, Colombia University, Massachusetts.

Labov, W. (1966a). 'Hypercorrection by the Lower Middle Class as a Factor in Linguistic Change'. In W. Bright (ed.), *Sociolinguistics – Proceedings of the UCLA Sociolinguistics Conference, 1964,* pp. 84–113. The Hague & Paris: De Gruyter Mouton.

Labov, W. (1966b). 'The Social Stratification of English in New York City', PhD thesis, Center for Applied Linguistics, Washington DC.

Labov, W. (1990). 'The Intersection of Sex and Social Class in the Course of Linguistic Change', *Language Variation and Change*, *2*, 205–54.

Labov, W. (2006). *The Social Stratification of English in New York City*. Cambridge: Cambridge University Press.

Lang, A. M. (2004). 'John, Ninth Earl of Rothes (1679–1722), Politician', *Oxford Dictionary of National Biography,* <https://www.oxforddnb.com/display/10.1093/ref:odnb/9780198614128.001.0001/odnb-9780198614128-e-16496>, accessed 1 Jan. 2023.

Lass, R. (1987). *The Shape of English, Structure and History*. London: J. M. Dent & Sons.

Lass, R. (1992). 'Phonology and Morphology'. In N. Blake (ed.), *The Cambridge History of the English Language. Volume 2: 1066–1476,* pp. 23–155, vol. 2. Cambridge: Cambridge University Press.

Lass, R. (2000). 'Phonology and Morphology'. In R. Lass (ed.), *The Cambridge History of the English Language: Volume 3: 1476–1776,* pp. 56–186, vol. 3. Cambridge: Cambridge University Press.

Lê, S., Josse, J., and Husson, F. (2008). 'FactoMineR: An R Package for Multivariate Analysis', *Journal of Statistical Software, 25* (1), 1–18.

Le Page, R. B. (1985). *Acts of Identity: Creole-Based Approaches to Language and Ethnicity*. Cambridge: Cambridge University Press.

Leslie, D. (2020). 'Perceptions of North East Scottish Speech', PhD thesis, University of Aberdeen, Aberdeen.

Leslie, D. (2021). 'What's in a Name? The Prevalence of the 'Doric' Label in the North-East of Scotland', *Scottish Language, 40*, 49–83.

Llamas, C. (2007). '"A Place Between Places": Language and Identities in a Border Town', *Language in Society, 36* (04), 579–604.

Llamas, C. (2010). 'Convergence and Divergence Across a National Border'. In C. Llamas and D. Watt (eds), *Language and Identities*, pp. 227–36. Edinburgh: Edinburgh University Press.

Llamas, C., Watt, D., and Johnson, D. E. (2009). 'Linguistic Accommodation and the Salience of National Identity Markers in a Border Town', *Journal of Language and Social Psychology, 28* (4), 381–407.

Macafee, C., & †Aitken, A. J. (2002). 'A History of Scots to 1700'. In *A Dictionary of the Older Scottish Tongue*, pp. xxix–clvii, vol. xii [online].

Macafee, C., & †Aitken, A. J. (2015a). 'The Phonology of Older Scots' [Originally published in J. Corbett, J. Derrick McClure and J. Stuart-Smith (eds), (2003). *The Edinburgh Companion to Scots*, 138–169. Edinburgh: Edinburgh University Press]; rev. edn, in C. Macafee (ed.), *Collected Writings on the Scots Language*, [online]: Scots Language Centre.

Macafee, C., & †Aitken, A. J. (2015b). 'Variation and Variety in Written Middle Scots' [Originally published in A. J. Aitken et al. (eds), (1971). *Edinburgh Studies in English and Scots*, 177–209. London: Longman]; rev. edn in C. Macafee (ed.), *Collected Writings on the Scots Language*, [online]: Scots Language Centre.

Macafee, C., and Ó Baoill, C. (1997). 'Why Scots is Not a Celtic English'. In H. L. C. Tristram (ed.), *The Celtic Englishes*, pp. 245–86, vol. 1. Heidelberg: Universitätsverlag C. Winter.

Macaulay, R. (1985). 'The Narrative Skills of a Scottish Coal Miner'. In M. Görlach (ed.), *Focus On: Scotland*, pp. 101–24. Amsterdam & Philadelphia: John Benjamins.

Macaulay, R. (2004). 'The Radical Conservatism of Scots'. In C. Fought (ed.), *Sociolinguistic Variation: Critical Reflections*, pp. 178–97. Oxford: Oxford University Press.

MacCormick, J. (ed.), (1774). *State-Papers and Letters, Addressed to William Carstares*. Edinburgh: John Balfour.

MacDonald, A. A. (2011). 'The Revival of Scotland's Older Literature'. In S. W. Brown and W. McDougall (eds), *The Edinburgh History of the Book in*

Scotland, Volume 2: Enlightenment and Expansion 1707–1800, pp. 1012–25, vol. 2. Edinburgh: Edinburgh University Press.

Macinnes, A. I. (1990). 'Influencing the Vote: The Scottish Estates and the Treaty of Union, 1706–07', *History Microcomputer Review*, *6* (2), 1–25.

Macinnes, A. I. (1996). *Clanship, Commerce and the House of Stuart, 1603–1788*. East Linton: Tuckwell Press.

Macinnes, A. I. (2007). *Union and Empire: The Making of the United Kingdom in 1707*. Cambridge: Cambridge University Press.

Macky, J. (1733). *Memoirs of the Secret Services of John Macky, Esq. During the Reigns of King William, Queen Anne, and King George I, 2nd edn* [s.n.]

MacQueen, L. E. C. (1957). 'The Last Stages of the Older Literary Language of Scotland: A Study of the Surviving Scottish Elements in Scottish Prose, 1700–1750, Especially of the Records, National and Local', PhD thesis, The University of Edinburgh, Edinburgh.

Maguire, W. (2012). 'English and Scots in Scotland'. In R. Hickey (ed.), *Areal Features of the Anglophone World*, pp. 53–78. Berlin: Mouton de Gruyter.

Maguire, W. (2015). 'The North Above the North: Scotland and Northern English'. In R. Hickey (ed.), *Researching Northern English*, pp. 437–58. Amsterdam & Philadelphia: John Benjamins.

Markus, M. (2006). 'Abbreviations in Early Modern English Correspondence'. In M. Dossena and S. M. Fitzmaurice (eds), *Business and Official Correspondence: Historical Investigations*, pp. 107–28. Bern: Peter Lang.

Martineau, F. (2013). 'Written Documents: What They Tell Us About Linguistic Usage'. In M. J. van der Wal and G. Rutten (eds), *Touching the Past: Studies in the Historical Sociolinguistics of Ego-documents*, pp. 129–47. Amsterdam: John Benjamins.

Mason, R. (1994). *Scots and Britons*. Cambridge: Cambridge University Press.

McArthur, T. (1979). 'The Status of English in and Furth of Scotland'. In A. J. Aitken and T. McArthur (eds), *Languages of Scotland*, pp. 49–67. Edinburgh: W&R Chambers.

McClure, J. D. (1983). *Scotland and the Lowland Tongue*. Aberdeen: Aberdeen University Press.

McElreath, R. (2020). *Statistical Rethinking: A Bayesian Course with Examples in R and Stan*, 2nd edn. Abingdon: CRC Press.

McGraw, K. M. (2003). 'Political Impressions: Formation and Management'. In D. O. Sears, L. Huddy, and R. Jervis (eds), *Oxford Handbook of Political Psychology*, pp. 394–432. Oxford: Oxford University Press.

McIntosh, A., Samuels, M., and Benskin, M. (1986). *A Linguistic Atlas of Late Mediaeval English [LALME]*. Aberdeen: Aberdeen University Press.

McMillan, A., and McLean, I. (2005). *State of the Union*. Oxford: Oxford University Press.

Mendoza-Denton, N. C. (1997). 'Chicana/Mexicana Identity and Linguistic Variation: An Ethnographic and Sociolinguistic Study of Gang Affiliation in an Urban High School', PhD thesis, Stanford University, California.

Meurman-Solin, A. (1989). 'The Helsinki Corpus of Older Scots'. In J. D. McClure and M. R. G. Spiller (eds), *Essays on the Language and Literature of Medieval and Renaissance Scotland*, pp. 451–58. Aberdeen: Aberdeen University Press.

Meurman-Solin, A. (1993). *Variation and Change in Early Scottish Prose: Studies Based on the Helsinki Corpus of Older Scots*. Helsinki: Suomalainen Tiedeakatemia.

Meurman-Solin, A. (1994). 'On the Evolution of Prose Genres in Older Scots', *NOWELE. North-Western European Language Evolution*, *23*, 91–138.

Meurman-Solin, A. (1995). 'A New Tool: The Helsinki Corpus of Older Scots (1450–1700)', *ICAME*, *19* (4), 49–62.

Meurman-Solin, A. (1997). 'Differentiation and Standardisation in Early Scots'. In C. Jones (ed.), *The Edinburgh History of the Scots Language*, pp. 3–23. Edinburgh: Edinburgh University Press.

Meurman-Solin, A. (2000). 'Change from Above or from Below? Mapping the Loci of Linguistic Change in the History of Scottish English'. In L. Wright (ed.), *The Development of Standard English, 1300–1800: Theories, Descriptions, Conflicts*, pp. 155–70. Cambridge: Cambridge University Press.

Meyerhoff, M. (2002). 'Formal and Cultural Constraints on Optional Objects in Bislama', *Language Variation and Change*, *14* (3), 323–46.

Millar, R. M. (2003). '"Blind Attachment to Inveterate Customs": Language Use, Language Attitude and the Rhetoric of Improvement in the First Statistical Account'. In M. Dossena and C. Jones (eds), *Insights into Late Modern English*, pp. 311–30. New York: Peter Lang.

Millar, R. M. (2004). 'Kailyard, Conservatism and Scots in the Statistical Accounts of Scotland'. In J. K. Christian, C. Hough, and I. Wotherspoon (eds), *New Perspectives on English Historical Linguistics vol II Lexis and Transmission*, pp. 163–76, vol. 2. Amsterdam & Philadelphia: John Benjamins.

Millar, R. M. (2005). 'Language and Dialect'. In R. M. Millar (ed.), *Language, Nation and Power*, pp. 31–58. London: Palgrave Macmillan.

Millar, R. M. (2007). *Northern and Insular Scots*. Edinburgh: Edinburgh University Press.

Millar, R. M. (2010). 'An Historic National Identity? The Case of Scots'. In C. Llamas and D. Watt (eds), *Language and Identities*, pp. 247–56. Edinburgh: Edinburgh University Press.

Millar, R. M. (2012). 'Social History and the Sociology of Language'. In J. M. Hernández-Campoy and J. C. Conde-Silvestre (eds), *The Handbook of Historical Sociolinguistics,* pp. 41–59. Chichester: John Wiley & Sons.

Millar, R. M. (2013). 'To Bring My Language Near to the Language of Men? Dialect and Dialect Use in the Eighteenth and Early Nineteenth Centuries: Some Observations', *Scottish Cultural Review of Language and Literature, suppl. Scots: Studies in its Literature and Language, 21* (31), 71–85.

Millar, R. M. (2018). *Modern Scots: An Analytical Survey*. Edinburgh: Edinburgh University Press.

Millar, R. M. (2020). *A Sociolinguistic History of Scotland*. Edinburgh: Edinburgh University Press.

Milroy, J. (2012). 'Sociolinguistics and Ideologies in Language History'. In J. M. Hernández-Campoy and J. C. Conde-Silvestre (eds), *The Handbook of Historical Sociolinguistics,* pp. 571–84. Chichester: John Wiley & Sons.

Milroy, L. (1980). 'Social Network and Language Maintenance'. In A. K. Pugh, V. Lee, & J. Swann (eds), *Language and Language Use,* pp. 35–45. London: Heinemann Educational.

Milroy, L. (1987). *Observing and Analysing Natural Language: A Critical Account of Sociolinguistic Method*. Oxford: Blackwell.

Milroy, L., and Gordon, M. (2003). *Sociolinguistics: Method and Interpretation*. Oxford: Blackwell.

Milroy, L., and Milroy, J. (1992). 'Social Network and Social Class: Toward an Integrated Sociolinguistic Model', *Language in Society, 21* (1), 1–26.

Mocholí Calvo, C. (2018). 'Development and Experimentation of a Deep Learning System for Convolutional and Recurrent Neural Networks', PhD thesis, Universitat Politècnica de València, Valencia.

Monod, P. K. (1989). *Jacobitism and the English people, 1688–1788*. Cambridge: Cambridge University Press.

Moore, E. (2004). 'Sociolinguistic Style: A Multidimensional Resource for Shared Identity Creation', *Canadian Journal of Linguistics/Revue Canadienne de Linguistique, 49* (3–4), 375–96.

Moore, E., and Podesva, R. J. (2009). 'Style, Indexicality and the Social Meaning of Tag Questions', *Language in Society, 38*, 447–85.

Moosmüller, S. (1989). 'Phonological Variation in Parliamentary Discussions'. In R. Wodak (ed.), *Language, Power and Ideology: Studies in Political Discourse,* pp. 165–80. Amsterdam: John Benjamins.

Munafò, M. R., Nosek, B. A., Bishop, D. V. M., Button, K. S., Chambers, C. D., Percie Du Sert, N., Simonsohn, U., Wagenmakers, E. J., Ware, J. J., and Ioannidis, J. P. A. (2017). 'A Manifesto for Reproducible Science', *Nature Human Behaviour, 1* (0021), 1–9.

Murdoch, A. (2006). 'Campbell, Archibald, Third Duke of Argyll (1682–1761), Politician', *Oxford Dictionary of National Biography*, <https://www.oxforddnb.com/display/10.1093/ref:odnb/9780198614128.001.0001/odnb-9780198614128-e-4477>, accessed 12 Jan. 2023.

Murison, D. (1964). 'The Scots Tongue – The Folk-Speech', *Folklore, 75* (1), 37–47.

Murison, D. (1979). 'The Historical Background'. In A. Aitken and T. McArthur (eds), *Languages of Scotland,* pp. 1–13, vol. 4. Edinburgh: W&R Chambers.

Murray, J. A. H. (1873). *The Dialect of the Southern Counties of Scotland*. London: The Philological Society.

Nevalainen, T. (1991). 'Motivated Archaism: The Use of Affirmative Periphrastic Do in Early Modern English Liturgical Prose'. In D. Kastovsky (ed.), *Historical English Syntax,* pp. 303–20, vol. 2. Berlin & New York: De Gruyter Mouton.

Nevalainen, T., and Raumolin-Brunberg, H. (1989). 'A Corpus of Early Modern Standard English in a Socio-Historical Perspective', *Neuphilologische Mitteilungen, 90* (1), 67–110.

Nevalainen, T., and Raumolin-Brunberg, H. (1994). 'Social Conditioning and Diachronic Language Change'. In D. Kastovsky (ed.), *Studies in Early Modern English,* pp. 325–38, vol. 13. Berlin: De Gruyter.

Nevalainen, T., and Raumolin-Brunberg, H. (1996). *Sociolinguistics and Language History: Studies Based on the Corpus of Early English Correspondence.* Amsterdam: Rodopi.

Nevalainen, T., and Raumolin-Brunberg, H. (2003). *Historical Sociolinguistics: Language Change in Tudor and Stuart England*. London: Pearson Education.

Nicenboim, B., Roettger, T., and Vasishth, S. (2018). 'Using Meta-analysis for Evidence Synthesis: The Case of Incomplete Neutralization in German', *Journal of Phonetics, 70*, 39–55.

Nicols, P. (1983). 'Linguistic Options and Choices for Black Women in the Rural South'. In B. Thorne, C. Kramarae and N. Henley (eds), *Language, Gender, and Society,* pp. 54–68. Rowley, MA: Newbury House.

Niedzielski, N., and Giles, H. (1996). 'Linguistic Accommodation'. In H. Goebl, Z. Stary and W. Wölck (eds), *Contact Linguistics: An International Handbook of Contemporary Research,* pp. 332–42. Berlin: De Gruyter Mouton.

Nordlund, T. (2007). 'Double Diglossia: Lower Class Writing in 19th Century Finland', *Multilingua, 26*, 229–46.

Nurmi, A. (2013). '"All the rest ye must lade yourself": Deontic Modality in Sixteenth-Century English Merchant Letters'. In M. J. van der Wal and G. Rutten (eds), *Touching the Past: Studies in the Historical Sociolinguistics of Ego-documents,* pp. 165–82. Amsterdam: John Benjamins.

Ó Ciardha, É. (2002). *Ireland and the Jacobite Cause, 1685–1766: A Fatal Attachment.* Dublin: Four Courts Press.

O'Connor, B., Taha, M., and Sheehan, M. (2008). 'Castro's Shifters: Locating Variation in Political Discourse', *University of Pennsylvania Working Papers in Linguistics, 14* (2), 120–29.

Oxford Dictionary of National Biography [ODNB], <https://www.oxforddnb.com/>, accessed 15 Feb. 2020

Oxford English Dictionary [OED], <https://www.oed.com/>, accessed 28 Mar. 2023.

Palander-Collin, M., Nevala, M., and Nurmi, A. (2009). 'The Language of Daily Life in the History of English: Studying how Macro meets Micro'. In A. Nurmi, M. Nevala and M. Palander-Collin (eds), *The Language of Daily Life in England (1400-1800),* pp. 1–23. Amsterdam & Philadelphia: John Benjamins.

Patrick, D. J. (2008). 'The Kirk, Parliament and the Union, 1706–7'. In S. J. Brown and C. A. Whatley (eds), *The Union of 1707,* pp. 94–115. Edinburgh: Edinburgh University Press.

Patrick, D. J., and Whatley, C. A. (2007). 'Persistence, Principle and Patriotism in the Making of the Union of 1707: The Revolution, Scottish Parliament and the "Squadrone Volante"', *History, 92* (2), 162–86.

Paul, J. B. (1904). *The Scots Peerage: Founded on Wood's Edition of Sir Robert Douglas's Peerage of Scotland. Containing an Historical and Genealogical Account of the Nobility of that Kingdom,* vols. 1–8. Edinburgh: David Douglas.

Pavalanathan, U., and Eisenstein, J. (2015). 'Audience-modulated Variation in Online Social Media', *American Speech, 90* (2), 187–213.

Pearce, M. (2001). '"Getting behind the image": Personality Politics in a Labour Party Election Broadcast', *Language and Literature: International Journal of Stylistics, 10* (3), 211–28.

Pearce, M. (2005). 'Informalization in UK party election broadcasts 1966–97', *Language and Literature: International Journal of Stylistics, 14* (1), 65–90.

Petré, P., and van de Velde, F. (2018). 'The Real-time Dynamics of the Individual and the Community in Grammaticalization', *Language, 94* (4), 867–901.

Phillips, J. D. (2012). 'Mutual Preservation of Standard Language and National Identity in Early Modern Wales'. In C. Percy and M. C. Davidson (eds), *The Languages of Nation: Attitudes and Norms,* pp. 83–98, vol. 148. Bristol: Multilingual Matters.

Pietsch, L. (2015). 'Archaism and Dialect in Irish Emigrant Letters'. In A. Auer, D. Schreier and R. J. Watts (eds), *Letter Writing and Language Change,* pp. 223–39. Cambridge: Cambridge University Press.

Podesva, R. J. (2006). 'Intonational Variation and Social Meaning: Categorical and Phonetic Aspects', *University of Pennsylvania Working Papers in Linguistics, 12* (2), 189–202.

Podesva, R. J. (2007). 'Phonation Type as a Stylistic Variable: The Use of Falsetto in Constructing a Persona', *Journal of Sociolinguistics, 11* (4), 478–504.

Podesva, R. J. (2011). 'The California Vowel Shift and Gay Identity', *American Speech*, *86* (1), 32–51.

Podesva, R. J., Jamsu, J., Callier, P., and Heitman, J. (2008). 'The Social Meaning of Released /t/ Among U.S. Politicians: Insights from Production and Perception'. [Paper presented in themed session *The Social Meaning of Linguistic Variation: Structure and Process*], *New Ways of Analyzing Variation (NWAV) 37*, Houston.

Podesva, R. J., Reynolds, J., Callier, P., and Baptiste, J. (2015). 'Constraints on the Social Meaning of Released /t/: A Production and Perception Study of U.S. Politicians', *Language Variation and Change*, *27* (1), 59–87.

Pollner, C. (2000). 'Shibboleths Galore: The Treatment of Irish and Scottish English in Histories of the English Language'. In D. Kastovsky and A. Mettinger (eds), *The History of English in a Social Context: A Contribution to Historical Sociolinguistics*, pp. 363–76. Berlin: Mouton de Gruyter.

Purnell, T. C. (2009). 'Convergence and Contact in Milwaukee: Evidence From Select African American and White Vowel Space Features', *Journal of Language and Social Psychology*, *28* (4), 408–27.

Purnell, T. C., Raimy, E., and Salmons, J. (2009). 'Defining Dialect, Perceiving Dialect, and New Dialect Formation: Sarah Palin's Speech', *Journal of English Linguistics*, *37* (4), 331–55.

R. (2020). A Language and Environment for Statistical Computing [software], R Core Team.

Raffe, A. (2010). 'Presbyterianism, Secularisation, and Scottish Politics After the Revolution of 1688–1690', *The Historical Journal*, *53* (2), 317–37.

Raffe, A. (2012a). *The Culture of Controversy: Religious Arguments in Scotland, 1660–1714*, vol. 28. Woodbridge: Boydell & Brewer.

Raffe, A. (2012b). 'Scotland Restored and Reshaped: Politics and Religion, c.1660–1712'. In T. M. Devine and J. Wormald (eds), *The Oxford Handbook of Modern Scottish History*. Oxford: Oxford University Press.

Raffe, A. (2022). 'Wodrow's News: Correspondence and Politics in Early 18th-Century Scotland', *Parliamentary History*, *41* (1), 135–49.

Raumolin-Brunberg, H. (1991). *The Noun phrase in Early Sixteenth-century English: A Study Based on Sir Thomas More's Writings*. Helsinki: Société néophilologique.

Raumolin-Brunberg, H. (1996a). 'Forms of Address in Early English Correspondence', *Language and Computers*, *15*, 167–81.

Raumolin-Brunberg, H. (1996b). 'Historical Sociolinguistics'. In T. Nevalainen and H. Raumolin-Brunberg (eds), *Sociolinguistics and Language History: Studies Based on the Corpus of Early English Correspondence*, pp. 11–38. Amsterdam: Rodopi.

Raumolin-Brunberg, H. and Nevalainen, T. (1994). 'Social Conditioning and Diachronic Language Change'. In D. Kastovsky (ed.), *Studies in Early Modern English,* pp. 325–38. Berlin: Mouton de Gruyter.

Rebeschini, P. and van Handel, R. (2015). 'Can Local Particle Filters Beat the Curse of Dimensionality?', *The Annals of Applied Probability, 25* (5), 2809–66.

Richardson, M. (1980). 'Henry V, the English Chancery and Chancery English', *Speculum, 55* (4), 726–50.

Rickford, J. R. (1986). 'The Need for New Approaches to Social Class Analysis in Sociolinguistics', *Language & Communication, 6* (3), 215–21.

Riley, P. W. J. (1978). *The Union of England and Scotland: A Study in Anglo-Scottish Politics of the Eighteenth Century.* Manchester: Manchester University Press.

Riley, P. W. J. (1979). *King William and the Scottish Politicians.* Edinburgh: John Donald.

Robertson, J. (1997). *Andrew Fletcher: Political Works.* Cambridge: Cambridge University Press.

Robertson, J. (2008). 'Fletcher, Andrew, of Saltoun (1653?–1716), Scottish Patriot, Political Theorist, and Book Collector', *Oxford Dictionary of National Biography,* <https://www.oxforddnb.com/view/10.1093/ref:odnb/9780198614128.001.0001/odnb-9780198614128-e-9720>, accessed 22 Nov. 2022

Robinson, M. (1973). 'Modern Literary Scots: Fergusson and After'. In A. J. Aitken and J. M. Templeton (eds), *Lowland Scots: Papers Presented to an Edinburgh Conference [12th–13th May 1972],* pp. 38–49, vol. 2. Glasgow: Association for Scottish Literary Studies.

Robinson, M. (1983). 'Language Choice in the Reformation: The Scots Confession of 1560'. In J. D. McClure (ed.), *Scotland and the Lowland Tongue: Studies in the Language and Literature of Lowland Scotland,* pp. 59–78. Aberdeen: Aberdeen University Press.

Robinson, M. (1985). *The Concise Scots Dictionary.* Aberdeen: Aberdeen University Press.

Roettger, T. (2019). 'Researcher Degrees of Freedom in Phonetic Sciences', *Laboratory Phonology: Journal of the Association for Laboratory Phonology, 10* (1), 1–27.

Romaine, S. (1980). 'Stylistic Variation and Evaluative Reactions to Speech: Problems in the Investigation of Linguistic Attitudes in Scotland', *Language and Speech, 23* (3), 213–32.

Romaine, S. (1982). 'The History of the Relative Clause/Markers in English with Special Reference to Middle Scots'. In S. Romaine (ed.), *Socio-Historical Linguistics: Its Status and Methodology,* pp. 53–80. Cambridge: Cambridge University Press.

Romaine, S. (1985). 'The Problem of Short /a/ in Scotland', *English World-Wide, 6* (2), 165–97.

Romaine, S. (1998). *The Cambridge History of the English language*, vol. 4. Cambridge: Cambridge University Press.

Records of the Parliament of Scotland to 1707 [RPS], <https://www.rps.ac.uk/>, accessed 10 Jan. 2023.

Russell, C. (1995). 'The Projected Settlement of 1641: January–March 1641'. In C. Russell (ed.), *The Fall of the British Monarchies 1637–1642*, pp. 237–73. Oxford: Oxford University Press.

Rutkowska, H. and Rössler, P. (2012). 'Orthographic Variables'. In J. M. Hernández-Campoy and J. C. Conde-Silvestre (eds), *The Handbook of Historical Sociolinguistics*, pp. 213–36. Chichester: John Wiley & Sons.

Rutten, G. and van der Wal, M. J. (2011). 'Local Dialects, Supralocal Writing Systems: The Degree of Orality of Dutch Private Letters from the Seventeenth Century', *Written Language and Literacy*, *14*, 251–74.

Sairio, A. and Palander-Collin, M. (2012). 'The Reconstruction of Prestige Patterns in Language History'. In J. M. Hernández-Campoy and J. C. Conde-Silvestre (eds), *The Handbook of Historical Sociolinguistics*, pp. 626–38. Chichester: John Wiley & Sons.

Sanchez, K., Hay, J. and Nilson, E. (2015). 'Contextual Activation of Australia Can Affect New Zealanders' Vowel Productions', *Journal of Phonetics*, *48*, 76–95.

Sandved, A. O. (1981). 'Prolegomena to a Renewed Study of the Rise of Standard English'. In M. Benskin and M. Samuels (eds), *So Meny People Longages and Tongues: Philological Essays in Scots and Mediaeval English*, pp. 31–2. Edinburgh: Edinburgh University Press.

Sankoff, G. (1980). *The Social Life of Language*. Philadelphia: University of Pennsylvania Press.

Schilling-Estes, N. (2002). 'Investigating Stylistic Variation'. In J. K. Chambers and N. Schilling-Estes (eds), *The Handbook of Language Variation and Change*, 2nd edn, pp. 327–49. Malden, MA & Oxford: Wiley-Blackwell.

Schilling-Estes, N. (2004). 'Constructing Ethnicity in Interaction', *Journal of Sociolinguistics*, *8* (2), 163–95.

Schlobinski, P. (1987). *Stadtsprache Berlin. Eine soziolinguistische Untersuchung*. Berlin & New York: De Gruyter Verlag.

Schneider, E. W. (2002). 'Investigating Variation and Change in Written Documents'. In J. K. Chambers, P. Trudgill and N. Schilling-Estes (eds), *The Handbook of Language Variation and Change*, pp. 67–96. Oxford: Blackwell.

Scobbie, J. M., Hewlett, N. and Turk, A. (1999). 'Standard English in Edinburgh and Glasgow: The Scottish Vowel Length Rule Revealed'. In P. Foulkes and G. Docherty (eds), *Urban Voices: Variation and Change in British Accents*, pp. 230–45. London: Arnold.

Scott, R. (1981). 'The Politics and Administration of Scotland, 1725–1748', PhD thesis, University of Edinburgh, Edinburgh.

Scott, R. (2006). 'Erskine, James, Lord Grange (bap. 1679, d. 1754), Judge and Politician', *Oxford Dictionary of National Biography*, <https://www.oxforddnb.com/display/10.1093/ref:odnb/9780198614128.001.0001/odnb-9780198614128-e-8861>, accessed 8 Mar. 2023.

Sharp, L. W. (1937). *Early letters of Robert Wodrow, 1698–1709*, vol. 24, 3rd edn. Edinburgh: T. & A. Constable.

Shoemark, P., Goldwater, S., Shrimpton, L., Murray, I., and Sur, D. (2017). 'Aye or naw, whit dae ye hink? Scottish Independence and Linguistic Identity on Social Media', *Proceedings of the 15th Conference of the European Chapter of the Association for Computational Linguistics*, *1*, 1239–48.

Shoemark, P., Kirby, J. and Goldwater, S. (2017). 'Topic and Audience Effects on Distinctively Scottish Vocabulary Usage in Twitter Data', *Proceedings of the Workshop on Stylistic Variation*, 59–68.

Simpson, J. M. (1970). 'Who Steered the Gravy Train, 1707–1766?'. In N. Phillipson and R. Mitchison (eds), *Scotland in the Age of Improvement: Essays in Scottish History in the Eighteenth Century*, pp. 47–72. Edinburgh: Edinburgh University Press.

Simpson, J. M. (2005). 'Ker, John, First Duke of Roxburghe (c. 1680–1741), Politician', Oxford Dictionary of National Biography, <https://www.oxforddnb.com/view/10.1093/ref:odnb/9780198614128.001.0001/odnb-9780198614128-e-15450>, accessed 25 Nov. 2022.

Smith, J. (2001). '"You ø na hear o' that kind o' things": Negative do in Buckie Scots', *English World Wide*, *21* (2), 231–59.

Smith, J. (2002). 'Negative Concord in the Old and New World: Evidence from Scotland', *Language Variation and Change*, *13* (2), 109–34.

Smith, J. J. (1996a). 'Ear-rhyme, Eye-rhyme and Traditional Rhyme: English and Scots in Robert Burns's Brigs of Ayr', *Glasgow Review*, *4*, 74–85.

Smith, J. J. (1996b). *An Historical Study of English: Function, Form and Change*. London: Routledge.

Smout, T. C. (1963). 'The Erskines of Mar and the Development of Alloa, 1689–1825', *Scottish Studies*, *7*, 57–74.

Sorensen, J. and Sorensen, H. V. (2000). *The Grammar of Empire in Eighteenth-Century British Writing*. Cambridge: Cambridge University Press.

Stephen, J. (2007). *Scottish Presbyterians and the Act of Union 1707*. Edinburgh: Edinburgh University Press.

Stuart-Smith, J. (2004). 'Scottish English: Phonology'. In B. Kortmann and E. Schneider (eds), *A Handbook of Varieties of English*, pp. 47–67, vol. 1. Amsterdam: Mouton de Gruyter.

Szechi, D. (1989). *Letters of George Lockhart of Carnwath 1698–1732*, vol. 2. Edinburgh: Pillans & Wilson.

Szechi, D. (2002). *George Lockhart of Carnwath 1689–1727: A Study in Jacobitism*. East Linton: Tuckwell Press.

Szechi, D. (2011). 'Lockhart, George, of Carnwath (1681?–1731), Jacobite Politician and Memoirist', Oxford Dictionary of National Biography (2011), <https://www.oxforddnb.com/view/10.1093/ref:odnb/9780198614128.001.0001/odnb-9780198614128-e-16902>, accessed 12 Nov. 2021.

Szechi, D. and Scott, P. H. (eds), (1995) *Scotland's Ruine: Lockhart of Carnwath's Memoirs of the Union*, vol. 25. Aberdeen: Association for Scottish Literature Studies.

Tabouret-Keller, A. (1997). *Les Enjeux de la Nomination des Langues*, vol. 95. Louvain: Peeters Publishers.

Tagliamonte, S. A. and Baayen, R. H. (2012). 'Models, Forests, and Trees of York English: Was/Were Variation as a Case Study for Statistical Practice', *Language Variation and Change*, *24* (2), 135–178.

Tajfel, H. and Turner, J. C. (1979). 'An Integrative Theory of Intergroup Conflict'. In W. G. Austin and S. Worchel (eds), *The Social Psychology of Intergroup Relations*, pp. 33–47. Monterey, CA: Brooks/Cole.

Tatman, R. (2015). '#Go awn: Sociophonetic Variation in Variant Spellings on Twitter', *Working Papers of the Linguistics Circle of the University of Victoria*, *25* (2), 97–108.

Tausczik, Y. R. and Pennebaker, J. W. (2010). 'The Psychological Meaning of Words: LIWC and Computerized Text Analysis Methods', *Journal of Language and Social Psychology*, *29* (1), 24–54.

Templeton, J. M. (1973). 'Scots: An Outline History'. In A. Aitken (ed.), *Lowland Scots*, pp. 4–13. Glasgow: Association of Scottish Literary Studies.

Thakerar, J. N., Giles, H. and Cheshire, J. (1982). 'Psychological and Linguistic Parameters of Speech Accommodation Theory', *Advances in the Social Psychology of Language*, *205*, 205–55.

Tieken-Boon van Ostade, I. (1996). 'Social Network Theory and Eighteenth-century English: The Case of Boswell'. In D. Britton (ed.), *English Historical Linguistics 1994: Papers from the 8th International Conference on English Historical Linguistics*, pp. 327–37, vol. 8. Amsterdam & Philadelphia: John Benjamins.

Tieken-Boon van Ostade, I. (1998). 'Standardization of English Spelling: The Eighteenth-Century'. In J. Fisiak and M. Krygier (eds), *Advances in English Historical Linguistics 1996*, pp. 457–70. Berlin & New York: De Gruyter Mouton.

Tieken-Boon van Ostade, I. (2000). 'Social Network Analysis and the Language of Sarah Fielding', *European Journal of English Studies*, *4* (3), 291–302.

Tieken-Boon van Ostade, I. (2003). 'Lowth's Language'. In M. Dossena and C. Jones (eds), *Insights into Late Modern English*, pp. 241–64. Bern: Peter Lang.

Tieken-Boon van Ostade, I. (2006). 'Eighteenth-century Prescriptivism and the Norm of Correctness'. In A. van Kemenade and B. Los (eds), *The Handbook of the History of English*, pp. 539–57. Oxford: Blackwell.

Tieken-Boon van Ostade, I. (2009). *An Introduction to Late Modern English*. Edinburgh: Edinburgh University Press.

Ting-Toomey, S. (1999). *Communicating Across Cultures*. New York: Guilford Press.

Trudgill, P. (1974). 'Linguistic Change and Diffusion: Description and Explanation in Sociolinguistic Dialect Geography', *Language in Society*, *3* (2), 215–46.

Trudgill, P. (1986). *Dialects in Contact*. Oxford: Blackwell.

Turner, J. C. (1999). 'Some Current Issues in Research on Social Identity and Self-categorization Theories', in N. Ellemers, R. Spears and B. Doosje (eds), *Social Identity: Context, Commitment, Content*, pp. 6–34. Oxford: Blackwell.

Turner, J. C. and Brown, R. J. (1978). 'Social Status, Cognitive Alternatives, and Intergroup Relations'. In H. Tajfel (ed.), *Differentiation Between Social Groups*, pp. 201–34. London: Academic Press.

Vandenbussche, W. (2002). 'Dutch Orthography in Lower, Middle and Upper Class Documents in 19th-century Flanders'. In A. Linn and N. McLelland (eds), *Standardisation: Studies from the Germanic Languages*, pp. 27–42. Amsterdam & Philadelphia: John Benjamins.

Vasishth, S., Beckman, M., Nicenboim, B., Fangfang, L. and Kong, E. J. (2018). 'Bayesian Data Analysis in the Phonetic Sciences: A Tutorial Introduction, *Journal of Phonetics*, *71*, 147–61.

Vosters, R. (2013). 'Dutch, Flemish or Hollandic? Social and Ideological Aspects of Linguistic Convergence and Divergence During the United Kingdom of the Netherlands (1815–1830)'. In E. Barát, P. Studer and J. Nekvapil (eds), *Ideological conceptualisations of language. Discourses of linguistic diversity*, pp. 35–54. Bern: Peter Lang.

Vosters, R. and Rutten, G. (2015). 'Three Southern Shibboleths: Spelling features as Conflicting Identity Markers in the Low Countries', *Written Language and Literacy*, *18* (2), 260–74.

Wagenmakers, E. J. (2007). 'A Practical Solution to the Pervasive Problems of p values', *Psychonomic Bulletin & Review*, *14* (5), 779–804.

Wal, M. J. van der, and Rutten, G. (2013). 'Ego-documents in a Historical-Sociolinguistic Perspective'. In M. J. van der Wal and G. Rutten (eds), *Touching the Past. Studies in the Historical Sociolinguistics of Ego-documents*, pp. 1–17, vol. 1. Amsterdam & Philadelphia: John Benjamins.

Wales, K. (1996). *Personal Pronouns in Present-day English*. Cambridge: Cambridge University Press.

Walker, A., Hay, J., Drager, K. and Sanchez, K. (2018). 'Divergence in Speech Perception', *Linguistics*, *56* (1), 257–78.

Wallace, V. and Kidd, C. (2018). 'Between Nationhood and Nonconformity: The Scottish Whig–Presbyterian Novel and the Denominational Press'. In G. Carruthers and C. Kidd (eds), *Literature and Union: Scottish Texts, British Contexts,* pp. 194–220. Oxford: Oxford University Press.

Watt, Dominic (2014). *Language, Borders and Identity.* Edinburgh: Edinburgh University Press.

Watt, Dominic, Llamas, C. and Ezra Johnson, D. (2010). 'Levels of Linguistic Accommodation Across a National Border', *Journal of English Linguistics*, *38* (3), 270–89.

Watt, Douglas (2014). *The Price of Scotland: Darien, Union and the Wealth of the Nations.* Edinburgh: Luath Press.

Watts, R. J. (1999). 'The Social Construction of Standard English: Grammar Writers as a "discourse community"'. In T. Bex and R. J. Watts (eds), *Standard English. The Widening Debate,* pp. 40–68. London: Routledge.

Watts, R. J. (2008). 'Grammar Writers in Eighteenth-century Britain: A Community of Practice or a Discourse Community?' In I. Tieken-Boon van Ostade (ed.), *Grammars, Grammarians and Grammar-Writing in Eighteenth-Century England,* pp. 37–56. Berlin & New York: De Gruyter Mouton.

Watts, R. J. (2015). 'Setting the Scene: Letters, Standards and Historical Sociolinguistics'. In A. Auer, D. Schreier and R. J. Watts (eds), *Letter Writing and Language Change,* pp. 1–13. Cambridge: Cambridge University Press.

Wenger, E. (1998). 'Communities of Practice: Learning as a Social System', *The Systems Thinker*, *9* (5), 1–10.

Whatley, C. A. (2006). *The Scots and the Union.* Edinburgh: Edinburgh University Press.

Whatley, C. A. (2008). 'The Issues Facing Scotland in 1707'. In S. J. Brown and C. A. Whatley (eds), *The Union of 1707: New Dimensions,* pp. 1–30. Edinburgh: Edinburgh University Press.

Wickham, H. (2016). *Ggplot2: Elegant Graphics for Data Analysis.* New York: Springer-Verlag.

Wilkinson, D. (2002a). 'Cochrane, William (aft.1659-1717), of Kilmaronock, Dunbarton', *History of Parliament Online*, <https://www.historyofparliamentonline.org/volume/1690-1715/member/cochrane-william-1659-1717>, accessed 17 Jan. 2023

Wilkinson, D. (2002b). 'Cockburn, John (c.1679-1758), of Ormiston, Haddington', *History of Parliament Online*, <https://www.historyofparliamentonline.org/volume/1690–1715/member/cockburn-john-1679-1758>, accessed 18 Jan. 2023

Williams, G. (1992). *Sociolinguistics: A Sociological Critique.* London: Routledge.

Williamson, K. (2002). 'The Dialectology of 'English' North of the Humber, c. 1380–1500'. In T. Fanego, B. Méndez-Naya and E. Seoane (eds), *Sounds, Words, Texts and Change,* pp. 253–86. Amsterdam: John Benjamins.

Włodarczyk, M. (2013). 'Self-reference and Ego Involvement in the 1820 Settler Petition as a Leaking Genre'. In M. J. van der Wal and G. Rutten (eds), *Touching the Past: Studies in the Historical Sociolinguistics of Ego-documents,* pp. 201–24. Amsterdam: John Benjamins.

Wodak, R. (1989). *Language, Power and Ideology: Studies in Political Discourse.* Amsterdam: John Benjamins.

Woesler, W. (1998). 'Editionsprinzipien für Deutsche Texte der Neuzeit II: Nichtliterarische Texte'. In W. Besch, A. Betten, O. Reichmann and S. Sonderregger (eds), *Sprachgeschichte. Ein Handbuch zur Geschichte der Deutschen Sprache und ihrer Erforschung,* 2nd edn, pp. 941–48, vol. 1. Berlin: Mouton de Gruyter.

Wolfram, W. A. (1969). *A Sociolinguistic Description of Detroit Negro Speech.* Washington DC: Centre for Applied Linguistics.

Woschitz, J. and Yağli, E. (2019). 'The Meaning Change of Hayır During the Turkish Constitutional Referendum 2017', *Language Sciences*, *72*, 116–33.

Yeoman, L. A. (2004). 'Wodrow, Robert (1679–1734), Ecclesiastical Historian', *Oxford Dictionary of National Biography*, <https://www.oxforddnb.com/view/10.1093/ref:odnb/9780198614128.001.0001/odnb-9780198614128-e-29819>, accessed 25 Nov. 2022.

Young, J. R. (1999). 'The Parliamentary Incorporating Union of 1707: Political Management, Anti-Unionism and Foreign Policy'. In T. M. Devine and J. Young (eds), *Eighteenth Century Scotland: New Perspectives,* pp. 24–52. East Linton: Tuckwell Press.

Young, J. R. (2004a). 'Hay, John, Second Marquess of Tweeddale (1645–1713), Politician', *Oxford Dictionary of National Biography,* <https://www.oxforddnb.com/view/10.1093/ref:odnb/9780198614128.001.0001/odnb-9780198614128-e-12728>, accessed 12 Nov. 2022.

Young, J. R. (2004b). 'Murray, John, First Duke of Atholl (1660–1724), Army Officer and Politician', *Oxford Dictionary of National Biography*, <https://www.oxforddnb.com/display/10.1093/ref:odnb/9780198614128.001.0001/odnb-9780198614128-e-19627>, accessed 17 Jan. 2023.

Young, J. R. (2006). 'Hume, Patrick, First Earl of Marchmont (1641–1724), Politician', *Oxford Dictionary of National Biography*, <https://www.oxforddnb.com/display/10.1093/ref:odnb/9780198614128.001.0001/odnb-9780198614128-e-14150>, accessed 18 Jan. 2023.

Young, J. R. (2008). 'Johnston, James (1655–1737), Politician and Government Official', *Oxford Dictionary of National Biography*, <https://www.

oxforddnb.com/display/10.1093/ref:odnb/9780198614128.001.0001/odnb-9780198614128-e-14941>, accessed 8 Mar. 2023.

Zai, R. (1942). 'The Phonology of the Morebattle Dialect, East Roxburghshire', PhD thesis, University of Lucerne, Lucerne.

Zimmermann, R. (2017). 'Formal and Quantitative Approaches to the Study of Syntactic Change: Three Case Studies from the History of English', PhD thesis, Université de Genéve, Geneva.

Appendices

Appendix 1

I would like to thank the following collection holders or archivists for their co-operation in kindly granting me access to these respective collections within the National Records of Scotland and Blair Atholl Archives.

Collection Holder	Collection Reference	Collection Title
The Earl of Eglinton	GD3	Papers of the Montgomerie Family, Earls of Eglinton
Mrs Gillean Smythe	GD190	Papers of the Smythe Family of Methven, Perthshire
Mr Will Anderson	GD248	Papers of the Ogilvy family, Earls of Seafield (Seafield Papers)
The Duke of Montrose	GD220	Papers of the Graham Family, Dukes of Montrose (Montrose Muniments)
James Peill	GD44	Papers of the Gordon Family, Dukes of Gordon (Gordon Castle Muniments)
The Earl of Leven and Melville	GD26	Papers of the Leslie family, Earls of Leven and Melville
Keren Guthrie, Archivist at Blair Atholl Estates	Blair MS Box 29.I, 44 and 45	Various Papers of the Atholl Estate

Appendix 2

Repository	Reference No.	Collection Title
National Records of Scotland	GD3	*Papers of the Montgomerie Family, Earls of Eglinton*
	GD26	*Papers of the Leslie family, Earls of Leven and Melville*
	GD29	*Papers of the Bruce family of Kinross (Kinross House Papers)*
	GD44	*Papers of the Gordon Family, Dukes of Gordon (Gordon Castle Muniments)*
	GD45	*Papers of the Maule Family, Earls of Dalhousie*
	GD112	*Papers of the Campbell Family, Earls of Breadalbane (Breadalbane Muniments)*
	GD124	*Papers of the Erskine Family, Earls of Mar and Kellie*
	GD190	*Papers of the Smythe Family of Methven, Perthshire*
	GD220	*Papers of the Graham Family, Dukes of Montrose (Montrose Muniments)*
	GD248	*Papers of the Ogilvy family, Earls of Seafield (Seafield Papers)*
	GD406	*Papers of the Douglas Hamilton Family, Dukes of Hamilton and Brandon*
	RH15	*Miscellaneous Papers (Formerly known as MP Bundles)*

Repository	Reference No.	Collection Title
National Records	GD40	*Papers of the Kerr Family, Marquises of Lothian (Lothian Muniments)*
	B34	*Records of Inverkeithing Burgh*
National Library of Scotland	MS.1248	*Letters and papers of clients or correspondents of the Mackenzies of Delvine, with the surname Carnegie*
	MS.1300	*Letters and papers of clients or correspondents of the Mackenzies of Delvine, with surnames from Len-Les, with papers of the 21st Earl of Crawfurd*
	MS.1403	*Letters and papers of Murray, Duke of Atholl, from the 1st Marquess to the 2nd Duke, including Tullibardine and Nairne*
	MS.2617	*Single manuscripts and small collections*
	MS.3112	*Miscellaneous letters and manuscripts*
	MS.3278	*Miscellaneous letters and papers*
	MS.3366	*Letters addressed to Lord Godolphin concerning Scottish Parliamentary affairs*
	MS.3648	*Single letters and small collections*
	MS.5136	*Miscellaneous correspondence of the family of Murray of Atholl*
	MS.7013	*Letters to the 1st and 2nd Marquesses of Tweeddale, with a few letters concerning them*
	MS.7031	*Letters of the 2nd Marquess of Tweeddale*
	MS.7104	*'Tweeddale Letters, 1869'. A volume of letters, 1631-1745, to the Earls and Marquesses of Tweeddale, compiled and arranged by Sir William Fraser*

Repository	Reference No.	Collection Title
National Library	MS.14418	*Miscellaneous business, estate and local affairs correspondence of the 2nd Marquess of Tweeddale*
	MS.16746	*Correspondence, undated, of the family of Fletcher of Saltoun*
	MS.20772	*Correspondence chiefly of the Earls of Wigtown on local and estate affairs*
	MS.25276	*Correspondence chiefly of Sir David Dalrymple, but also including letters to his wife, Lady Janet Dalrymple*
Blair Atholl Archives	NRAS234/Box 45/2	BA.45(2).4
		BA.45(2).66
		BA.45(2).155
		BA.45(2).235
	NRAS234/Box 45/6	BA.45(6).3
		BA.45(6).42
		BA.45(6).56
		BA.45(6).57
		BA.45(6).58
		BA.45(6).59
		BA.45(6).65
		BA.45(6).66
		BA.45(6).85
		BA.45(6).90
		BA.45(6).100
		BA.45(6).104
		BA.45(6).106
		BA.45(6).108
		BA.45(6).110
		BA.45(6).113
		BA.45(6).121
		BA.45(6).124
		BA.45(6).125

Appendix 3

Lexical Features	'Other' Category
adoeing, advertish, ae, alenarlie, anent/annent, approwen, arent(s), attaint(ed), attegue, atteigue, aye, barrous, bedellus, beik, beis, bigging, bisket, boaking, bra', brae(s), braeface, brok, bruckle, brucklness, cabaling, cabals, casten, cesse(s), clog-bag, cognosce, coldrife(ness), Commissar(s), commissariat, commontie, comontie, commonty, compartnery, compear, complean(ed), contrair, contraire, corkie, corkie-lit, cotter, craige-pick, creil, darties, dead-chack, decreet, difficulted, dilator(y), demitt, deput(e), dimitt, dipping, drumly, dyet, dytment(s), evite(d), excambion, exime(d), exped, expiscate, faill, fale, ffaill, firmance, flyting, forfault(ing), frae, frite(s), frush, gaet, gars, goand, hain'd, haining, harangue(s), harrangue(s), hereaway, heughhirnes, homologate, hurtcheoun, infeft, infeftments, judicatory, judiccatories, Justiciorie, keil, ken, loch(s), lochan, lou, lugs, lymmer(s), lymmers, liver, liver'd, livered, macer(s), mae, maelin, mank, mart(s), maun, meikle, mettle, minch(ed), minch'd, mind(ing), minding, moyen, muckle, mump(ing), mure, nae, nolt, outmake, outmaking, outreek, outreik(e), outreiking, overtour, nae, Pech(s), Pecht, pickle, platt, powny, praejudge, praelimiting, precognition, prelimit, prelimitation, propale(ing), prorogation, rawen, repulls, repone(d), rexive, roop, roup(s), rouping, scrufe, sederunt, sen, sensyne, shotle, siller, slap, sneck, sned(ing), subscryve(d), subtile, superplus, syke, syre, saugh, saughs, sclate, theick, theranent, therannent, Thesaury, Thraesurie, Thrasurie, thray, thir, thire, thirr, throng, tirring, tost, trafect(ing), treater(s), treatters, tye, umquhill, vocable(s), whin(s), wordle	ane, airth, brack, carring, catell, fan (when), fat (what), ffrayday, frayday, gad, gefe, graafe(s), jokky, miscarring, steipend, suk(ed), suking, sweem(s), ware, wark, weel(l), weet, wictuall(ers), wreat(s), wreating, writt, wrot(t)

Appendix 4

Year	Word Count	Anglicised features	Scots features
1689	1,085	7	105
1690	1,040	90	13
1691	6,405	544	38
1692	10,461	797	72
1693	14,262	1,058	105
1694	6,568	494	40
1695	1,732	166	2
1696	3,553	261	32
1697	4,660	363	19
1698	5,041	299	67
1699	9,198	532	314
1700	27,459	1,617	859
1701	20,996	1,231	544
1702	30,305	2,001	783
1703	25,461	1,789	445
1704	37,378	3,367	362
1705	62,076	4,982	898
1706	64,658	4,940	583
1707	1,301	106	17
1708	8,099	668	42
1709	11,700	836	134
1710	1,857	119	9
1711	5,319	382	16
1712	2,399	195	7
1713	9,970	711	33
1714	21,015	1,719	186
1715	3,198	230	8
1716	1,840	139	20
1717	7,422	705	36
1718	8,454	862	22
1719	1,193	131	2
1720	4,247	511	24
1721	8,315	756	36

(Continued)

Year	Word Count	Anglicised features	Scots features
1722	6,931	604	20
1723	8,072	633	22
1724	5,722	490	6
1725	15,811	1,299	36
1726	17,864	1,477	29
1727	11,931	1,024	47
1728	2,463	234	9
1729	927	88	3
1730	327	31	1
1731	5,223	515	32
1732	1,503	138	10
1733	0	0	0
1734	3,302	286	10
1735	10,572	1,106	10
1736	0	0	0
1737	330	26	1
1738	0	0	0
1739	3,420	348	10
1740	6,303	631	12
1741	2,603	268	14
1742	3,876	39	14
1743	748	85	2
1744	1,068	120	9
1745	0	0	0

Appendix 5

Output of the first brms model (which included all factors) in log-odds. Looking at the credibility intervals (CI), we can see that almost all effects are spread largely around zero, indicating a portion of the probability is at zero, suggesting most predictor levels have little-to-no probability in conditioning the use of written Scots.

```
 Family: bernoulli
  Links: mu = logit
Formula: Scots_English ~ Party + Polit_Affl + Religion + Jacobite + Address + Relationship
   Data: Scots (Number of observations: 47169)
  Draws: 4 chains, each with iter = 3000; warmup = 1500; thin = 5;
         total post-warmup draws = 1200

Group-Level Effects:
~Author (Number of levels: 33)
              Estimate Est.Error l-95% CI u-95% CI Rhat Bulk_ESS Tail_ESS
sd(Intercept)     1.22      0.26     0.80     1.83 1.00     1085     1117

Population-Level Effects:
              Estimate Est.Error l-95% CI u-95% CI Rhat Bulk_ESS Tail_ESS
Intercept        -3.10      0.54    -4.15    -1.99 1.00     1238     1098
Party1            0.03      0.62    -1.21     1.33 1.00     1232     1059
Party2           -0.00      0.61    -1.27     1.26 1.00     1144      986
Party3            0.57      1.10    -1.56     2.64 1.00     1147     1095
Polit_Affl1       0.23      0.52    -0.81     1.19 1.00     1255     1260
Religion1        -0.66      0.54    -1.67     0.46 1.00     1130      912
Jacobite1        -0.04      0.66    -1.29     1.31 1.00     1192     1212
Jacobite2        -0.13      0.53    -1.12     1.02 1.00     1140     1135
Address1         -0.17      0.08    -0.33    -0.02 1.00     1066     1052
Address2          0.19      0.04     0.12     0.27 1.00     1180     1174
Address3          0.11      0.04     0.02     0.19 1.00     1441     1170
Address4         -0.40      0.06    -0.51    -0.29 1.00     1196     1128
Address5         -0.07      0.07    -0.22     0.07 1.00     1138     1163
Address6         -0.01      0.07    -0.15     0.12 1.00      973      967
Address7          0.11      0.05     0.01     0.22 1.00     1195     1070
Relationship1     0.08      0.02     0.04     0.11 1.00     1212     1099
Birthplace1       0.87      0.65    -0.34     2.09 1.00     1021     1046
Birthplace2      -0.12      0.65    -1.49     1.09 1.00     1176     1131
Birthplace3      -0.72      0.65    -1.92     0.60 1.00     1233     1258
Birthplace4       0.06      0.78    -1.50     1.53 1.00     1249     1177
Birthplace5      -0.37      0.57    -1.45     0.74 1.00     1106     1057
Location1        -0.21      0.15    -0.50     0.08 1.00     1223     1017
Location2         0.14      0.09    -0.03     0.30 1.01     1099     1082
Location3         0.13      0.09    -0.05     0.30 1.00     1236     1208
Location4        -0.23      0.11    -0.46    -0.00 1.00     1078     1074
Location5         0.02      0.32    -0.65     0.67 1.00     1102     1087
Profession1       1.19      0.93    -0.68     2.97 1.00     1269     1175
Profession2      -1.40      0.93    -3.18     0.52 1.00     1176     1213

Draws were sampled using sampling(NUTS). For each parameter, Bulk_ESS
and Tail_ESS are effective sample size measures, and Rhat is the potential
scale reduction factor on split chains (at convergence, Rhat = 1).
```

Figure A.1: Log odds of all effects in full brms model.

Appendix 6

The graphs below show two different pieces of information. The plots on the left indicate the probability distributions of all three independent effects and their interaction, indicating where probability is spread. These we have already seen in Chapter 6. On the right side the plots reflect the MCMC chains in the model. There were four chains included in the model and successful convergence toward the highest probability region looks like a 'Hairy Caterpillar', in which the chains are well mixed into each other, rather than remaining distinct or with large gaps between them. Examining these plots, it is clear that these chains are well-mixed and behaving as expected.

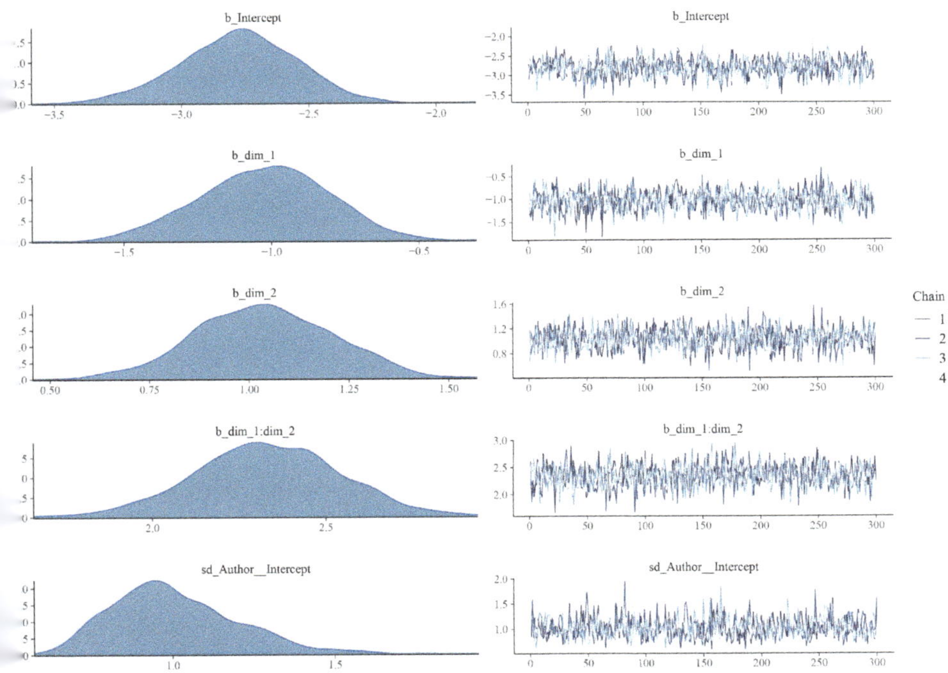

Figure A.2: Posterior distributions and MCMC chains for final model.

Index

HISTORICAL SOCIOLINGUISTICS

Studies on Language and Society in the Past

SERIES EDITORS

The interdisciplinary field of Historical Sociolinguistics seeks to reveal the impact of language development on society and the role of individuals and society in the changing forms and usage of language. This book series is aimed at sociolinguists and social historians who are keen to publish studies on the social history of languages, the interaction of linguistic practices and society, and the sociological significance of linguistic variation with a historical dimension. The purpose of the series is to provide empirically supported studies that will challenge and advance current language historiographies, which often continue to present the history of particular languages as necessarily leading to the creation of a standard or prestige variety. Of particular interest are topics such as the following: language myths and language ideology, historical multilingualism and the formation of nation-states, the sociolinguistics of minority and regional languages, the rise of urban vernaculars, immigrants and their languages, the role of prescriptive grammarians, and the social history of pidgins and creoles.

Book proposals from historians and linguists working on any language in any period are welcome, in particular those that include a comparative dimension as well as those with a strong empirical foundation. The language of publication is primarily English, though other languages may be considered. The editors guarantee that all publications in this series have been subjected to external and anonymous peer review. The four series editors and twenty-six members of the advisory board are all members of the Historical Sociolinguistics Network (HiSoN).

ADVISORY BOARD

Vol. 1 Vladislav Rjéoutski, Gesine Argent and Derek Offord (eds):
European Francophonie: The Social, Political and Cultural History of an International Prestige Language
2014. ISBN 978-3-0343-1703-0

Vol. 2 Anna Havinga and Nils Langer (eds):
Invisible Languages in the Nineteenth Century
2015. ISBN 978-3-0343-1968-3

Vol. 3 Luis Andrade Ciudad:
The Spanish of the Northern Peruvian Andes: A Sociohistorical and Dialectological Account
2016. ISBN 978-3-0343-1790-0

Vol. 4 Gijsbert Rutten and Kristine Horner (eds):
Metalinguistic Perspectives on Germanic Languages: European Case Studies from Past to Present
2016. ISBN 978-3-0343-1853-2

Vol. 5 Markus Schiegg and Judith Huber (eds):
Intra-Writer Variation in Historical Sociolinguistics
2023. ISBN 978-1-80079-703-1

Vol. 6 Sabrina Freund:
Lexikalische Variation in Patientenbriefen des 19. und frühen 20. Jahrhunderts
2024. ISBN 978-1-80374-271-7

Vol. 7 Samantha M. Litty and Nils Langer (eds):
Language Ideology, Policy, and Practice: Focus on Minoritized Languages Past and Present
2024. ISBN 978-1-80374-556-5

Vol. 8 Sarah van Eyndhoven: 'Ane end of an auld song?':
Macro and Micro Perspectives on Written Scots in Correspondence during the Union of the Parliaments Debates
2025. ISBN 978-1-80374-501-5

www.ingramcontent.com/pod-product-compliance
Ingram Content Group UK Ltd.
Pitfield, Milton Keynes, MK11 3LW, UK
UKHW021843100926
8556IPUK00019B/1029

9 781803 74501